RESUMED INNOCENT

RENE FOMBY

Book Ness
Monster
Press

Book Ness Monster Press
4530 Blue Ridge Drive
Belton, Texas 76513

Paperback ISBN: 9780998755519

Cover design by BespokeBookCovers.com

Visit us on the World Wide Web: http://www.renefomby.com

Fomby, Rene. Resumed Innocent. Book Ness Monster Press. Paperback Edition.

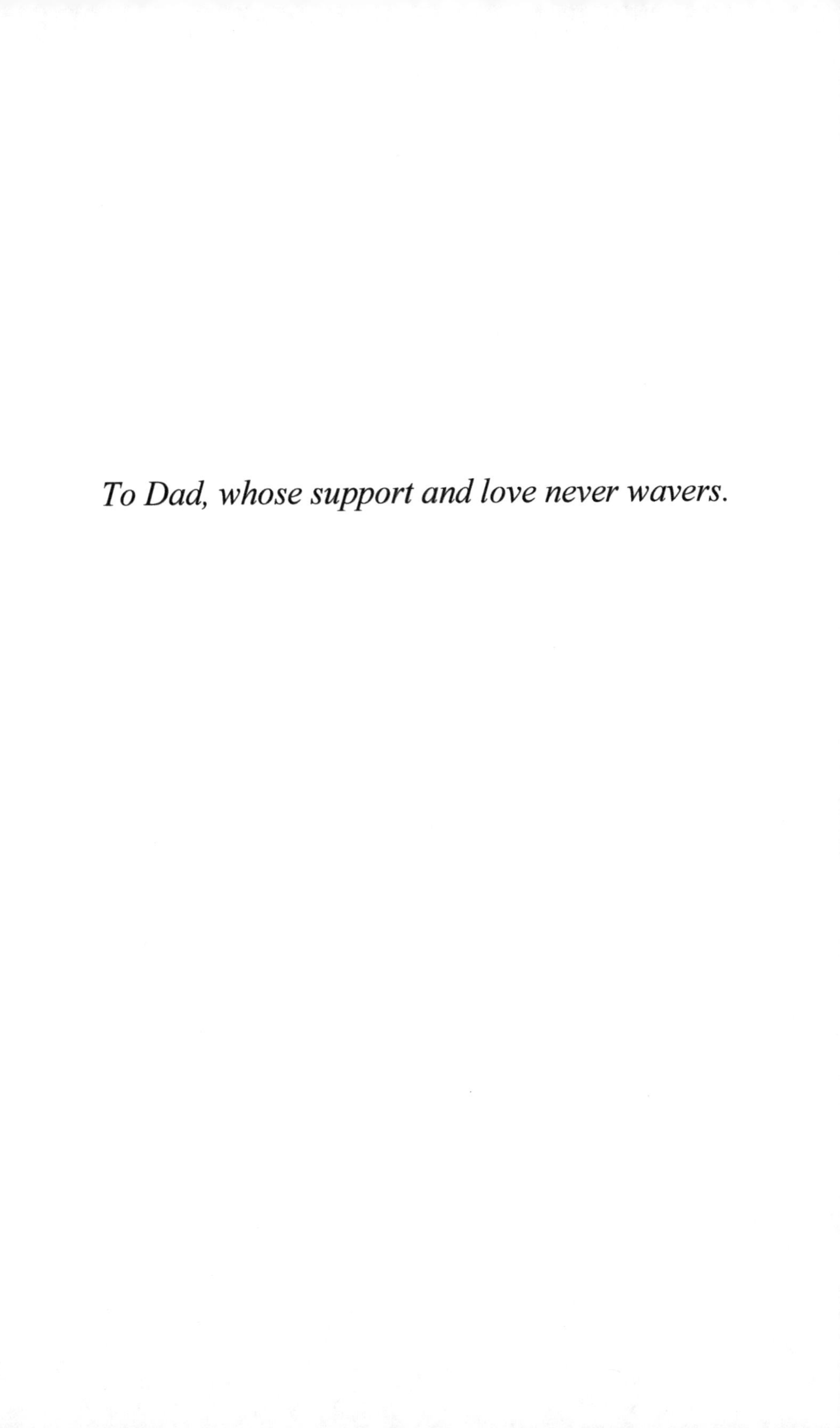

To Dad, whose support and love never wavers.

foreword

True crime fiction has always been focused on the blood and guts, crimes so lurid that the reader is drawn to the action like a driver staring at severed heads on a roadway. But in reality, true crime is far less dramatic. Almost every crime that pops up around us is a minor crime, important to the victims and defendants but irrelevant to the rest of us who slog though our lives intentionally ignorant of the everyday mishaps that can disrupt or destroy the lives of people almost identical to ourselves. I live this dichotomy every day of my life. I live being an integral part of a justice system that is designed to create the opposite of justice. And it rips me apart.

Conventional wisdom tells us that we authors should always write about what we know, and this book, being semiautobiographical, certainly fits that bill. As you read this book, it may strike you that these cases, the people and the trials, are too farcical to be believable, and in fact that is exactly the feedback that I have gotten from several literary agents. But the sad truth is, other than the triple murder that bookends this story, every bit of this book is pulled directly from my own case files, and even that one murder case turns on an issue that I came across several years ago in a different case. If anything, instead of pushing these stories to the extreme to maximize their entertainment value, I've actually left out some of the more outrageous details. The reality of day to day criminal practice in Texas is simply too unreal to be believed.

One liberty I did take in telling this story is in making the protagonist a single mother, and Jewish at that. In my experience, women are generally better lawyers than their male counterparts. They work harder and care more intensely for their clients than us guys, and they tend to take far more seriously the tremendous duties and responsibilities criminal lawyers assume when we take the oath. And, of course, the last thing this world needs is one more book about a middle aged, middle-class white male lawyer. Like Samantha, though, I'm what we in the profession call a "baby lawyer." Even though I'm now pushing sixty years old, I graduated law school only seven years ago, and the cases in this story cover the last four years of that stretch. So, unlike many of my colleagues, I haven't yet reached the tipping point for my

cynicism. I like to think I still have some of my innocence left.

the lawyer letter

1

Blair County, Central Texas

It was well past midnight, and the sky was shrouded with low lying clouds, pregnant with rain. A stranger to the area couldn't have made it down the pitch-black alleyway without stumbling over all of the trash cans and related debris littering both sides of the alley and spilling out across his path. But he was no stranger, and moving slowly in the dark, feeling his way step by excruciating step, he made his way through a gathering mist to the back gate, now nearly invisible in the gloom. He reached out and opened it cautiously, careful not to let the sound of the latch or the slight squeak from the hinge awaken the neighbors. Or, worse, the inhabitants of the little white wood-frame house. He left the gate open and crept silently to the back door. Testing the knob and finding it locked, he pulled out a key, unlocked the door and gently pushed it open.

The kitchen was even blacker than the outside, but he had long learned how to wind his way around the center island and back out into the hallway in the dark. Kicking off his shoes, he slipped down the hall to the back master bedroom. The door was slightly ajar, left that way in case one of the children woke up and cried out in the night. He paused for a moment just outside the door and pulled on a pair of blue surgical-style gloves. Easing the door open, he tiptoed to the left side of the bed where she lay sleeping, her mouth barely open, her auburn hair floating upon the pillow. He stood staring at her for well over a minute, her face scarcely visible in the dark.

It is time, Katherine.

He threw his left hand over her mouth to cover her screams as he reached down and dragged the blade of his box cutter raggedly across her throat. He was forced to drop the box cutter to fight off her flailing arms for the few short moments it took for her to finally lie still, her blood quickly soaking into the pillow and bed sheets.

Now that she was quiet, he needed to finish the job. He snatched up the bloody box cutter, wiping it on the clean sheets at the foot of the bed, then stole back down the hall toward the children's bedrooms. The little boy went easily, his throat slashed just like his mother's. But the sister put up more of a fight, and when he failed at his first attempt to quiet her, he buried the tip of the box cutter into her belly just below her sternum and ripped downward, spilling her viscera out across the blanket and sheets. Like her mother, the five-year-old refused to cooperate, and once again he had to drop the box cutter to hold her still.

Finally finished with the children, he returned to the master bedroom. The night was not yet over.

2

For Samantha Tulley, it seemed like the faster she raced ahead, the further she fell behind. One particularly cold January morning she woke up to realize that she'd been handling low-paying misdemeanor cases for well over a year, but had almost no net income to show for it. On the plus side, she was working out of her house and didn't have any legal assistants to feed, so at least she wasn't hemorrhaging money. And now she was starting to pick up a few promising felonies, so her long-term plan was working. But the money Luke had left her in the bank wouldn't last forever.

She glanced down at her list of court appearances for the day. Seven pleas set for the morning, and five pretrials right after lunch. Her best bet for seeing the new client was right after the pretrial announcements, but she would have to hustle to get over to the county jail before they shut down for shift change. Right now, though, she needed to slog through the pleas, a task that would likely take all morning. She searched the faces of the rowdy mob of defendants who had lined up to check in, but didn't see any of her clients, so she headed to the county clerk's office to pull the plea paperwork, ready to shove her clients in front of a judge just as soon as they showed up. She also had seven continuances ready in her briefcase for her clients who decided to sleep in and miss their court dates. Which usually meant most of them.

"Sam!"

She glanced around for the face behind the voice and spotted him immediately, a tall, lanky red-head towering over the throng of miscreants like a tree rising out of an African savannah. "Evan!" she called out. "Are you having any more luck than I am locating your wayward wards?"

"Actually, Sam, I don't want to brag, but I'm already at two. Out of ten. Might even be able to afford the gas to get home." Evan Murphy was one of the few good guys in the local criminal bar, who like Sam refused to sell his clients down the river just to make more money. And she seemed to remember that he was happily married, unlike some of the other men lounging around the courthouse. Emphasis on happily.

"I hear that," she laughed, turning to walk with him toward the clerk's office. "So, what's new with you?"

"Not much," Evan answered. "Heard about the hot new case in McDaniel's court?"

"No, I'm pretty much out of the loop on court gossip. What's it about?"

Evan stopped to open the door for her, then followed Sam into the lawyer's work room. The place was packed, with lawyers already lining up for their shot at the computer terminals. "The police are keeping a lid on most of it right now, but as you know, things leak out. Judge McDaniel pulled a special and assigned it to Rock the Boat, and you know *he* leaks like a newborn baby."

Sam laughed. 'Rock the Boat' was the criminal bar's unofficial nickname for Charlie Bower, because out of all the attorneys practicing criminal law in the county, he would be the very last to rock the boat. "Go along to get along" was his motto, and all the judges knew that he was the man for the job if a case needed to be pushed through the system with no wrinkles. But Bower loved to hear himself talk, and he could easily eat up half your day with chitchat if you weren't careful. "So what's the case about?"

Evan lowered his voice and leaned in closer. "It's the triple murder that's been in the news the last week or so. Woman in her late twenties and her two children, boy and a girl, both under six years old. The mother and the boy got their necks slashed in bed. The little girl got her belly ripped open. The cops on the scene said it was the worst crime scene they'd ever worked."

Sam nodded. "So since it's a case, they obviously caught the killer. Anyone we know?"

"No, I don't think so. As it turns out, it was her ex-husband. They'd been estranged, and he moved out to a cheap apartment over on East First several months ago. The police aren't sure what spooked him into doing it, but I hear they found the murder weapon in a dumpster bin just outside his front door. They pulled a warrant and emptied out the apartment. Then that techie guy in forensics, Ray whats-his-name, he found something on the husband's computer that evidently nailed the guy to the wall. No doubt he was the one who did it."

"Right. Ray Wallace. He handled the black box download from Luke's car." Sam stared down at the ground, frowning. "Well, I know from personal experience that losing someone you really care about can make you crazy, but this is *way* over the top. The guy must have been unhinged to begin with."

"Yeah, Sam, I think that's the consensus. But you and I both know this county's full of nut jobs. PTSDs, schizos, bipolars. It's just a matter of time before one of them snaps."

"Makes me think I should get that concealed carry permit after all," she said to herself. "By the way, you said McDaniel pulled a special. What's that? I don't think I've ever heard that term, at least not in that context."

"Sorry. It's easy to forget you're pretty new around here. A 'special', well, you know how the wheel is supposed to keep judges from cherry picking lawyers for their cases…"

"Yeah, every case gets assigned to the next lawyer on the list."

"Right. Well, in the felony courts, the judges sometimes dodge the wheel for special cases – cases they need to have sail through the system with no waves, nothing stirred up in the courtroom that could make the papers or the evening news. And if any case was special, this looks like the poster child. Gruesome murders, children slashed, psycho killer, it has all the markers. The press is going to be watching this one very closely, so McDaniel wants to choreograph the guilty verdict like a Russian ballet."

Sam was just starting to catch on to how the game was really played at the Justice Center. A game within a game, all designed to maximize convictions and send a strong message to the voters that these judges and prosecutors were tough on crime. "So that's why the judge picked Rock the Boat."

"Exactly. Make it look kosher on the surface, like the guy's getting a fair shake, but in reality you're just pushing him one step closer toward the needle. The question's not if, but when. To tell you the truth, I'm perfectly happy not to get assigned to that one. I'd have had to play it straight up, and that wouldn't be very popular around here. The last case I saw like this, the defense lawyer spent the entire time dodging death threats."

"I'm with you on that. I wouldn't touch that case with a ten foot pole. Really, at this point in my career, I don't think I'd even know where to start." Sam hooked a thumb toward the clerk's office. "Look, I'm swamped today, but why don't we grab lunch one day this week. I'd love to try that new Mexican restaurant down by the river."

"Hey, great idea, Sam. How does tomorrow sound? Around noon? I could round up some of the other guys, and we can catch up on all the courtroom gossip. Bash a few judges behind their backs…"

Sam laughed. "Sounds like a plan, Ev. See ya there!"

Shooting her a quick parting smile, Evan grabbed some blank continuances and snagged a seat in front of a terminal that had just opened up. Sam headed toward the piles of plea paperwork as she checked her watch. Fifteen minutes lost. But making friends at the courthouse was critical to figuring out the game. She could memorize the Rules of Criminal Procedure all day long, but those weren't the rules that truly mattered. The rules that spell the difference between a one word verdict and a two word verdict. Not guilty. The two sweetest words in the world.

3

Only four of her seven plea deals bothered to show up for court. Two of those didn't have their money together to pay court costs, much less their fines, so that left only two of the seven cases to actually make it before the judge, adding up to a total haul of six hundred dollars for the week. And even then she had to sweet talk the prosecutors to get them to sign off on the continuances for her other clients.

By rights, Sam could have let those clients default and lose their bonds. That would land them back in jail to pay off their debts to the county — including her court-appointed fee — at the rate of one hundred dollars a day. She would get paid, regardless of what happened to her deadbeat clients. It was tempting, and it was certainly the route chosen by almost every other lawyer in the county, but Sam had a soft heart. Even though her family had never been poor, she knew what it was like to suffer through a lean Christmas because the family minivan needed new tires. So Sam refused to join a system where justice existed only for the rich.

She polished off the sandwich she had packed for lunch and just as quickly disposed of her pretrial announcements. By 1:45 she was out the door and racing for the jail. She had fifteen minutes to get there before shift change kicked in and she was forced to cool her heels for an hour. Sam tucked an errant lock of her short auburn hair back in place and picked up the pace.

4

She made it just in time, slipping into the "Attorneys Only" line and moving straight to the front, handing her request to the deputy who had pulled jail call duty that day. Looking it over, he made some entries into his computer, then pointed to an open door behind him. "Attorney Three. You cut it pretty close."

"Yeah, luckily I wore sensible shoes today for the hike over." Sam thanked him and headed for the room set aside for private conferences between attorneys and their clients. The buzzer went off as she ducked through the metal detector, but the deputy waved her on. She didn't look like much of a threat, and the conference rooms weren't set up to allow anything thicker than a sheet of paper to pass between lawyers and defendants.

Sam's client today was Andrea Owens, who despite the Caucasian-sounding name was actually full blooded Native American. She had been arrested almost four months earlier, but didn't have the money to make bail. Her court-appointed lawyer went through all the motions of a bail hearing, but his heart wasn't in it, particularly since he knew she'd be more receptive to taking a plea deal sitting inside the jail than walking around on the outside. About a week ago he came to Owens with a sweet offer. Ten to fifteen in state prison, insisting that her alternative, if she decided to reject the plea and take it to trial, would almost certainly be life. And since Owens was clearly guilty, that was exactly what would happen. "Save your skin and take the deal," he begged her. "It's your only chance."

The charge was attempted murder, plus aggravated assault with a deadly weapon. In reality, just two ways to characterize the same event, but prosecutors loved to pile on charges when they could. It tended to encourage quicker plea deals.

The police reports said Andrea stabbed her boyfriend five times with a butcher knife during an alcohol-fueled domestic disturbance. The boyfriend was hospitalized but survived, and Andrea was arrested on the spot. Sam had learned about Andrea's case from one of her clients, Tanja Meadows, who had a blue warrant and was therefore barred from getting out on bail. Tanja had been around and knew the score with court-appointed lawyers. Some, like Sam, had their hearts in the right place and could be trusted. Most of them, though, only wanted to flip the case quickly, grab their money and move on to the next sucker.

Tanja had sworn Andrea was innocent, a fact Sam found significant, because people with as much jail time as Tanja had heard it all, and knew that very few prisoners ever admitted to being guilty. They had all been framed.

Sam entered the tiny room and closed the door behind her. The cubicle was about five feet wide and six deep on her side of the security window, and roughly the same on the other side. Even though the county's Justice Center and jail were fairly new, the room already had a well-worn look to it. The peeling linoleum floors didn't help.

A few minutes later, the door on the opposite side of the conference room opened and Sam got her first look at her new client. Andrea was short, about five foot two, and a little on the pudgy side. It was clear that at one point in her life she had been something of a looker, with well-chiseled Native American features, rich black hair and a nice natural tan. It was equally obvious, though, that years of heavy drinking had taken their toll, and Sam noted the deep vertical creases around her lips that told of a lifetime of smoking. Her teeth were good, though, and together with the lack of emaciation, Sam could easily rule out a meth addiction, a problem alarmingly common among her other female clients. Andrea was dressed in the same baggy orange pants and shirt worn by all of the county inmates.

"Ms. Owens, allow me to introduce myself. I'm Sam Tulley. Tanja Meadows suggested I should come over and talk to you about your case."

"Nice to meet you, Miz Sam. Can I call you that? You can call me Andrea. Tanja says you're the best lawyer in the county."

"Miz Sam is just fine, Andrea. And Tanja is overly kind. I just wish I had some way of getting her out of here, but with the blue warrant my hands are pretty tied." A blue warrant is an arrest warrant issued after a parole officer decides to revoke a defendant's walking papers. As long as the blue warrant was in place, bailing Tanja out on any new charges was impossible.

"Okay, Andrea, I trust Tanja's insight into the case, but I've had a chance to look over the police reports from that night, and they look pretty bad for you." Andrea looked like she was going to protest, but Sam held up a hand to cut her off. "No, I get it. I've read a lot of police reports, and I know the cops tend to lie about things. Or, more to the point, they come on the scene and make up their minds too quickly, before they have all the facts."

Sam paused for a moment to let that sink in. "That problem is compounded by the prosecutors. Unless an arrest is clearly wrong, and unless even the police reports themselves make that pretty obvious, prosecutors take the reports as gospel and make very little effort to look any deeper for the truth. They don't want the truth, in fact. They just want a conviction. So the only person in the entire system who cares about the truth, in the end, is your lawyer."

"And even they don't care, Miz Sam. They just want to get their money and sell me down the river. Except you, of course."

"Well, I try to take good care of my clients, to make sure you get at least some shot at fair deal. Whether you pay me a million dollars or I take on your case for free."

"You know I don't have a million dollars, Miz Sam. I don't even have what's left of the ten thousand I got four months ago.

Robbie found that money after the po-lice left and took off out the state with it. But if you can get me out of here you can have the next check I get from my tribe next fall. All ten thousand of it."

"Okay, Andrea, I'll take your word on that, but for now let's move on and focus on your case." Sam knew that she would never see a dime of the money even if she found a way to get Andrea released, but for now she was happy just to pick up a high-profile felony case and use it to build on her reputation and experience. The money could come later. "With that in mind, Andrea, why don't we go back to the start, and tell me what you remember from that evening."

Andrea nodded okay, closing her eyes and trying to remember all the details. "Some of it is kind of fuzzy, Miz Sam. I had a lot to drink that night."

"That's okay. Just tell me what you remember for now. We can go back later and try to flesh out any details if we need to." Andrea nodded again, then slowly began to tell the story of what had happened that evening.

Earlier that day, Andrea had received a ten thousand dollar check from her tribe, paid for by its casino earnings. Flush with cash, she and Robbie, her boyfriend, headed straight to the liquor store and then back home to celebrate. But later that evening, the celebration turned ugly as Robbie started searching for where Andrea had hidden what was left of the cash. In a drunken rage, he started turning over mattresses and pulling out drawers. Finally, frustrated that he hadn't found the money, he turned on Andrea, slapping her several times on the side of her head – hard – then punching her and pushing her around the apartment. Backing away from him and holding up her hands to ward off his blows, Andrea finally wound up in the kitchen. There was a butcher knife lying on the counter, and she snatched it up to defend herself. But Robbie kept coming at her. She held the knife up in front of her in a raised fist, the blade pointed away from her at Robbie's chest. "Stay away from me!" she screamed. The neighbors, hearing the loud disturbance next door, must have picked up the phone and called 911. Robbie lunged at Andrea. She held the knife out in front of her, and it stuck him lightly on his upper left breast. "You bitch!" he yelled, and lunged again. This time she made an effort to stick him with the knife, but once again the wound to his chest was superficial. He backed away, the blood from his cuts starting to soak through his T-shirt. "I'm going to kill you, you goddamn bitch!" He lunged again, grabbing for the knife, but missed as she stuck the blade an inch or so into his side.

By this time they could hear the sound of police sirens. Robbie pulled back, blood spurting from the wound on his left side. He walked to the front door, and Andrea thought he was going to try to make his escape before the cops arrived. He had a warrant out for his arrest in Dallas on a felony charge, and if caught was facing fifteen to twenty in the state pen. Andrea let out a sigh of relief, but then tensed up again as she saw him double-lock the door and come back toward her again, a deadly look showing on his face.

She was almost out of the kitchen at that point, but with Robbie suddenly in her face, she backed up, the knife still held firmly in her fist and pointed at his chest. "Stay away from me, Robbie! I'll stab you if I have to! Stay away!" Robbie didn't seem to hear her, his blood and anger boiling over with murderous intent. He came at her once more, grabbing for the knife. She stabbed him again, once in the stomach, deep. He drew back, blood now gushing from his belly, and Andrea thought he had finally decided to give up. The police were pounding on the front door, trying to break in. Suddenly, like a snarling animal, Robbie jumped at her. She fell back against the kitchen pantry, the knife held in front of her with both hands. As he leaped on her, grabbing again for the knife, he slipped on his own blood and lost his balance. He landed heavily on her, the knife plunging into his stomach up to the hilt. He screamed and pulled back, giving Andrea a chance to roll away and race for the door. She flipped the locks and the police poured in. Andrea, standing in the living room covered in blood from the neck down, pointed mutely toward the kitchen. Seeing all the blood, one of the officers shouted "Are you hurt?" She answered, "No," in a small voice, and almost immediately was thrown to the ground and handcuffed. The EMS arrived, and Robbie was taken to the hospital for emergency surgery. Andrea was arrested and taken to the county jail.

23

<h1 align="center">5</h1>

After her talk with Andrea, Sam went straight to the courthouse and filed a Motion to Substitute Counsel, making her Andrea's attorney of record in the case. Armed with that, she called up the assistant district attorney assigned to the case, John Dubcek, and asked him to put together a complete copy of the State's file for her. Tanja had given her Andrea's copy of the initial police report, but it was missing all of the crucial details as to what had happened after the arrest, details Sam knew would be the key to establishing Andrea's innocence. Dubcek's assistant suggested the file would be ready in two days.

Sam cleared her calendar to make sure she wouldn't have any conflicts when the file finally arrived. By that time it was five o'clock and the courthouse was shutting down. She gathered up her things and headed home, stopping briefly at the grocery store to pick up fresh milk and diapers for the baby, a big bag of dog food for Barley, and a small bottle of wine for herself.

Arriving home by six, she stepped into the kitchen to unload, putting the milk and wine away in the refrigerator and stuffing the diapers into an ancient dumbwaiter built into the kitchen wall. One press of a button later and the diapers were on their way up to the bedrooms on the third floor, just one less thing for her to haul up and down the steps or try to squeeze into the elevator.

Her babysitter, Stella, gave Sam a quick rundown of the day's activities and left for home, dinner for Sam and her daughter already finished and waiting for them in the oven. After a quiet evening with Maddie, reading to her until the three-year-old's eyes finally began to droop, Sam finally slipped her into bed and poured herself a third glass of wine. *Time to get it over with*, she thought. During what Sam's father had called her "trip down the rabbit hole," her parents had gone through Luke's desk, paying bills, tossing anything even remotely resembling trash, and boxing up everything that was left. The boxes were stored in the basement, where they had remained undisturbed since his death. Sam finally thought she had the strength to deal with them. She grabbed a trash bag from underneath the kitchen sink and dragged a box up to the study.

The first items she came to were a stack of greeting cards she had given Luke over the years, covering everything from birthdays to Valentines to I-just-want-to-say-I-love-you moments. Sam thought it was sweet that he had kept all of them, but they didn't hold any particular sentiment for her. She had her own stack of treasures from Luke stored carefully away in a desk drawer beside her, so these she just dropped into the trash bag. Next up was a pile of papers Luke had been using as background for his research on new techniques in pediatric cardiology. He had always hated reading these on a computer screen or tablet, and instead preferred printing them off so he could scribble his thoughts across them, or spread pages out on the dining room table to help organize his thoughts. Sam tossed those into the trash bag as well.

Near the bottom, though, she stumbled across a box, wrapped clumsily in red gift wrap. Despite his many talents, Luke had never mastered the arcane art of wrapping presents, she remembered warmly. She checked the small tag taped to the top of the box. Scrawled across the tag in perfect schoolboy cursive was a single word: *Samantha.* She paused for a moment, wondering what was inside the package, and for what occasion Luke had been saving it to give to her. Slowly she started peeling away the gift wrap, exposing a simple white box underneath. Sam held her breath and pried open the lid.

Inside was a framed Winnie the Pooh print. Winnie and Tigger were walking down a long path leading into the woods. Scrolled in small type across the top of the print was a simple inscription:

If ever there is a tomorrow when we're not together... there is something you must always remember. You are braver than you believe, stronger than you seem, and smarter than you think. But the most important thing is, even if we're apart... I'll always be with you.

It was a quote to Pooh from Christopher Robin. For what seemed like the millionth time that year, Sam burst into tears. But this time, for once, they were tears of joy. Even in death, dear

Luke had found a way to reach out to her, to try to help her heal from all the searing pain of losing him so suddenly. "Yes, Luke," she whispered quietly. "I will be brave. I will be strong. For our baby. For you. You haven't truly left us, as long as you are up in Heaven, watching over us. And I will always be here for you. I love you, Luke. I will always love you."

6

Sam's legal calendar was pretty clear the next day, so she decided to spend most of it with Maddie. They had finger sandwiches at a little English bistro downtown, then walked down to the river, where Maddie unsuccessfully but enthusiastically chased the ducks and geese prowling along the water's edge.

After dinner, she curled up with Maddie on the living room couch, humming soft tunes to her as she poured over her notes on the Tanja Meadows case. Sam was still amazed that the DA's office was pursuing it, but, as usual, whenever a police officer gets hurt somebody has to pay. Even if the police officer was entirely at fault.

The case was set for trial in a few weeks, and her stomach was tied up in knots at the thought of it. This would technically be only her second trial. The first had been a silly little case in municipal court over a public intoxication arrest. Even though it was just a Class C misdemeanor – essentially a traffic ticket – her client insisted on fighting it. The trial started early in the morning and ended just after lunch. The case came down to a damning police cam video of the officer detaining her client for forty minutes at two o'clock in the morning, just fifteen feet from his front door. On cross examination, the officer tried to explain that he arrested her drunken client in order to protect him, because a car could have raced down the street at any moment, veered into the front yard and struck him dead. Sam played that video to the jury during closing arguments, pointing out that the only vehicle seen on that street for the entire forty minutes was the police car. It took the jury just five minutes to return with a Not Guilty verdict.

But in the end, all that was at stake in that trial was around three hundred dollars in fines and court costs, and Sam's client wound up shelling out over a thousand dollars to fight and win it. Justice doesn't come cheap.

Tanja's case, on the other hand, was for all the money. Tanja already had two felony convictions on her record, so under the state's three strikes law she was looking at a mandatory sentence of life in prison. Quite literally, her entire future rested on whether Sam could convince twelve jurors that Tanja was innocent.

Maddie had fallen asleep in her arms, so Sam eased gently off the couch and carried her upstairs to her bedroom, taking the elevator to the top floor. Maddie had recently graduated from her crib to a bed, made up like a fairy castle with diaphanous pink and green streamers. Unlike Sam, who had always been something of a tomboy, Maddie loved to dress up in Disney princess outfits and hold court over an endless array of dolls and stuffed animals. And poor Barley was forced to suffer through seemingly infinite indignities as her fifty pound canine Prince Charming.

Sam tucked the three-year-old into bed, pulling the covers up over her chest and pausing to brush an errant strand of blonde hair from her little pink cheeks. A unicorn night light was plugged in to the opposite wall to provide some comfort in case the toddler woke up during the night, and Sam checked to make sure the baby monitor was on before easing the door almost shut and tiptoeing down the stairs.

A fresh glass of wine in hand, Sam picked up the Meadows file and spread the evidence out on the dining room table, her trial notepad in front of her. The police reports weren't all that useful – the cops had been careful to coordinate their stories before putting anything down on paper, and they had made sure to color all of Tanja's actions that day in the worst possible light. Once again, the only real evidence was buried in the police videos, and Sam had two of them – one from each of the two police cars at the scene – plus a third video of Tanja's interrogation days later. That last video was a problem, because the interrogator had skillfully manipulated Tanja into making statements that Sam knew would be real trouble when played out of context before the jury. She was pretty sure after watching the video that the interrogator was not only a cop but a trained psychologist. Without a lawyer present to intervene, Tanja didn't stand a chance. And that's why judges never appointed a lawyer until after the interrogation was finished and the defendant was hung out to dry.

The other two videos, in contrast, were far more positive. Sam decided to watch them again, looking for any small detail that would prove her client didn't intend to run over the officer that day. There was a disc already loaded up in her laptop, left over from another case she was reviewing, so she pulled it out and inserted the DVD from the first police car, the one driven by the injured officer.

Like most Texas counties, the local cops used custom software to store and run police cam videos. That software let you switch between multiple perspectives, such as the front-facing camera and another camera pointed at the back seat of the cruiser, and you could monitor the status of various radios and lights, as well as the speed of the cruiser if it was in motion. Sam selected the front camera, turned off the microphone from inside the car, and hit Play.

The scene on the laptop showed the police car traveling down a neighborhood street. The clock at the bottom of the screen indicated it was almost three in the afternoon on Friday, August 13. Friday the thirteenth. Suddenly, the driver switched on his siren and overhead lights. Sam knew from experience that this was what triggered the recording, the start of the tape automatically backing up sixty seconds to establish important context. The police car picked up speed, racing past surrounding houses and through stop signs and red lights with barely any regard to other motorists. A little over a minute later the officer pulled in to a convenience store parking lot, stopping his cruiser at a slight angle, roughly twenty feet behind and just to the left of a gray Toyota Camry.

Tanja is sitting in the front seat of the Camry, facing the double glass doors leading into the store and waiting for her passenger to return from buying a Big Gulp. On the far right edge of the video, a second police car pulls up and stops, also at an angle to the Camry and slightly to the right. A young black man exits the store with a drink in his hand. Seeing the two police cars, he walks over to the passenger side of the Camry and reaches out with his right hand to open the door.

"ON YOUR KNEES!" A female officer rushes toward him from the right side of the screen. The man looks back, perplexed for a moment, then obediently drops to his knees, sets the Big Gulp on the ground, and places his hands behind his head in a classic gesture of surrender. The female police officer races up behind him and immediately throws him to the ground, digging her left knee into his back and planting his face firmly onto the hot asphalt. She grabs his right hand and cuffs it, then the left. Finally, she forces him to his feet and leads him back to her car.

Watching all this, Tanja finally notices the other police officer, a man, standing just behind her car on the driver's side, talking into his radio. The video shows her rolling down her window and turning toward the officer. "Sir, what's going on?"

she asks in a polite but obviously disturbed tone. "Can you tell me what's going on?"

The officer pulls the radio from his mouth. "SHUT UP AND TURN AROUND," he orders, his right hand moving to the gun holstered on his right hip. Tanja turns around and rolls up the window.

Sam knew from her interview with Tanja that the engine was still running at this point, the car's transmission in park. It was summertime in Texas, and the outside temperature was well over a hundred and five degrees, so she had the air conditioner going full blast. After talking to the cop, Tanja rolled up her window to keep the cold air in the car. Not knowing what was happening, and seeing her companion being shoved in the back seat of the police cruiser to her right, Tanja called her friend's mother to let her know her son had been arrested. She was still on the phone when the male officer stalked up to her door and threw it open, his gun drawn and pointed at her.

"PUT THAT DOWN AND EXIT THE VEHICLE!" he orders. Startled, Tanja lowers the phone. "Sir, I..." she manages to stammer before he lunges at her, grabbing her left arm and pulling her violently from the car.

Given the angle of the video, it wasn't clear what happened next, but Tanja had explained that, as she was being yanked from of the car, she instinctively reached back with her right hand to grab something, anything, to break her fall. Unfortunately, what she grabbed was the gear shift handle. Without meaning to, she pulled the gear shift all the way back and into drive.

On the video, the car lurches forward toward the front door of the convenience store, then just as abruptly lurches to a stop. Tanja said that when she felt the car move forward she immediately stomped her right foot back down on the brake. Her left leg was almost completely out of the car at this point. The male officer shouts to his female partner, crouched just to his right and slightly behind Tanja. "TASER HER! TASER HER!" His partner shouts back at Tanja, "PUT IT IN PARK!" The officers clearly know at this point that the car is in gear. The male officer screams again, "TASER HER! TASER HER!" And then the female officer fires her Taser at point blank range right into Tanja's left side. The period of time from when the officer first opened the door to the point where Tanja gets tased covers just under three seconds.

Sam paused the video at this point. There was so much going on in so little time it was hard to figure out exactly how and when the car was shifted into reverse. Tanja's memory was unclear on that point, with everything happening so fast, but she seemed to remember her right foot starting to slip off the brake pedal as she was being pulled from the driver's seat, and trying to get the car out of drive before it went out of control and plunged through the front of the convenience store. Sam knew that the key to an acquittal in this case would be proving Tanja put the car into reverse for all the right reasons, and not because she was trying to escape. But how? She took a sip of wine and clicked the play button to restart the action.

Tanja screams in agony. Her entire body goes rigid as the Taser instantly fires all of the voluntary nerve synapses in her body. Unfortunately, as Tanja's legs stiffen, the foot that has been on the brake since the initial lurch forward slips off and lands on the accelerator, depressing the gas pedal. The car, which never made it all the way to park, suddenly starts to move in reverse. Alarmed that the car is rapidly hurtling backward, the female officer drops her Taser and bolts away, toward the camera. The male officer, though, is still trying to drag Tanja from the car. He runs alongside the Camry as it speeds up in reverse, gripping her left arm and trying to pull her out. Finally, he decides to plant his heels into the asphalt in a vain effort to stop the car, pressing his back into the open driver's door. At this point the action moves off the video to the right, so the camera doesn't catch what happens next, when the car door slams him to the ground and shatters his shoulder.

Sam didn't bother watching the other video again. Other than being from a different angle, it didn't have much to add to her understanding of what happened. She took a big gulp of wine and decided it was time for bed. She was still no closer to figuring out how to convince a jury that Tanja had never intended to put the car into reverse, and that the officer was injured because of his stupidity in ordering his partner to Taser the driver of a car that was clearly in gear. And, in the end, that was the key to whether Tanja went free, or spent the rest of her life in state prison.

7

Sam got the call from the DA's office that the Owens file was ready for pickup, just four days later than promised. Barley sensed that she was leaving and raced out the doggy door to sit patiently by the car, his large, soft Australian Shepherd eyes silently begging her to let him come along for the ride. "Okay, Barley, it's a nice day for an outing. You deserve a little break from the baby." She opened the front passenger door and he bounced in eagerly, immediately settling into his place on the passenger seat facing forward. Sam shut the door and walked around the back of the car to get in herself. Starting the car, she lowered the passenger window just enough so Barley could stick his head out into the wind, then opened the electric gate out front and headed toward the courthouse.

Parking the car at the Justice Center, she left Barley behind with the windows cracked and headed inside to retrieve the file on Andrea. It took the girl at the front desk almost twenty minutes to locate the file, but Sam finally signed the paperwork acknowledging she had received the package and headed home.

When she walked in, Stella was in the sunroom with Maddie, reading a book out loud and patiently pointing out the words that went along with the illustrations. It had only taken Sam a few weeks after starting the law firm to realize that she needed someone to help out with the baby, someone with a flexible schedule and low income needs, and Stella fit that job description perfectly. A grandmother herself, Stella lived just a few houses down the street, in a neat little gingerbread cottage with carefully tended rose bushes out front and a roomy yard out back, complete with a vegetable garden, swing set and lots of space for her grandbabies to play when they came for a visit. She was financially comfortable, but had grown lonely in the little house ever since her husband had passed on, so she welcomed the opportunity to dote over Maddie anytime Sam got too busy with her legal work. Which, to Sam's chagrin, was almost all the time now. Stella gave her a small wave and continued on with the gripping tale of The Lonely Unicorn, with Maddie in rapt attention. Barley ran to his play box to pull out a large bone, then trotted to the dining room to sit with his mistress while she poured over the file.

Sam spread the contents of the folder in a wide arc across the dining table, a yellow legal pad planted in front of her for her notes. She poured over the pictures first. The crime scene photos she flipped through quickly. There wasn't anything on them that stood out at this point, but she would study them more carefully later on, once she got a better understanding of what to look for. She paused, though, when she got to the picture of the knife that Andrea had used that evening. Sam had assumed that when Andrea described the weapon as a "butcher knife" that it was long and broad, maybe six inches long. But the blade in the picture, conveniently photographed next to a ruler, was barely three inches long. More like a paring knife than a butcher knife, she thought. It wasn't all that surprising that Andrea had gotten that detail wrong – in the heat of the moment, it probably seemed much larger to her at the time. But Sam made a note that Andrea's memory couldn't really be trusted, and she'd have to be careful to verify all of her facts.

Putting the knife picture down, she moved on to the photos the hospital had taken of Robbie's injuries. Just as Andrea had described, the first two wounds appeared to be fairly minor, and the doctors at the hospital had closed them up with butterfly bandages. The third wound, on his left side, was a little worse, but still only needed a few stitches as far as she could tell. The fourth wound looked much deeper, and judging from the width of the knife and the size of the wound, the blade had apparently sliced a little downward after it entered the body. Finally, Sam turned to the fifth wound, which was photographed individually in a close-up. It wasn't really possible to tell from the picture how much damage had been done to the wound site by the kitchen knife, and how much by the surgical scalpels as they opened him up to repair the internal damage to Robbie's organs and blood vessels. But cross-referencing the picture with the post-surgical reports from the hospital suggested that he was very lucky the blade had been so small. If the cut had been any deeper, he almost certainly would never have made it to the ER in time.

The last pictures in the stack were of Andrea Owen, including photographs taken at the scene and her mug shots from booking. Sam examined the pictures carefully, and even with the blood smears in the first photos, it was clear that Andrea had suffered numerous blows to both sides of her face, injuries that had begun to bruise over by the time she got to the jail.

Done with the pictures for now, Sam skimmed the police reports, both the initial reports from the crime scene and the follow-up reports from interviews with neighbors and with Robbie at the hospital. All of the reports were consistent, characterizing the incident as a one-sided, alcohol-fueled assault on Robbie by his mentally unstable girlfriend. There was no mention in any of the reports of the injuries to her face, injuries that had to have been visible to the officers at the scene, or to the widespread bruising on her front and sides that were apparent in later photographs taken at the jail.

The case sheets listed Robbie as a black male, six foot two inches tall and about 225 pounds. The only address listed for him was Andrea's apartment, and the only contact the DA's office had with him since he left the hospital was through his cell phone. Sam made a note on her legal pad to try and find out his current location, particularly since he still had an outstanding warrant for his arrest out of Dallas. A fact that neither the police nor the DA's office had noted.

Andrea was listed in the reports as five foot one inch and about 105 pounds. The apartment was also listed as *her* last known address. Other than county jail.

Finally, Sam turned to the victim interview, the official statement Robbie made to the police about what had happened at the apartment. It was several pages long, so she grabbed her legal pad and a pencil and headed toward the easy chair in the study. Picking apart Robbie's story would be critical to proving that he was lying, that Andrea had only been trying to defend herself that evening.

It was clear from the beginning of the handwritten statement that Robbie was only partially literate. His statement was filled with spelling and grammatical errors, and with places where he had scratched out what he originally wrote and filled in something else. In almost every case, though, even where he had scratched out parts of the statement, it was still possible to determine what he had originally written, and the differences were often very telling. She skipped ahead to where he said she stabbed him.

At this point I was afrade she would fall down and hert hersef with the knife, so I reaches over to try and ~~grab~~ hold her up sos she won fall, and thats wen she pokes me in the chess with the knife.

That suprise me, and there was some blood where she poke me, ~~an I was pissed off~~ but I was okay. I say to her, stop pokin me that knife, and I try to take it away from her agin sos she won get hert, sos she pokes me agin. I says dam! that herts! Give me that knife, girl!

"I'll bet that was exactly what he said to her," Sam murmured to herself.

Sos at this point she pokes me agin, this time in the stomach. And shes yellin, all crazy and shit, and I think maybe Ill call the hospital and git her some medisin or some shit. That's when I hears the police, and I walk over to the front dore to unlock it.

Sam looked back at the police report, which said there was blood on the doorknob, dead bolt and chain lock. *If he was trying to unlock the door he was doing a piss poor job...*, she scribbled onto her notepad.

Sos Im tryin to unlocks the dore for the police when she says come here, I was just foolin roun, so I turn roun and head back to the kichen.

Sam carefully underlined the words "just foolin roun".

Shes holdin the knife down at her side, sos I say give me the knife. She says she sorry, she loves me, so I gos in the kichen to hep her agin and thats when she pokes me agin in the stomach. There was blood everwhere so I slips on the blood and fall down on the flore. That's when the police comes and kicks in the dore. Thats all I remembers, sept goin to the hospital.

I is in the hospital a week or so, then they let me go. I gos by the apartment to get my shit, then I desides to go stay with my mama til I could get better. When I went to the apartment there was no money there. I ~~looked around to find it for her~~ didn't look for it. Maybe somebody took it. Im sorry if Andrea loss her money. I still love her, even after she stab me and shit.

The other police man I talk to ax what I do. I do this and that, enuff to get by. Mosly I jus hep my frens when they need hep. Cuz thats how I roll. Im a good fren.

Sam paused to record that on her notepad. *Uh-huh. The best friend money can buy. How could the DA's office read this bullshit story and believe a word of it?* Setting the notepad aside, she reached down and dug a business card out of her purse, then dialed the number for "Randy Martinez, Private Eye" on her cell phone.

He answered on the third ring. "Randy here. How can I help you?"

Randy had given her his card when she first started handling misdemeanor cases a year earlier. There was no money in those cases to pay for a private eye, and little chance of finding anything that would make a difference even if there was, but she desperately needed some help on this one. Even if the case was pro bono, so the money would come out of her own back pocket. "Yes, Mr. Martinez, this is Samantha Tulley. I'm a criminal defense lawyer. You and I met about a year ago…"

"Sure, I remember you, Ms. Tulley. You're a good friend of Evan Murphy's, working the minor crime circuit, as I recall. Evan and I go way back, served in the Army Rangers together back in the early days of the Iraq war. He speaks pretty highly of you. You have a little girl at home, don't you? What's her name… Maude?"

"Oh, yes, my little Madeleine. We call her Maddie for short. She's quite a handful, especially with my schedule, but I wouldn't trade her for the world. Anyway, Mr. Martinez, I have something a little bigger than my usual cases that just got dropped in my lap, a felony assault, and I need your help tracking someone down."

"It's just Randy to my friends. And I'd be happy to help out. Whatcha got on it? Looking for a witness?"

"No, actually, Randy, it's the victim. Or the so-called victim, as it is. He's really just a low-life piece of shit who attacked my client to try and steal some money from her. And it looks like he got away with it. Both the money and the attack. Anyway, the police report shows no forwarding address, and my client says he has an outstanding felony warrant out of Dallas, so I'm thinking he may have skipped the state. The report suggests he might have headed out to stay with his mother, but I don't have anything on her. He might also be doing time in Huntsville or one of the other state units, assuming they caught him between then and now. The point is, I need to know whether he's out of state, since there's almost zero chance he'd come back to testify and face getting arrested. Oh, and by the way, you can call me Sam."

"Got ya. Sure, I'll give it a shot. As I always say, any friend of Evan's is a client to me." He let out a low snort. "You know, when even a criminal lawyer says you're a low-life piece of shit, you've got to be pretty bad. You guys see 'em all."

"That's for sure," Sam agreed. "Very few solid citizens in my line of work."

"Well, you have to take 'em as you get 'em, Sam. Thanks to the Constitution, we all deserve our day in court. Anyway, you still have my fax number and e-mail address? Shoot me what you got and I'll get right on it."

"Thanks, Randy. Oh, and by the way, my girl is a pro bono case, stuck behind bars with no cash for bail, and the judge has already waived on a PR bond, so sooner would be better than later. I'll be glad to pay extra to speed things up."

"Don't worry about it. I'll get right on it. Is this a good number to reach you when I find out something?"

"Absolutely. I have your name in my contacts so I'll know it's you when you call. If I don't pick up, you know the drill. I'm in court or the jail, but leave a message and I'll get right back to you."

"Sure. Does this number accept texts? I can text you first and you can call me back when you're free."

"Sounds great, Randy. And thanks!"

"Don't mention it. I should have something for you in a day or so."

"Super. I really appreciate it." Sam hung up, glad she had remembered to keep his card all this time. Everyone she had talked to in the local criminal bar seemed to think Randy was a miracle worker, and she could use a few miracles for a change. She gathered up what she had on Robbie from the dining room and headed for the fax machine. She'd send what little she had on the case to Randy, then send Stella home and spend the rest of the evening playing with Maddie. Barley had fallen asleep on the floor, his nose perched protectively atop the bone. Sam envied him. All he needed was a car ride and a bone, and life was good. She could certainly use a bone right about now.

8

The sun was just coming up and Sam was finishing off her first cup of morning coffee when her phone suddenly buzzed. She glanced down and saw it was Randy Martinez. She hit the answer icon so quickly she spilled some of the coffee on her house robe. "Randy! How pleasantly unexpected! You got some answers already?"

"Haha!" he replied with a hearty chuckle. "Right to the point, Counselor Tulley. And I hope it's not too early. I just assumed I would get your voicemail and leave a message…"

"It's just Sam, remember? And, no, it's not too early. I'm always up with the chickens. Get a little me time in before the baby wakes up." She shifted the phone to her other ear and set her coffee down on the kitchen counter. "So, what's going on? Did you find him?"

"I did, as a matter of fact. It appears that Robbie Johnson is comfortably settled into his mother's house in Little Rock, Arkansas, and isn't headed back to Texas any time soon."

"Really! How did you find that out?"

"I know a fellow who knows a fellow who knows some of Robbie's friends back home in Little Rock. No way he wants to come back to Texas to do a dime or two for that burglary in Dallas.”

“That’s fabulous news, Randy! If he doesn’t come back for trial, they don’t have a case. Anything he told the cops is hearsay, and other than Andrea there were no other eye witnesses.”

“Sounds cut-and-dried, Sam. Glad I could help out.”

“Boy, everything they say about you is true, Randy. You really *are* a miracle worker. So how much do I owe you for this?”

“You don’t owe me a thing. I know you’re just getting your feet under you, plus you’re taking on this case pro bono, to boot. Let’s just call it my New Customer Loyalty Program. Free for now, and I’ll be sure to charge you double when you’re rolling in the big bucks.”

“Well, thanks tons. And you can charge me triple for results like this.”

Sam hung up, checking the clock. It was still way too early to call John Dubcek at the DA’s office, so she bided her time impatiently, feeding and changing Maddie and starting a fresh pot of coffee. Finally, the clock hit nine and she grabbed her phone, dialing the number she had compulsively memorized while she waited.

It rang twice on the other end. “Dubcek here. How can I help you?”

"Yes, Mr. Dubcek, this is Sam Tulley. I have the Owens case?"

"Yeah, got you, the crazy Indian lady with the attempted murder. What's up?"

"I have some new developments in the case, Mr. Dubcek, and I wondered if you had some time for us to sit down and go over them."

"Uh, sure. Let me check my calendar" He paused briefly. "Okay, I'm set for trial the beginning of next week, so my schedule's pretty tight after today. And this afternoon I need to try and line up my witnesses. Any way you can get over here this morning? I can squeeze you in just before lunch."

"Sure! Eleven sound okay?"

"Better make it closer to eleven-thirty. We have a staff meeting at ten, and they usually run a little long."

"Eleven-thirty it is. Thanks, I'll see you then."

Sam hung up, refilled her coffee and cheerfully headed upstairs. She could drop Maddie off at Stella's around eleven, then be back in time for lunch. Maybe she could even convince Stella to join her at the new Thai restaurant she had been dying to try. It would do the old bird some good to get out on the town for a change…

9

The district attorney's office was like a rat maze, with piles of paper and assorted litter lying all around. The front desk receptionist guided Sam through the mess and into the back, finally ushering her into John Dubcek's crowded office. Dubcek looked up from a file he was studying. "Ms. Tulley. Do sit down." He motioned toward two chairs perched just inside the door.

Dubcek plopped the file down on his desk as she was getting seated. "Just looking over what we have on the case. Seems pretty straight forward from where I sit." Dubcek tapped the file. "Woman gets drunk, gets mad at her boyfriend, maybe finds out he's cheating on her. Next thing you know, she's going after him with a kitchen knife, puts him in the hospital. No serious injuries to her, her prints on the weapon, his blood all over the place. I'm not even sure this is a case we'd want to plea out. I think a jury would hand me a guilty in a heartbeat."

"Well, I appreciate that, Mr. Dubcek." Sam had pulled out her notes and was checking her talking points for the meeting. She had to be very careful here. Several of her colleagues had warned her that Dubcek was concerned about one thing and one thing only: winning. The pursuit of justice be damned. And they assured her he wasn't afraid to color way outside the legal lines if he felt boxed into a corner on a case. But she was ready for him today. If Dubcek tried to get shifty on her, she had a plan to keep him in line. And if he decided to venture *way* off the reservation – if he was willing to break the law just to win the case – then she was ready for that, too.

She looked up from her notes. "The thing is, sir, there are a few things wrong with that picture you just painted." She checked off the first item on her list. "First of all, while it's true she was drunk, it's also true he was equally as drunk. And we both know that almost all alcohol-related assaults of this magnitude are conducted by the man at the scene, not the woman."

"Most, but not all. We have assault cases come through here all the time where the woman is the aggressor. And she was the one with the knife."

"Yes, that's true, but the numbers tell us that it's much more likely that Johnson was the bad guy in this case, not Andrea Owens. Particularly since he had a good foot of height on her, and well over a hundred pounds. With that kind of size difference, he didn't need a weapon. The knife just evened things out, gave her a fighting chance to protect herself. And that's exactly what she did. Plus, if you look at the pictures, she still got the hell beat out of her that night, even with the knife."

"We'll have to disagree on that, but go ahead. What's your next point."

"Okay, you say she was the aggressor, that she attacked *him*. But that isn't consistent with the wounds. Look at the medical records. The first two wounds were shallow, with no vertical tearing. That tells me they were defensive wounds. Not consistent with an attempt to stab him, but only with how she described it, poking at him to try to get him to back away. In fact, that's even how *he* described those wounds in his statement. 'She poked me,' he says. Not 'she stabbed me'."

"That doesn't explain the other wounds, which were much deeper. Particularly the last wound, the one that almost killed him."

"No, but what they show is a gradual escalation of violence, when the first shallow cuts didn't seem to stop him. I mean, think back to his statement. Does it make any sense at all? She stabs him two or three times with a knife, and he says he's just trying to protect her from falling down and getting hurt? Who would do that?"

"Someone who is stinking drunk."

"Not even a drunk. Even a drunk would have had the sense to back away from a crazy woman stabbing him with a knife. And that brings me to point number three: his statement. There is absolutely nothing believable in that entire statement. It's the biggest cock-and-bull story I've ever read. It's clear that he's trying to put a good slant on what happened. The problem is, no matter how hard he tries, he just can't get there. Check out the bit about trying to unlock the door. The police report shows that his blood was all over the chain lock, the dead bolt, and the button lock on the doorknob. But when the police first arrived at the front door, all of those were still locked. Until Andrea Owens unlocked them herself. How is it he had time to touch all three of those locks, but failed to unlock a single one?"

"He *was* drunk…"

"Again, that excuse just doesn't fly. I could see being so drunk that you fumble with one of the locks, trying to get it open. But not all three. The only possible explanation here is that he was *locking* the door, not *unlocking* it. He was trying to keep the police out, not letting them in. And that fact is only consistent with him being the aggressor that night."

"You make some good points, but you weren't on the scene that night. The police were. And I have to lean in the direction of what the boots on the ground say happened."

"Look, Mr. Dubcek. You know very well that the police tend to jump to conclusions almost immediately, and then never go back to reconsider. They let their instincts, their gut feel cloud them to the facts. Here I am showing you how the *facts* tell a completely different story from those first impressions, and you still refuse to face those facts. Well, let me give you just one more fact. One the police never bothered to check on. Your so-called victim, Robbie Johnson, was a two-time convicted felon, wanted out of Dallas on a brand new charge. Felony burglary. The whole time the local police were politely taking his statement at the hospital, Johnson had a warrant out for his arrest in Dallas."

"You can't really blame the police for that," Dubcek said, clearly shaken by the new revelation.

"I can, and I will. It's sloppy, and sloppy is what's putting Andrea Owens' entire future in jeopardy. But that isn't what I'm driving at here. The point is, Andrea cashed a royalty check for ten thousand dollars that day. They spent less than a hundred of it on food and liquor. That left almost the entire wad of cash still intact. But now it's gone. She's been in jail, and I don't think you'll try and pin the theft of the money on the police…"

Dubcek shook his head no, agreeing that he wasn't interested in making that claim.

"So where did the money go? Easy. Johnson went back to the apartment after he got released from the hospital. He ransacked the place and found the money."

"So what? So he takes some of her money. That has no bearing on whether or not she stabbed him. And after what she did to him, I might argue that he deserved every dime of it."

"Doesn't matter. What matters is that your 'victim' fled the state. Took the money and got out of town before the police could connect him with the outstanding arrest warrant."

"So what's your point?" Dubcek impatiently checked his watch. It was almost noon.

"My point is that I hired Randy Martinez to track him down. To find out if Johnson had any interest in coming back to Texas and testifying for you at Andrea's trial. Coming back to Texas, where as soon as he finished testifying he would be handcuffed and shipped off to Dallas to face his own trial, and maybe life in the state slammer. I think you know the answer to that question. My *point*, Mr. Dubcek, is that you don't have a victim, and you don't have a witness. You've got bupkis, as my grandfather used to say. Case closed."

Dubcek finally looked worried. "Okay, say I look into this and find out you're right. What do you expect me to do about it? Just because he doesn't show doesn't prove that she's innocent."

"No, maybe not to you. But you're not the jury in this case. Twelve fine men and women have that distinction. And if you insist on taking this case all the way to a jury trial, you're going to lose big time. It'll hit the front page of every local paper. Maybe, if I'm lucky, even some of the big city papers. Just another example of small-town injustice, prosecuting a woman for the vile act of defending herself. And your shining face in the middle of all of it."

Dubcek stared at her across his desk. Still defiant. "So what the hell is it you want?"

Sam leaned back over his desk, returning the stare. "Look, I'll make this easy for you. Give me a simple Class A misdemeanor assault, time served, and we'll all shake hands and go about our business. My client doesn't really care about her record, she just wants to smell fresh air again. You get a conviction. I get my client freed. Everybody's happy."

Dubcek chewed on his lower lip a moment. "Okay, I'll check in with Martinez to confirm what you're telling me. I still have Johnson's cell, so I'll buzz him and see what I can find out from that direction. Assuming you're right, and he refuses to show up for trial, maybe I can get my boss to agree to a reduction."

"Make it quick, Mr. Dubcek. Every day you delay is one more day she has to stay locked up in that cell. I'll give you till the start of your trial to sign the paperwork for the misdemeanor plea and get her before a judge. That's one and a half days, plus the weekend. More than enough time for a couple of phone calls."

"And what are you going to do if I refuse?" Dubcek looked defiant again. "I can just keep putting off a trial for quite a long time, and meanwhile she stays safely locked away. She can't get a PR bond, and she doesn't have the money to bond out otherwise. And there's absolutely nothing you can do about it."

"But you and I both know that's illegal. You can't punish her just because she's standing up for her rights –"

"It's only illegal if you can *prove* that's why I did it. And you can't, so I'm the one holdin' all the cards, here. She better get comfortable, 'cause I'm not buying off on letting her walk. I may not be able to get ten years out of her, but she's looking at one or two at the least."

"That's where you're wrong, Mr. Dubcek. Because I learned long ago the hard way to make sure and check my shoes for scorpions before I slipped them on. To check my McDonalds drive through order before I left the window. And, of course," she smiled at him venomously, holding up her phone, "to record any and all discussions I have with slimy assistant district attorneys. Quite clearly, that includes you."

"You can't do that –"

"Actually, Mr. Dubcek, I can, and I did. A moment ago, I was willing to give you the benefit of the doubt and a few days to sign off on this. Now, given your threats, I've changed my position. I want a signed dismissal in this case by the close of business today. Or else I go public with your threats, and take this tape to the judge. Either way my client walks out of jail first thing in the morning. Your choice, sir. And now I must bid you good day. I know my way out."

10

Her phone was buzzing before she even got to her car. It was Randy Martinez. Sam quickly put down her briefcase to answer it.

"Randy! How nice to hear from you. Twice in one day. What's up?"

"You sure don't pull your punches, do you, Sam?" She could hear him faintly chuckling to himself on the other end. "I just hung up from talking to Dubcek. The man sounded like he was having a stroke! What happened between you two?"

"I just laid out my case, which he refused to listen to, and then I dropped the bomb that Johnson will be a no-show for trial."

"Yeah, he asked for confirmation on that. But that can't be what set him off. He's faced no-shows before. Part of the job."

"W-e-l-l." Sam laughed nervously. "I think he overplayed his hand a bit, thinking that because I'm a girl, and new to the felony game, he could get away with threatening my client."

"What kind of threat, Sam?"

"He said he'd play the old delay game to leave Andrea in jail for a while, and there was nothing I could do about it. You and I know both that could mean a year, maybe two."

"How could he pull off two years? I thought there was a speedy trial law, especially for inmates."

"In theory, that's true, Randy. But he could stretch it out until I filed for a speedy trial dismissal, then simply drop the existing indictment and replace it with a new charge, resetting the clock. And there are dozens of similar tricks. The gist of it is, if you're willing to be crooked and you have the power of the state behind you, you can pretty much get away with murder in these small Texas counties."

"Okay, I get it. But from the sound of it, that ploy didn't work out like he wanted it to. What did you do to piss him off?"

Sam laughed. "I simply taught him a little lesson about modern technology. I showed him that cell phones don't just make calls, anymore. They can also record conversations."

Randy whistled softly. "I'll bet that went over like a fart in a spacesuit."

"He was pretty steamed about it, for sure. But he knew I was right, that he doesn't really have a choice. What he threatened to do was illegal, and he knows it."

Randy was quiet for a moment. "I hear you, and I can't tell you how much I respect your standing up for the little guy against the machine. But this may wind up being a case where you won a battle but started a war."

"I've fought these same battles downstairs in the county attorney's office for over a year now, and in the end they just wound up respecting me and backing down. I know what I'm doing."

"But the county attorney is the junior varsity, Sam, and these guys are the pros. You can beat the misdemeanor guys because they play by the rules, and they don't have your brains and your work ethic. But it's just the opposite with the DA's office. They're hired specifically because they're willing to fight dirty. Do anything to win."

"I think I can hold my own with them, Randy."

"And that's where you're dead wrong. When I say they're dirty, I don't mean just pulling legal tricks, like Dubcek tried on you today. These guys are in deep with the police and the sheriff's department. They all have each other's backs. So Dubcek makes a call, and in a month or three you get pulled over for speeding, or failure to signal, or a tail light that's out. Cop says he smells 'the distinctive odor of marijuana emanating from your vehicle,' and initiates a spot search. Lo and behold, he 'finds' a joint and a bag of cocaine in the glove compartment or the middle console. You go to jail, and your license to practice law is old news."

"You're just being paranoid."

"Yeah? Tell that to Tyler Andrews, the last hot shot like you to stir up a hornets nest with these guys. You'll find him at the

Vance Unit down in Fort Bend County, near Houston. Didn't even let him be housed where his family could easily visit him. Not that his wife cares. She committed suicide right after the trial. I guess after what happened to her Sir Galahad, she just lost her faith in Camelot."

Sam drew a deep breath. Having lived in the big city for so long, she had always imagined life was much simpler in the sticks. Now it seemed like she may have miscalculated. "Okay, so what do I do about it? I can't play the game, it's just not in me. Somebody has to draw the line."

"I agree, Sam. And from what Evan says, nobody is better equipped than you to change things around here, to go toe to toe with those bastards. I just want to warn you about what you're getting into." Randy paused. "Look, I've got a friend who's into really sophisticated personal security technology. Car cams, home monitors, the whole enchilada. Let me give him a call, get him to set you up. He owes me, so he'll give it to you at cost. That way, if they try to pull any shit on you, you'll have a fighting chance at proving your innocence."

"Well, thanks. You're probably right. But I don't want to drag *you* into my battles."

"Trust me, Sam, I'm already there. Tyler was – is – one of my best friends. I loved his wife like a sister. Protecting you is the least thing I can do to honor her memory. Tell you what. Put a link to me on the front screen of your phone. You see anything suspicious, call me. You get pulled over by a cop, call me and set the phone to the side. My cell is set to record anything and everything that comes in. And I will move heaven and earth to get to you before they can screw up your life.”

“Do you really think that’s necessary?” Sam didn’t want to impose, but Randy was beginning to scare her.

“Let’s hope it isn’t, but make sure just in case it is. I let my buddy down. I don’t want to make that same mistake twice.”

“Okay, Randy. I’ll fix my phone, and wait for your friend to call. And… thanks. I’m kind of all alone these days, just me and Maddie. I appreciate someone watching out for us. I owe you big time.”

“You don’t owe me a thing, Sam. Just stay safe. I don’t want to have to attend another funeral, another failure. And, by the way, make sure to keep a close eye on your daughter. I wouldn’t put it past them to try to hurt you by getting to her. You have no idea what these guys are capable of.”

Sam was suddenly ice cold. She hadn’t even thought about Maddie, about what could happen to her little princess. “Oh my God,” she whispered under her breath, “what have I gotten us into?”

11

Sam found it completely by accident. She was Googling "Texas mens rea conjunctive," trying to find articles explaining the difference between "intentionally, knowingly *and* recklessly" and "intentionally, knowingly *or* recklessly." In the process she came across a blog written by a criminal lawyer from Houston that included several well-researched articles on the issue, all of which simply proved that Texas courts had not yet decided the issue.

But it was another post in the Houston attorney's blog that really caught her eye. A discussion of Texas Code of Criminal Procedure Article 21.15. After reading the article, Sam suddenly realized that she really knew very little about criminal law, at least when it came to defending clients charged with serious crimes. She was still very much what they call a "baby lawyer," and while she had a pretty good grasp of the Texas Penal Code, of *what* constituted a crime, she was completely hopeless when it came to the Code of Criminal Procedure, the handbook for exactly *how* the justice system worked. She had spent her career learning Civil Procedure, and her ignorance of criminal law might just cost her clients their freedom. It was time for her to buckle down and catch up. Before she ran out of time and made a critical mistake in a major case. She just felt lucky she had stumbled onto this one before it was too late.

And she couldn't help but feel that her luck was indeed beginning to run out. She'd had the dream again the night before. The dream where she was back in law school, and suddenly remembered that she had a final exam scheduled in a class she had forgotten about all semester. She raced down the hall and made it into the classroom just in time, but as she sank down into her seat she realized she didn't have a stitch of clothing on. She was sitting there completely naked, and everyone in the class was staring at her, laughing. That was how she was starting to feel every single day, now. Completely exposed, a fraud. Both as a mother and as a lawyer. She was trying to juggle both careers, but wasn't sure she could truly manage even one. Not that she really had a choice.

Sam checked the clock. Still enough time to swing by the jailhouse before lunch, then hopefully back home to draw up a motion to quash for Tanja and get it filed before the courthouse closed down for the day. She smiled to herself. At least this time she was lucky enough to pass the test. And, smiling even more broadly, she knew that this was really going to piss off the good old boys back at the DA's office.

12

Even dressed in the standard-issue oversized prison orange, Tanja Meadows was a striking young black woman. She was careful to keep her hair clean and pulled neatly back, showing off her flawless skin and sharp cheekbones. In any other setting she could have been a model. But the county had other plans.

"I hope I'm not keeping you from lunch, Tanja." Sam had almost no inkling of what life was like on the other side of the glass barrier separating her from Tanja. Her clients assured her that, for a jail, this one was fairly nice. At least the guards didn't make overt efforts to stir up trouble, and the inmates with mental health issues – generally about half the population – were carefully segregated and monitored.

"No, ma'am, I'm fine. It's Thursday, so my group had lunch early today. They rotate us through the dining area so we don't have too many people in there at one time. I guess the guards worry that we might turn dangerous, and use our plastic sporks on them. Or on each other."

Sam smiled at Tanja's ability to still manage a sense of humor, despite her circumstances. "Well good then. Look, I need to be pretty quick today. I stumbled upon a legal wrinkle that may help your case, and I want to get it written up and filed before the end of the day."

"A legal wrinkle?" Tanja was suddenly very interested. Unlike most inmates, who prided themselves on being experts in a form of street law that had little in common with actual legal practice, Tanja always struck Sam as amazingly bright and eager to learn. If she could ever find a way to bust Tanja out of jail on this case, Sam thought she might make a great low-cost legal assistant. And Tanja seemed to have a unique knack for finding the true diamonds in the great pile of filth called criminal law. Clients that actually deserved to be defended. "You got something for me to look at?"

Sam passed a single sheet of paper through the crack at the bottom of the glass screen. "It's Article 21.15 from the Texas Code of Criminal Procedure."

Tanja looked down at the sheet:

```
Art. 21.15. MUST ALLEGE ACTS OF
RECKLESSNESS        OR      CRIMINAL
NEGLIGENCE. Whenever recklessness
or criminal negligence enters into
or is a part or element of any
offense, or it is charged that the
accused acted recklessly or with
criminal   negligence    in    the
commission of an offense, the
complaint,    information,      or
indictment    in   order   to   be
```

sufficient in any such case must allege, with reasonable certainty, the act or acts relied upon to constitute recklessness or criminal negligence, and in no event shall it be sufficient to allege merely that the accused, in committing the offense, acted recklessly or with criminal negligence.

"Okay, I get it, Sam. But what does all this mean?"

"All right, to begin with, you and I have talked about the concept of mens rea, the guilty mind. Well, in your case the DA charged you with intentional, knowing and reckless conduct. The first two of those are fairly easy for jurors to understand, and they usually get those two right. In contrast, though, reckless is a real problem."

"Why's that?" Tanja asked, leaning forward intently.

"The first two require you to have some form of clear criminal intent, to take some action that is clearly wrong and dangerous. Reckless, on the other hand, is a fairly murky concept. And the legal definition of reckless is far different from the way we usually use the term."

Tanja considered that. "I would say reckless means not being careful when you should be. Not taking the right steps to make sure something bad doesn't happen."

"And you would be right about that, in the normal way that the word is used. But in the law, what you're describing is actually much closer to the mens rea we call criminal negligence. That you failed to exercise proper caution in what you were doing, and someone got hurt. For example, you were handling a loaded pistol and it went off accidentally, killing someone. The fact that it was pointed at someone when it discharged could be seen as negligent behavior, instead of just an accident."

"Okay, I get that. So what is reckless, then?"

Sam paused a moment to think about how to explain it. "Reckless is behavior that is much more dangerous. One of the best explanations I've heard is that a reckless person understands that what he is doing is dangerous, but continues to do it, anyway. One court said it shows that the defendant displayed an 'I don't give a damn' attitude. For example, driving erratically and at high speed without paying attention to the impact your driving might have on other cars and pedestrians."

"So reckless would be putting my car in reverse and then stomping on the pedal."

"Exactly, Tanja. And this law says, if you charge someone with reckless behavior, you have to spell out precisely how that behavior was reckless. You can't just claim the behavior was reckless because someone got hurt. The DA has to identify something else that, in fact, made it reckless."

"Okay, Sam, I think I understand. But what does that mean to my case?"

"It means they screwed up with the indictment, because they can't meet the requirements imposed on them by twenty-one fifteen. So by the end of the day I'll be filing a motion to quash the indictment, and we'll set it for a hearing the next week or so."

Tanja looked thoughtful. "I can see what you're getting at, but why does it matter? I have a blue warrant, so I can't get released. And if the judge dismisses this case, they'll just turn around and reindict me, fixing the language so it sticks."

"The reason it matters, Tanja, is that it forces them to prove up one more issue, an issue that is very important to our case." Sam glanced down at her copy of the code. "You see, it's kind of like poker. It forces the prosecutor's hand. He can't just vaguely state that you were acting recklessly, and then try to confuse the jury into going along with him. Believe me, that would be a big problem for us. A cop got hurt, and they're going to want to hang it all on you. So we need to nail the DA down on exactly what they claim you did wrong. We may still lose on that, but at least we've narrowed down what we have to defend. If we can establish reasonable doubt on that, then the jury can never get to knowing or intentional. This is the key to our case. This is our only possible path to a not guilty."

"I'll have to trust you on that. But, under any circumstance, I can't see where it could hurt us. As usual, you're thinking way outside the box. You can't know how much I appreciate you fighting so hard for me."

"My pleasure, Tanja. You know that. But now I have to scoot. I've got to get this written up and filed before the end of the day. Every day I delay is just another day you have to stay on that side of the glass. I'm burning daylight on this."

"Okay, but before you go, listen, I've got another client for you."

Sam was all ears. Most of the in-house "referrals" Tanja had sent her way wound up being pro bono, but they were all slam-dunk wins, and Sam could feel her confidence growing with every case. "Sure, Tanja. What you got?"

"A girl who's been in here a while. Her name is Cynthia Rollins. She's wanted on attempted murder, and assault with a deadly weapon." Tanja had a slip of paper with the contact information already scribbled on it in prison pencil, and passed it through the slot. "You know the routine. Her court-appointed left her in here for several months, and now he wants her to cop a plea. But he's talking eight years, and she needs to be out of here tomorrow if she can."

"Other than the usual reasons, why the hurry?"

Tanja had a pleading look in her eyes. "Look, Cindy's a single mother with two small boys. A friend is watching them now, but that can't go on forever. Pretty soon the state is gonna step in and grab them – send them off to foster care. And if she winds up taking the plea, that is guaranteed. So you're not just saving her, Sam. You're saving her kids. You know I've been in foster care, I know what it's like. You gotta do something for her."

Sam took a long moment to consider it. "I don't know. Attempted murder, assault. Those are pretty serious charges. What makes you think she's not guilty?"

"Because she's *not*. She's just being charged because she's poor and black. If some rich white guy did what she did, they'd pin a medal on him."

"Okay. I trust your judgment. But why don't you just tell me what happened and let me work out whether she was right or wrong."

Tanja nodded. "All right. Well, to start with, she was working as a night manager at a fast food joint over on Highway 12. It was her second job that day, she was working two jobs to pay the bills and try to get her family ahead a little. It was last Halloween night, around ten, and she was getting ready to shut down for the day and head home. Suddenly she got a call from her babysitter — the same friend who has her children right now —

telling her she thought someone had broken into Cindy's home. So Cindy races home, and when she gets there she finds her ex-boyfriend and some of his buddies clearing out her house, and putting all of her stuff in the trunks of their cars. She told me she did everything to stop them, but they just kept on loading up their cars like she wasn't even there. That's when she ran into the house and got her gun."

"She had a gun?" Sam felt this story was going south in a hurry. "Why would a single mother have a gun in the house with two young boys running around?"

"I don't know. I never asked her. But it's not all that unusual when you live in her part of town to keep something around for protection. *Especially* if you're a single mother."

"Okay, I'll buy that for now." Sam had a skeptical look on her face, and was taking notes on a legal pad she had pulled from her briefcase. "Go on. What happened next?"

"I'm not really sure of the details. When I talked to Cindy, she seemed a little confused herself. But I read a copy of the police report her court-appointed dropped off for her, and it said she fired the gun at her ex and his friends, trying to kill them. Some neighbors confirmed hearing gunshots. But the gun was never found, and Cindy says she never owned a gun, and never fired one that night."

"So what you're telling me is, her story's a little shaky." Not the first time a defendant did a little creative editing to try and save her skin. But it usually wound up hurting them more than helping. Honesty was always the best policy when you're talking with your lawyer. And silence was always the best policy when talking to the police.

"Well, she was pretty scared, and my take on it is she might be afraid to cop to the gun. It might not be legal, if you know what I mean. But the important thing is, she didn't shoot anyone, even though she was standing right next to all three of them."

Sam considered that. "So, I guess the next part of the story involves the police showing up on the scene to investigate the shots fired."

"Right. And the ex and his friends told the cops he was leaving her, and they were just moving his stuff out of the house when she came home and shot at them, tried to kill them. The ex claimed she said that if she couldn't have him, no one else would either. It was their word against hers, three to one. The cops handcuffed her immediately, then brought her over here to county and booked her."

"What happened to the ex and his friends?" Sam asked, even though she already knew the answer.

"When the babysitter checked on the house the next day, it was completely wiped out. They even took the baby's clothes and the crib."

On the surface, this case sounded like it was right up Sam's alley, but she still had serious reservations. "To be honest, Tanja, a lot of this story just doesn't add up. If what Cynthia told you is true, then what she did isn't a crime. The Castle Doctrine says you can shoot to kill in Texas if you find someone burglarizing your home, or even causing criminal mischief in the middle of the night on your property. In fact, just a few months ago, a farmer in Kerr County shot and killed a teenager who was doing donuts out in front of his house, and the sheriffs just interviewed the guy and closed the case. There's got to be more to this case than she's letting on."

"I hear you," Tanja agreed. "But I'm telling you, in this county there's one law for whites and another for blacks and browns. If you're black and you fire a gun for some reason, *any* reason, you're going away for a long time. That's the system. That's just how it works for folks like me. For folks like Cindy."

"Okay, I'll look into it. But I'm not promising anything." Sam looked down at the piece of paper that Tanja had slipped through the slot. "By the way, do you happen to know the name of her court-appointed?"

"Yeah," Tanja replied immediately. "He's that old dude, Charlie Bower, but inside the jail people just call him Rock the Boat."

13

Before meeting with Collins at the county jail, Sam knew she needed to take a peek at the DA's file on the case. The defense copy of that file was at Charlie Bower's office, so she made an appointment to meet with him in two days to review the case and decide whether she wanted to take it on.

In the meantime, she needed to draft the 21.15 motion and get it filed. But on the drive back home to pound that out, with the windows rolled down and singing along at the top of her voice to an old Vince Gill song, she had an epiphany. Maybe she shouldn't rush that filing, after all. Sometimes a little delay can be a good thing. After all, timing is everything.

14

With all of the new felony cases piling up, Sam knew she couldn't put it off any longer. She had to bite the bullet and hire an assistant.

Almost all of the "legal assistants" working for other criminal lawyers in the county were really not much more than glorified gofers, paid to keep track of cases and clients and run the occasional motion over to the Justice Center. But Sam needed something more, an assistant who could actually help her with legal research and draft motions and briefs. The problem was, that kind of legal talent just didn't exist anywhere in the county. Sam needed to look elsewhere. And she knew just where to start.

The drive over to Baylor Law School in Waco had been uneventful, and since school was in session and the parking lot was full to bursting, she decided to park her Volvo at the Mayborn Museum next door and walk over.

The law school was situated on the Brazos River, just across the river from the new Baylor Bears football stadium. At first glance, the Sheila and Walter Umphrey Law Center was architecturally striking, with red brick walls that clearly and intentionally connected the school to its Southern Baptist heritage. A sprawling courtyard separated two large three-story classrooms, attached along the back at the river's edge by a long two-story structure that held most of the law school's offices. Walking up to the school, Sam wasn't sure whether she felt attracted to the building or repelled. It held many memories for her, but very few of them were happy. Shrugging that feeling away, she headed straight to the office of the director of admissions and financial aid.

"Samantha! So good to see you again." Janice Ellis had seen her coming down the hall and met her at the door. "Come in to my office. Have a seat. Can I get you anything?"

Sam could barely stifle a laugh. Baylor had long been adamant that no food or drink other than bottled water could leave the small cafeteria tucked into the northeast corner of the building. That was one way to keep the facility spotless, and spotless appearances were very important at Baylor. "No, thanks, Ms. Ellis. I'm good."

"It's just Janice, now, Samantha," the director suggested. "And look at you! All grown up, with your own practice. And showing some *style*, girl!"

Sam had to admit that she had learned to pay more attention to her looks since leaving law school. Luke had been a big part of that, giving her a compelling reason every day to put an effort into looking nice. Like a girl, for a change. And now, with Maddie around, like a woman. "Well, yes, blue jeans and a T-shirt really don't cut it at this point in my life," she admitted. "And, as for having my own practice, well, as we discussed on the phone, that sword cuts both ways. I kind of have way more work than I can handle these days."

Janice had settled into her chair behind a massive mahogany desk. A picture window behind her provided a perfect panoramic view of the river and the new stadium. Sam wondered why she didn't move her desk around to take advantage of the view, instead of spending the day with her back to the window. "Well, maybe I can help you a bit with that problem," Janice offered. "But first, catch me up on what's going on in your life. Last I heard, you were setting the woods on fire in Houston chasing civil litigation. Now I hear you're involved in small-town criminal law. What in the world convinced you to make that switch?"

Quickly, and somewhat painfully, Sam outlined what had happened in her life since graduating from law school, dancing around the story of Luke's death as much as she could. It was all still too soon, too raw to share. Wrapping up, she brushed a stray hair from her eyes and leaned back in her chair. "So now I have a sweet little daughter, and my criminal practice is finally starting to take off. And, actually, living in a small town is a bit refreshing, in its own way. So innocent, really, so very different from the dog eat dog world of big cities like Houston. I find it all quite intriguing, fighting the good fight in a part of the state that still hasn't realized we've moved into the twenty-first century. Really, to be honest, I think they missed most of the last century, as well. So I seem to spend most of my days dragging them kicking and screaming into the reality of modern law. It's kind of funny – I walk into a courtroom with a stack of case law to support my arguments, just like I was taught, and the prosecutors just stare at me like I have two heads. And the judges are no different. I had a DWI case where the prosecutor objected that certain testimony was hearsay. When I responded that it was an exception to hearsay, the judge yelled 'There *are* no exceptions to hearsay!' I mean, what do you say to that?"

Janice was smiling and nodding. "I can't believe that still goes on. So what happened with that case?"

"There were dozens of judicial errors that the court of appeals would have had a field day with, so at the end of the trial, the prosecutor just handed me a dismissal and stalked out," Sam explained. "I don't think he had any interest in fighting my appeal, just to lose in the end and have to do it all over again in front of the same judge."

"Cut your losses and run. I must say, you've picked up a lot of patience since your law school days. I remember a Samantha Goldberg that would have sliced a courtroom to ribbons over such nonsense."

"Maybe I *have* finally grown up," Sam responded with a laugh. "But enough about me. You said over the phone that you might have a good candidate for my legal assistant opening. Or, at least for now, a promising intern."

"Right." Janice pulled out a file from a tall stack on her desk. "As you know, Samantha, financial aid covers a wide range of options. We have scholarships, like the one we gave you. The one you earned, I should say. But those are generally reserved for applicants who bring good numbers to the school. High GPAs and LSATs."

"Because those scores affect the school's overall rankings compared to other law schools."

"That's correct. It's an ugly situation, but those are the cards we're dealt. The problem is, sometimes a student misses out on a scholarship but shows real promise once he or she hits campus. They make great grades, but those grades don't show up in the rankings. So my office gets pressured to save the scholarship money for the numbers kids, and very little of it trickles down to the late bloomers."

"And so the late bloomers have to squeak by on student loans. I saw a lot of that when I was here. Kids walking out of graduation with two hundred grand in loans and no real way to pay them."

"Exactly. And the problem is only getting worse. So my office is trying to come up with creative ways to stretch our financial aid dollars, to target some money to the kids we think will best represent our Baylor values and reputation after graduation."

"So you think you've identified a top-tier student you can swing my way, and the money I'm paying can help her hold off on taking on so much debt."

"That's right," Janice answered. "But that's only half of it. In more ways than one." She pulled out a blank piece of paper and pushed it in front of Sam. "We've started a new program that helps augment the money that legal employers pay to their interns. It's pretty simple." Writing upside down, she spelled out "10 + 10 = 20" on the blank sheet of paper. "You pay a certain hourly salary to the intern, and we match it, up to ten dollars per hour. That means they end up getting paid a total of twenty per hour. During the school year we limit the match to twenty hours per week, to keep them focused on classes. During Christmas and summer break we kick that up to forty hours. I can go sixty if they are buried in a trial."

"That makes a lot of sense. Double your money, double your fun for everyone involved. And meanwhile the intern gains some valuable legal experience."

"That's the plan, Samantha." Janice leaned back in her chair. "So, what do you think? Interested?"

"I must say I like the financial game, but the key question is still the person playing that game."

"I think that's the best part, at least for you." Janice pushed a resume and photo across the desk. "His name is Harrison Crawford, Harry for short. He has a sister who's a lawyer, went to UT, I think, and helps him out with some of his bills. We've cut him some slack on tuition his second year, based upon his performance the first year. No grade less than an A, and top scores in most of his classes."

Sam was impressed. "So what's the deal? Does he look like Quasimodo or something? Why isn't he being picked up by the big firms?"

Janice nodded. "It's because he's damaged goods. First off, he's a little older than usual. He worked for a few years before applying to law school."

"Okay," Sam replied. "Not a problem for me, but I understand the age issue with the big law firms. They like their meat fresh so they can pound them flat with no push back. Been there, done that. What else?"

Janice leaned forward suggestively. "Something *really* bad. He likes criminal law."

"Ah," Sam noted. "Quasimodo, indeed. So the kid's got brains off the charts, but none of the big firms want to play in the criminal law cesspool. I get it now. There's no money in criminal. Or at least, no big money. So they avoid criminal law like the plague."

"And on top of that, almost all of the criminal law firms are lone wolves. One wolf per firm. But lots of low-cost research assistants and gofers."

So it isn't just my little neck of the woods, Sam thought. "Okay, you've piqued my interest. Where do we go from here?"

Janice pointed to the resume. "His contact info is all there. Touch base with him, see if he's a match. We have interview rooms here, if you'd like, or you can meet him at your office, or wherever. Just give me a buzz and let me know what you think." She paused, turning to look directly into Sam's eyes. "I like this guy, Samantha. I think he can make a real impact for you, if you give him a chance. He just seems like the perfect match for your needs."

Sam glanced down at the photo. Something about him looked familiar, but she couldn't quite place it. "What have I got to lose?"

<h1 style="text-align:center">15</h1>

Charlie Bower's office was downtown, on Main Street. Maybe at one point it had been impressive, Sam thought, walking up to the entrance, but now it just looked depressing. Kind of like Charlie. She turned the knob on the front door and thought at first the door was locked, but a vigorous shove kicked it open and Sam stepped into the anteroom.

Peeling yellow linoleum covered the floor, and a nondescript brown desk swallowed most of the room. Behind the desk sat a grossly obese woman with stringy gray hair, intently engaged in a game of solitaire on a ten-year-old CRT computer display. A haze of old smoke hung in the air. "Solitaire" seemed put out at having been interrupted.

"Yeah. What do you want?" A cigarette butt was smoldering down to the filter in a glass ashtray to the woman's right.

"I have an appointment with Mr. Bower."

"He's running late. Have a seat." Solitaire indicated one of the threadbare side chairs shoved to the right side of the room.

Sam shot a look at the cigarette, which had just given up the fight with the filter. "You know, it's such a nice day. I'll wait for him outside, if you don't mind."

"Suit yerself, sugar. He's sleeping one off, most likely, so I'd find somewhere to cool your heels if I were you. Could be a while."

Sam sat down on a wooden bench outside and started checking her e-mails on her tablet. Thirty minutes went by before she finally spotted her target shuffling down the street toward her, still a block away. A rotund old man in a tight brown suit. A suit that looked like it was about to give up the fight. "Charlie!" She stood up and waved to him, then walked down the street to meet him halfway.

"Sorry," he muttered. "I… got tied up."

"No need to apologize. Let's go inside and see what we can do to get Ms. Collins a fair shake." They walked together to the front door of his office. She shoved it open and motioned him inside. Solitaire barely looked up as they brushed past her on the way to Bower's private office.

Sam had never seen so much clutter in her entire life. She wondered how Charlie ever got anything done, surrounded by all this mess. Then she remembered that getting things done wasn't really Bower's forte. More like getting things buried. She moved some files off a chair and sat down, opening her briefcase to pull out a notepad.

"I don't want to eat up too much of your time, Mr. Bower. I know you've got that triple murder to deal with, so if you don't mind, let's get down to business." Bower slumped down in his desk chair with a loud 'oomph.' "As I told you on the phone, I've been asked to represent Cynthia Rollins in her assault case. Before I take that on, however, I wanted to find out what I was getting into. Whether there were some hidden alligators in the water I should know about."

Bower rubbed a reddened, fleshy hand across his mouth. "Yeah, well, I don't know why you're trying to jump into her case at this point. I've got her all set up to plead out next Friday morning."

"Right. Eight years straight up." Sam was wondering whether Bower could even find the Rollins file in all this chaos.

"Best deal I could get. Frank wanted fifteen to twenty, but I jewed him down to less than half that."

Sam ignored the racial slur, knowing that ignorant old Southern men like Bower probably never even put a thought into the real meaning of what came out of their mouths. "I get that. For what she did, that's probably a great resolution to the case. But I've been asked to look into it, so I was just wondering if I could get a peek at the file. See if there is anything in there that I should care about."

"Sure, if you want to waste your time..." Bower pulled himself up and lumbered over to a four-drawer file cabinet, gray but with the paint beginning to flake off with age. Like Bower himself. He pulled out the second drawer from the top. "Should be in here…" It took over a minute for him to slowly thumb through the files, stuffed tightly into the drawer like sardines in a tin can. "Ah. Found it." He pulled out a thick manila folder and brought it over, dropping it onto the desk in front of her. She immediately snapped it up and starting speed-reading through the police reports.

"Girl tried to kill her boyfriend and a bunch of his buddies," Bower explained, waving his hands for emphasis. "She's lucky they didn't load her up with attempted murder. Hell, for that matter, if she'd been any kind of a shot, she'd probably be sitting there for murder one." He plopped back down into his chair.

In stark contrast to Bower's view of the case, Sam couldn't find anything that conflicted with a basic Castle Doctrine defense of home scenario. Late at night. Check. Taking things from her home. Check. Wouldn't stop when she told them to. Check. Other than the fact that she was black and a woman, this case should have never been filed. Tanja was right. And Bower clearly didn't realize that his client *had* in fact been charged with attempted murder. Just more proof to Sam that he wasn't really paying any attention to the case.

"You know, Mr. Bower, you've been at this a lot longer than I have, so you're probably right about eight years being a sweet deal. But, to tell you the truth, I really need the experience, and the DA has already signed off on the deal, so if you don't mind, I think this is one I would like to sub in on. Plus, I know you're pretty busy with that triple murder case –"

"If that's what you want, then I'm not going to stop you. But, look here, I've already got a lot of time invested in this case." Bower was pointing at the case file with his fat and stubby right index finger. "You remind your girl that, no matter what happens, I still get my court-appointed fees."

"Sure, Mr. Bower," Sam replied. "That will just come out of her eight years, anyway, so the county will pay that out to you, no problem. But do you mind if I keep the file for now?"

"Nah, keep it. Although you won't find anything in there that will help you. It's pretty cut and dried at this point." Bower paused. "Oh, one other thing."

"Yes," Sam answered, already tucking the file into her briefcase and standing up to leave.

"That girl is a big liar. You can't trust her a minute. She won't even admit to having a gun that night, and the cops have five witnesses that say she shot it." Bower wasn't making any effort to stand and see her out. "You been doing this as long as I have, you lose that girlish enthusiasm over your clients pretty quickly. They all say they're innocent, but the truth is, they're all guilty, every one of them. If they didn't do this, then they did something else. Probably something much worse. So don't go feeling all sorry for them. They chose to be lowlifes, it's the world they live in. Just don't make the mistake of crawling down into that gutter with them."

"I'll try to remember that, Mr. Bower." Sam waved sweetly at him and headed quickly for the door. "Thanks again for the file."

16

Based upon how he sounded over the phone, Sam expected Huber Kennedy to be a big fellow, and was surprised when she was escorted to his office in the DA rat maze to find that he was actually pretty tiny. He stayed seated as she entered his office, but Sam's initial guess was that he couldn't be any taller than five foot four. Including the risers in his shoes. That could be a real problem, she thought as she took a seat in front of him. Little guys often tried to play extra tough to compensate. The old Napoleon complex.

"Mr. Kennedy! Nice to finally meet you in person." The desk was too wide to try and reach across to shake hands, so Sam didn't try.

"Sure. What you got?"

"Right. Let's get straight to business." Sam took an immediate dislike to the guy, but tried not to show it as she pulled out her notes for the meeting. "As I mentioned, I've subbed in on the Cynthia Rollins case, and I just have a few questions for you. See if there is something to this case that I'm missing."

"Seems pretty straight forward to me," Kennedy responded, slumping back in his chair arrogantly. "Girl comes home, finds boyfriend moving out. Decides that if she can't have him, no one else will, so she opens fire. Open and shut case. What's to discuss?"

Once again, Sam was astonished at the way prosecutors saw the world. Even the most innocent thing to them always seemed to translate into a crime. "I can see your point of view on this," she said. "But here's the thing. When I read through the file, I kept wondering what part of the case didn't fit the old Castle Doctrine defense. Girl comes home late at night to find an ex boyfriend and his amigos pilfering her stuff. She can't get them to stop, so she fires a gun in the air to get their attention. Which worked, because when she fired the gun they all took off running."

"Who's saying he was an ex?" Kennedy shot her a condescending look. "My take on it is, she's a clinging vine and he just decides it's time to move on. Time to be free. She's a big drama queen, so he does the smart thing and waits for her to be stuck at work to make his move. Happens all the time."

Sam shook her head, exasperated. "But you've got several witnesses that say they broke up months before."

"People move out, people move in. The heart is fickle. If he wasn't living with her at the time, then why was his stuff still there? Does that make any sense to you?"

"Who says any of that was his stuff? And for that matter, some of what they packed into those cars were clothes for the baby. How in the world can you say the baby clothes were his?"

"Maybe he paid for them and decided to take them back. Or maybe he didn't take the clothes in the first place. We don't have a complete inventory of what was in those cars. So it's just your girl's word against the police. And I'm going to take the word of a police officer against a crazy woman every day of the week."

"So you're saying a young black mother has no right to defend her home, but old white men can shoot people dead in their front yards and everyone just looks the other way."

"No, what I'm saying is, people shouldn't be trying to take the law into their own hands." Kennedy leaned forward, both palms flat on his desk. "It's as simple as this. If she thought she was being robbed, then she should have called 911 and let the police handle it. But shooting at people with a gun, I'm not going to let that slide. We've got a basic rule around here. Show a gun, you get two years. Fire a gun, five to ten. Shoot someone, then you get the long ride."

"Well, then, I guess that means we're at an impasse. We'll just have to set this one for trial."

"You do that, Ms. Tulley. But before you make that call, you better have a long heart to heart with your client. After all, you're not the one who's going to do the time for this. She is. And the bottom line is, she either takes the deal and pleas out on Friday, or the deal's off and we'll push for the whole enchilada.

Twenty years. You have a couple of days to think that over. See you on Friday. You know the way out."

17

The telephone interview had gone very well, so now all that was left was a face-to-face meeting to consummate the deal. Harry showed up a few minutes early, which Sam took as a good sign. Her law school professors had always emphasized that she should *never* be late for a court appearance, and they felt the best way to establish that habit was to never be late for class. Late meant absent, and every unexcused absence translated into a letter grade reduction at the end of the semester. Sam remembered Janice Ellis' comment that Harry had never made less than an A in any of his classes. That meant he had never been late once in three semesters of law school.

"Come on in." Sam steered Harry into the entryway and back toward her office, Barley tagging along beside them. "You've had a long drive. Can I get you something?"

"No, thank you. I had a Diet Coke in the car on the way over." He stopped for a moment and gazed around the living room. "Wow. This place is amazing. It reminds me a lot of pictures I've seen of the house my parents lived in about the time I was born."

Sam nodded. "It is *large*, I'll grant you that. But a little *too* large for just the two of us, my daughter and me. It was built by a railroad baron in the early part of the last century, back when this area was one of the major hubs for the railroads in Texas. He took advantage of free shipping on the rail lines to bring in materials you couldn't otherwise buy back then, including an honest-to-God Otis elevator, a real life saver for a three story house, plus a humongous dumbwaiter in the kitchen to move stuff like clothes and food up and down, so you don't have to haul it all up by hand. And the view from the third floor terrace is to die for. Unfortunately, the realtors around here say there's no market for mansions these days, and hasn't been for a very long time. So in the end we're kind of stuck with it. I guess the only other alternative would be to burn it down."

"Oh, don't say that! That would be a real crime. They just don't make grand houses like this anymore."

"Well, one way I try to make it more livable is by hiding away in some of the smaller rooms." Sam opened the door into her study. "This is one of my favorites. Nice and cozy, and it even has a fireplace with gas logs. Barley here loves to curl up in front of the fire and snooze." Hearing his name, Barley looked up with a small 'woof.' "Why don't you grab a seat on the couch, and I'll grab a chair and we can talk a bit."

Once they were settled, Sam started the conversation off by explaining a little more about the job. "The biggest things I need right now are legal research and help with some of my briefs. Unlike most of the criminal lawyers around here, I like to build my legal fights on a solid foundation of case law. But researching the law is eating up a massive amount of my time. Some days I get started looking up cases on Westlaw and suddenly realize most of the day has slipped away."

"I'm pretty good with all that, Ms. Tulley. As you can tell from my transcript, I got top marks in my legal writing class, including training on Westlaw and several of the other research tools." He glanced around at the piles of paperwork and files that were beginning to clutter up her office. "By the way, from the looks of things, I get the impression that you haven't gone to digital filing."

"No, I've been meaning to but something always seems to get higher priority…"

"Okay, I can definitely get going on helping you organize. But that may have to wait until June. Right now I'm heading into finals and can't spare that much time."

"I'm glad you brought that up, Harry. In addition to working out *what* you'll be doing, we need to decide *where* you'll be doing it. My thought is, as long as we're just talking research and writing, you can do that from school, and we can conference on Skype. You keep track of your hours, and I'll trust you to be honest. How does that sound?"

"That would work out great, Ms. Tulley."

"And, while we're on *that* subject, you should just call me Sam. Except in the courtroom, where everybody gets a little more formal about names."

"That works for me. Sam it is. So, if you don't mind, I also have a question for you."

"Fire away."

"After finals are over I'll be free to work all summer, since I'm not signing up for summer classes. That means I'll be available full time, but from what we discussed over the phone I'm not sure there will be enough research and writing to keep me busy. I'd love to come here and put in some hours organizing your office and, ideally, getting involved in your cases and trials, but there is the distance problem."

"You mean the daily drive back and forth from Waco."

"Exactly. I mean, I'm not one to complain about the twenty dollars an hour, but I don't know if my old truck can handle the wear and tear of such a long commute, and on one sixty a day minus taxes, I'm not sure I can afford to rent an apartment here. I'm stuck with the one I have in Waco, because all the apartment complexes force students to take on a full year lease. So paying for two places might be a bit of a stretch."

Sam nodded, smiling. "I know what you mean, and I think I might have just the solution." She glanced down at his resume.

"You and I are not that different age-wise, so it wouldn't do for you to stay inside the main house. People would start talking, and although I don't give a hoot, it might cause problems for Maddie when she gets older. Gossip dies very slowly in these small towns. On top of that, I *am* your employer –"

"I agree with all of that."

"That being said, I do have a guest house out back that is fully furnished and has its own private access to the kitchen. My husband and I fixed it up for my parents, but it turns out they prefer to stay in the main house when they visit, closer to my daughter. You could stay out there as much as you want, and either join us for meals or make your own meals. However that works out. The place is completely private, so you could come and go as you wish. You could even have a *guest* over every now and then –"

"That sounds perfect, Sam. This job is starting to sound better and better! But as far as the guest thing goes, unless something miraculous happens over the next few weeks, that won't be an issue. I broke up with my girlfriend at the beginning of this semester, and I'm just too darn busy with school to worry about it right now. Lots of time for that later."

Sam nodded. "I took pretty much the same path in law school, focusing on my grades and not on my love life. Though, to be fair, by the time I was your age I was already married and had a kid. It's amazing how life can somehow sneak up and upset all of your carefully laid plans." She paused thoughtfully. "Well, it's settled, then. As far as I'm concerned, you're hired. I'll start sending you work right away, and you can somehow squeeze it in to your studying for finals. In the meantime, do you have any more questions for me?"

"Well, one right off. It's actually just a bit of a personal question. After we talked on the phone, I decided to Facebook stalk you a bit to get some background info on who you were, and I saw on your LinkedIn page that you worked at Truman Walker for several years."

"That's right. I started there right after my clerkship on the Supreme Court, and stayed on with them until my husband stumbled into his dream job out here."

"Okay, so I was just wondering if you knew my sister, who worked there at about the same time. Hailey Crawford."

Suddenly Sam knew exactly why Harry looked so familiar. "Hailey! Of course! She was one of my bridesmaids. In fact, Hailey was the reason I met my husband. She lured me to a birthday party at a bar in Houston, and he turned out to be the birthday boy. Wound up sweeping me off my feet, the bastard. What a small world!"

"Oh, then you must…" Harry's voice dropped off, suddenly embarrassed.

"What were you going to ask me, Harry? It's okay. What is it?"

"Well, Hailey told me a while back she had a friend who had lost her husband in a car accident… and then you said you live here alone with your daughter…"

Sam nodded. "It's been over a year now, Harry, and I'm past it already. Or almost past it. But let's talk about happier things. Hailey always said she had a younger brother, but by my calculations you two are pretty much the same age. How does that work?"

Harry relaxed, feeling better about his earlier faux pas. "That 's kind of an inside joke between us, actually. We're twins. Fraternal, obviously. She beat me out into the world by a matter of minutes, so ever since then she made sure everyone knew she was the older, wiser sister."

"Didn't you two have some kind of plan to help each other pay for school? I seem to recall Hailey saying something about that…"

"As a matter of fact, we did. My family was pretty rich when I was born, but something happened and it all fell apart. We lost our house in Dallas and had to move to a smaller place near Austin. My parents helped us out through undergrad, and we both went to UT, so we minimized our living costs, but there just wasn't enough left over for law school. Hailey and I didn't want to graduate with a massive debt load on our backs, so I got a job designing web pages and helped pay for her to get through law school. When she got the job at Truman Walker, it was my turn."

"Wow. That's a really sweet story."

"I guess it's just part of being twins. We're a lot closer than your average brother and sister."

"Isn't she still at Truman?" Sam had been busy lately and was falling behind on keeping up with old friends, but she seemed to recall a Facebook or LinkedIn posting of Hailey getting a big promotion from the firm.

"Yeah, in fact, she's on track for full partner status. She'll wind up making all the money in the family, and I'll have to learn how to get by on peanuts. But my Dad survived without money, and he and Mom are pretty happy together, so I guess I'll be fine, too."

"You mentioned you were originally from Dallas. I seem to remember hearing about that from Hailey, although I always pictured her as more of an Austin kind of girl. A little more down to earth than the Dallas types." Sam looked thoughtful. Getting together with Harry to discuss the new job had started out pretty routine but had suddenly taken a sharp left turn. "That big house you mentioned. Where was that in Dallas? Preston Hollow, maybe?"

"No. Highland Park. On Oak Tree Lane."

It hit Sam like a swift blow to the head. Crawford. "Tell me it's not 300 Oak Tree Lane."

"Why, yes," Harry agreed. "Have you seen it? It's pretty famous, even by Highland Park standards."

"Yes, I have," Sam replied slowly. She was about to open up a very dark and dangerous door. "William Tulley lives there now."

"William Tulley? He's the son of a bitch who –" Suddenly Sam could see it all click in Harry's mind. "You're a Tulley…"

"My husband was. Luke Tulley, William's son."

"Oh my God!" Harry's right hand darted straight to his mouth, his eyes dancing about wildly. "He completely destroyed my family, stole my father's company. Our *house!* "

"Harry, he did pretty much the same thing to us." Sam swung over to the couch and sat beside him, trying to think of a way to work through what they had both just discovered. "William Tulley is a wrecking ball that has swung through a great many lives. He's an evil man, the very essence of evil. I can assure you my husband wanted nothing to do with his father by the time he died. Luke hadn't even spoken to him since well before our marriage."

"Can I ask why?" Harry was watching her face with a wary look.

"Well, it's pretty complicated, but I guess it's something we both need to deal with, if we're going to wind up working together." Sam glanced across the room at a small portrait of her husband she kept in a silver frame on her desk. "So, to start with, I grew up Jewish. Not that I'm all that religious. Kind of like a lot of Christians who only go to church on Christmas and Easter. But yeah, it's my heritage, it's a big part of who I am. Of what I am." She paused, turning back to face Harry. "Luke, on the other hand, was raised Catholic. And not just Catholic lite. He got the whole freaking enchilada shoved down his throat."

Harry looked bewildered. "But didn't Vatican II make that alright? I mean, Jews and Catholics getting married?"

Sam shook her head. "Well, yes and no. But that wasn't really the problem. You see, Luke's family didn't acknowledge Vatican II. Or any of the other church reforms, for that matter. Their take on Christianity was very different from mainstream Catholicism."

"You mean like Protestants? Seven thousand ways to worship God, and only one of those ways will get you to heaven?"

"Not exactly, Harry, but close. You see, the way Luke explained it to me, most people think of the Catholic faith as one monolithic entity, all run from Rome. But that really isn't how it works. Just like with Protestants, or even Judaism, there are smaller subsets of the overarching religion. Almost all of them clustered on the radical conservative side."

"Right, like the Jews with the crazy hair up in New York City."

"Yeah, something like that. Anyway, apparently, in Catholicism, there's a rapidly growing radical group called the Catholic Traditionalist movement that, among other things, rejects the reforms of the Second Vatican Council and the abolition of the Latin Mass. That crazy action movie star who got arrested spewing anti-Semitic nonsense is a prominent leader of that movement, or, to be accurate, of an even more radical subset, the 'sedevacantist' movement. That word comes from a Latin phrase meaning 'empty seat' – they believe the Pope isn't the legitimate heir to the papacy, and hasn't been so since around 1960. That actor's father is even more extreme, and believes that the Church in Rome has been taken over by some weird coalition of Jews and Freemasons acting under the orders of Satan. He even once claimed in a radio interview that there were never any Nazi extermination camps, that the Jews just got up and left Germany and then spread throughout the world. Apparently following Satan's orders. Luke told me that his father had become a big believer in all of that. A leader of the movement, not just a follower. He sees Jews as being the henchmen of Satan, sent to destroy the only true Christian faith."

Harry was looking even more confused. "So how did that work out between you and your husband? Did he believe any of that? And how could you get along if he did?"

Sam smiled. "Nah, he thought it was all just a bunch of horse shit. But no matter how hard Luke tried, he could never win his father over to the idea of our getting married. And the problem just seemed to get bigger over time. When he found out that Luke defied his demands and married me anyway, then again when our daughter was born. And all of that came to a roaring climax after Luke's accident, during the funeral. I really can't repeat any of the nasty things that came out of his mouth that day, the filthy things he had to say about me, and about Maddie. Right to my face. If my father hadn't been there to come to my defense, I honestly don't know what I would have done. Even then, heaped on top of losing Luke so suddenly, so horribly, I completely lost it. I had a nervous breakdown of sorts, buried myself in my room and didn't come out for almost two months. If it hadn't been for all the love my parents showered on me at the time, I might never have emerged from that."

"Ms. Tulley... Sam... I'm so sorry. Did... have things gotten any better between you and the Tulleys?"

"No, Harry, they haven't. William Tulley has made it clear that Maddie and I are not ever going to be a part of his family. And I'm okay with that. Some kinds of evil... just can't be forgiven.

And I don't want Maddie to grow up exposed to that kind of hate. She never really got a chance to know her father, and I don't want her ever thinking that Luke was anything like William Tulley. Or like Luke's sister, for that matter. Evidently they are just two peas in a pod."

"So you've met all of them?" Harry had become very quiet.

"Yes, once before we got married, and then once more at the funeral. And believe me, that was enough. More than enough. I'm just amazed Luke ever emerged from that world."

"What about his mother? Is she a part of all that?"

"No, not at all. She's very much the opposite. She divorced William Tulley soon after they moved into the mansion. Your family's old house. Took the kids and moved home to her family in Italy."

"That makes sense," Harry said. "My mom once told me that she and Margaret Tulley were best friends, that our two families did everything together – holidays, vacations, everything. But that was before William Tulley swindled my father out of his half of the company, his half of Tulley Crawford. And then managed to get control of the mortgage on our house. He quite literally kicked us into the street and moved his own family in. I guess your husband would have been a part of that."

Sam nodded. "He moved in with his parents, but I wouldn't say he was a part of it. He was just a little boy at the time, the same as you."

"No, I get it. I'm fine with that." Harry looked away, still seeming to be struggling with taking it all in. "But, Sam, I guess the thing about it is, when everything collapsed back then, so did my Dad. He started drinking. Heavily. Mom had to work two jobs just to keep us afloat, because he kept getting fired from every job he could land. Because of his drinking. Then one day he just... stopped. He joined an AA group, and started pulling himself back together."

"How is he now?" Sam asked softly.

"He's in pretty good shape, considering. He got a job overseeing some major construction projects and morphed that into his own business. With no partners, this time. He's finally starting to pull ahead financially. And, even more important, he and Mom are still deeply in love. I think the strain of what they went through may have somehow made their love even stronger."

Sam knew what that felt like. "My parents had a similar experience. For them it was my baby brother, who died a few days after his birth. It's been a long path for them, but I think they've finally made it through to the other side. As I said before, I know I wouldn't have survived my husband's death – and the thing with the Tulleys – without all of the love Mom and Dad had in store for me." She smiled at him wryly. "Very few of us are lucky enough to get through life without taking on collateral damage, without experiencing the painful fact that life can sometimes be totally unfair. But there's nothing we can do about that, so in the end it doesn't matter. What matters is what we do going forward, how we channel our pain into something positive." She rubbed at a tear that was threatening to escape. "For me, part of that is the impact I have on my clients' lives, trying every day to save them from a *justice* system that can be extremely cruel and extremely unjust. Just like the Tulleys. I have to be strong for them, and in the process I've discovered an inner strength in myself. So maybe that's why you're here today, Harry. What little I know of you, it seems there's something about criminal law that stirs your soul, that gives your life meaning and direction." She paused to give him a curious look. "I'll tell you what. Why don't we head down that path together, at least for this summer. I could certainly use a fresh face around here, a little raw innocence. I'm starting to feel like I'm becoming a part of the whole dirty system, in a way. Like I've given up some big chunk of my old Fort Worth values. And of the things I shared with Luke."

Harry turned to face her, and she saw that his eyes had reddened, too. "Lose your values? From what I've heard today, there's a fat chance of that." He brushed his curly brown hair back and looked down at his hands, pensive. "Sam, the thing is, I've never told anyone before today how I truly felt about Tulley, about all the anger. Not even Mom and Dad, who I suppose must be holding in some level of anger and frustration that makes mine look like nothing. But you're right, it feels good to let it out, to walk away from all that. And I just want you to know I feel truly blessed to have this job. Even if it only lasts a summer. To be realistic, I don't know a whole lot about criminal law, other than the handful of classes I've taken. But I'm ready to learn."

"I can't say I'm much further down that road than you are, Harry. But it will be fun to learn together, to have someone to make mistakes with. To share victories with."

Harry glanced away for a moment, nodding to himself. After a moment he looked back, a big smile showing on his face. "Hey, Sam, I just had the craziest idea. If this works out between us, maybe we could wind up as law partners. You and I are – were – both at the top of our classes. As partners, we would be totally unstoppable!"

Sam answered with a crooked grin of her own. "Not a bad idea, Harry. It'd be Tulley Crawford all over again."

"Nope," he corrected her, playfully wagging his finger. "This time it's gonna be Crawford Tulley. We go alphabetically. And I get to hold the mortgage on the house!"

"As I already told you,," Sam responded with a laugh. "You want this old ball and chain, you can have it. Good riddance! I'll have the paperwork to you in the morning."

18

After her fruitless meeting with Huber Kennedy on the Rollins case, Sam had no choice but to set it for trial. Even if by some crazy measure she lost, the worst punishment Rollins could expect given the facts of the case would be some form of probation. Cynthia could keep her kids and get on with her life. Taking an eight year deal would throw both of those away for good.

Besides, it was a gun case, tried in the gun-loving Bible Belt of Texas. Sam sometimes thought these people loved guns more than they loved God. She just needed to play up the Second Amendment angle, and there was no way at least one of the twelve jurors wouldn't hold out for acquittal.

In the meantime, she had a trial to run. It was a silly little criminal trespass misdemeanor, and the plea offer she had negotiated was more than fair, but her client insisted he was innocent and wanted to tell his story to the world. Or at least to six jurors, a judge and anyone else bored enough to wander into the courtroom.

According to Russell Taylor, his girlfriend got pissed at him because he was drunk very early on a Sunday morning. It wasn't that he had *started* drinking early that morning, he just hadn't stopped from the night before. So she called the cops and had him thrown out. Then, later in the day, she called him on his cell phone and told him she loved him, she was sorry she called the cops, please come back home so they can talk. And that's exactly what he did. But when he got there, she secretly called the police on him again and had him arrested. That story might have seemed a bit fishy, other than the fact that Sam had seen it repeated at least a dozen times since she had started practicing criminal law. And it was always the women who pulled it on their boyfriends, almost never the other way around.

The real key to the case, though, was the fact that Taylor insisted that he was back together with the old girlfriend. Now she wanted to drop the charges, but the county attorney refused to go along. The trial was moving forward, but up to this point the girlfriend had managed to dodge the subpoenas. The "victim" was going to be a no-show at the trial. As a result, on the very first day of trial Sam managed to throw a wrench into the state's case by getting the arresting officers to admit that they never checked the girlfriend's ID, so they couldn't be sure she had any legal right to ban Taylor from the house.

Walking into court the next morning, Sam saw that Sanders, the prosecutor, had already arrived. Seated behind him in the audience gallery was a mousy looking middle-aged man in a cheap, ill fitting brown suit. *Who the heck is that?* she wondered as she started to unload her trial box. Sanders stood up and walked over, dropping a photograph onto the table in front of her. "Her driver's license," he muttered, returning to his place at the prosecution table.

Sam examined the photo closely. She had never met the mystery lady, nor had she ever seen any pictures of her, so this was the first time she could put a face to the person at the center of the trial. She held up the picture so her client could see it. "This her?" she asked in a low voice.

"Yeah," Taylor answered. "That's her."

Sam went back to studying the photo. She assumed the man in the audience was there to authenticate the picture. That meant Sanders had called someone at the DPS in Austin after hours the night before and arranged for the picture to be copied from the driver's license database, and for this guy to drive it up from Austin very early this morning. She considered, not for the first time, the vast discrepancy between the resources employed by the state and the resources that were available to her. Even ignoring the fact that the DPS would never had responded so quickly to a request from her, Sanders had thousands of dollars in taxpayer money he could direct toward winning his case. She just had her court-appointed fee, plus any extra money the judge might approve for exhibits, investigators and expert witnesses. Extra money that was rarely, if ever, approved.

But the photo held one big surprise. The address listed on the license was not the house on West Eighth Street where her client had been banned and later arrested. It was actually just a few doors down from Sam's own house. Now that she thought about it, Sam remembered seeing this woman in the neighborhood. Along with a husband and three kids. No wonder she was fighting so desperately to steer clear of this trial. It wasn't about helping out her boyfriend. It was about not making a public record of her infidelity that could be used against her in a divorce. Sam signaled to Sanders that they needed to talk, and they both headed to the back of the courtroom.

"You ready to deal on this?" he asked.

Sam smiled at his arrogance. "Sure. I assume you're bringing the cop back to prove up the fact that you now have a solid ID on the woman."

"Yep. So now you're nailed seven ways to Sunday. What's your offer?"

Sanders was smiling like a Cheshire cat. Sam grinned back. "How about you give me a dismissal, and in return I let you keep your dignity."

The smiled faded. "What do you mean, a dismissal? You're boxed in on this. I was thinking maybe probation –"

"And that would be wishful thinking." Sam handed him her copy of the driver's license photo. "Check out the address on the ID. She doesn't live on Eighth Street. As a matter of fact, she's my neighbor. Happily married, or close enough, I suppose. Drives a BMW station wagon, just roomy enough for hauling the three kids to soccer practice."

Sanders looked at her like his breakfast has suddenly gone bad. "Are you shittin' me on this?"

Sam nodded across the room toward her client. "He don't look like much, but for her I guess it was enough. Who can understand the mysteries of love?"

Sanders gave her a long, hard look, then finally mumbled something about a dismissal and stalked out of the courtroom to gather the forms. Fifteen minutes later the judge was releasing the jurors and Sam was packing up and heading out the door herself.

Even though the case had been about a relatively minor crime, Sam still felt the glow of victory as she left the courtroom, her trial box clasped before her in both arms and her client trailing along behind. She was just congratulating him when she saw Evan Murphy striding down the hall.

"Sam! How'd it go?" His booming voice carried all the way down the hall.

"Still the undefeated champion."

He finally caught up to her. "Boy, I wish I could say that," he noted admiringly. "Hey, I heard through the grapevine you've got a big trial coming up in the felony courts. How did you manage to shag that?"

Sam waved it off. "Just a referral from one of my clients. Charlie Bower had the case and was botching it up as usual, so I just took it off his hands."

"Bower? He was taking it to trial?"

"Nah, he was pushing for a plea deal, and a really bad one at that. But once he realized I wasn't asking for any of his court-appointed money, he dropped it like a hot potato."

Evan nodded. "I guess he needs every spare moment he can get these days, boning up on his lines for the Jordan trial."

"The Jordan trial?" Sam looked confused. "They're really going to take that nasty thing to trial? I thought for sure they'd just plea it out for life no parole. Why in the world would they put everyone through that awful mess? Didn't I read something about her parents? Why would they want to relive any of that?"

"Yeah, her parents live out on a nice little farm just south of town, the one with a herd of Oreo cows out front. But you gotta remember, Missy, it's an election year, so the DA is gonna make sure this trial is the greatest show on earth. I wouldn't be at all surprised if he didn't get the Ringling Brothers to pull some of their elephants out of retirement and trot them through the courtroom."

"I guess I shouldn't be surprised," Sam agreed. "Just more of the same, people's lives being bandied around like it's all just one big game. But enough with all that. What's going on in your life?"

"Pretty much just pleas and paperwork. And waiting for the rain to let up so I can spend more time outdoors with the kids." He paused, a pleading expression suddenly playing across his face. "By the way, I wouldn't mind sitting second seat on your trial if you need some help. I could use the trial practice. It's been a while, well over two years now."

Sam felt her cheeks begin to redden. She hadn't even considered asking Evan when she offered the job to Harry. "Well, unfortunately, I think that seat is already taken. I just hired an intern for the summer, a third year out of Baylor who is specializing in criminal law. We already filed the application for a temporary trial card with the state bar, so he's set from that end. But, you know, there's a chance that he won't be up to the challenge, so if you're open ended on that, I'd love to be able to count you in if he washes out."

"That would be swell, Sam. And I get where he's coming from. We've all been there, hankering for our first shot at a real courtroom. Just give me a call if you need me. I'd also be willing to help out if you want to run it past a mock trial to test your ideas. And to see how he holds up under fire, even if the fire is fake."

"Super. I appreciate that more than you know, Evan." Sam's phone was buzzing, and she fished it out of the side pocket of her black Henri Bendel briefcase, a birthday gift from Luke. "Speak of the devil. It's my intern." She thumbed the green button to answer. "One second, Harry," she said, waving goodbye to Evan and heading for a quiet spot in the hall. Stepping into an empty alcove, she eased her briefcase to the floor and turned her attention to the call. "Hey, Big H, what's up?"

Harry's voice sounded pretty pumped over the phone. "Hey back atcha, Sam. I just got off the phone with the court coordinator for the DA's office. I gave her a line about being a UT Law student and wanting to sit in on some courtroom action, and she wound up emailing me Kennedy's schedule for the whole summer, including his vacation schedule. We're in luck. He's planning to take a trip out to Disneyworld with his kids almost as soon as school lets out. Second week in June."

Sam sorted through the date math in her head. "That will give us barely enough time to get rid of the blue warrant. And we still have to get our brief put together. But if we can pull it off, that'll work out perfectly." She paused for a second, thinking through the complications. "But now that the DA's office has your e-mail address, when we pull the trigger on this, they can go back and see that someone was clearly planning a setup on Kennedy –"

"Give me a little credit, Sam! I actually asked for the schedule for the entire department, a little bit of misdirection. And I gave them a Gmail account I just created today, so they'll never be able to track that back to me. It's all dark ops…"

Sam was glad Harry was on *her* side in this battle. "Harry, I'm beginning to think that hiring you was one of the most brilliant decisions I have ever made."

Harry rewarded her with a snort of laughter. "Well, I still think we need to count our chickens once they're good and cooked, but I'm enjoying being in the middle of the fight for a change. I grew up being one of the victims of the system, so it feels pretty sweet to be able to finally push back now. To give the little guy a chance."

"You and me both," Sam said, looking out across the sea of underdogs littering the court house hallway, waiting for their fleeting shot at justice. "You and me both."

19

Now armed with Kennedy's summer schedule, Sam officially filed her Motion for Dismissal with the district clerk and set the hearing for the Friday just before Kennedy's departure for Orlando. Her brief on the motion would be dropped on him at the last possible moment, late in the day on the Friday one week before the hearing. That would give Kennedy very little time to figure out all of the implications of the motion. To catch on to all the nuances of the game she had set in motion.

Sam called Stella to let her know that her trial had ended early, and for once she'd be home in time for Maddie's midday meal and nap. Stella suggested she might stick around the house a little longer, anyway. Maddie adored her granny nanny, and the feeling was mutual. Once again, Sam felt a familiar sting of jealousy. And frustration. As much as she tried, she just couldn't be two places at the same time. And that meant missing out on most of her daughter's most magical moments.

Finally arriving home, Sam grabbed the mail from the mailbox before she drove through the electric security gate. Most of it was junk mail and catalogs, but she noticed one particular envelope that had been sent to her from a law firm in Dallas. That wouldn't have been unusual for a lawyer involved in civil litigation, but for a criminal defense attorney it was extremely peculiar. Intrigued, Sam swept into her office, grabbed a letter opener from her desk and sliced it open. Pulling out a two-page letter, she dropped into her desk chair and skimmed through the contents. The meat of the letter was contained in the second paragraph.

Sam was completely floored. She read it again, just to be sure. *What the f-?*

the smoking gun

20

Sam caught Evan on his cell phone, driving back to his office from the Justice Center. "Don't worry, Sam. I'll handle it all for you." Even though he was making every effort to reassure her, internally Evan Murphy was spinning. *A paternity test? Who the hell* are *these people?*

Sam was in scarcely better shape. The letter had come completely out of left field. "Thanks, Ev. And don't worry about the cost. I can cover it. Also, just so you know, I don't give a tinker's dam about getting my hands on any of their money. I just want to make sure Maddie is protected."

"I hear you, Sam. I'll get on the line with their lawyer as soon as we hang up and see if I can figure out what they're really up to." Evan paused. "Look, Sam, I hate to ask this, but…"

"I understand why you have to ask, Evan, but the answer is, yes, Maddie *is* Luke's daughter. No doubt about that."

Evan was perplexed. None of this made any real sense. "What has me completely befuddled, Sam, is *why* they are doing this. I mean, if Luke's father just wants to make sure that none of his money ever makes it to you or Maddie when he dies, then he can spell that out in his will. I'm sure he has probate lawyers on tap that make the two of us look like total amateurs. So why press a paternity suit?"

Sam was equally at a loss to explain the maneuver. "Maybe it's just one more aspect of this whole Catholic/Jew thing he has floating around in his head. Maybe he's in denial, and wants to cling to the idea that Luke wasn't Maddie's father. God knows Tulley has the money to chase down every possible angle on that to fuel all of his fantasies. But I've already sent him a formal renouncement of any claim Maddie and I might have to the Tulley fortune."

Evan considered that. "Hmmm. That might just be part of it, Sam. The thing is, as long as Maddie is a minor, you can legally make that call for her. But as soon as she hits eighteen, she can change all that. She can renounce your renouncement. And, even as a minor, a probate court could appoint a guardian ad litem to challenge your decision."

Sam glanced down at a picture on her desk of Luke holding his daughter in his arms at the hospital, shortly after her birth. Even that young, Maddie already had whispers of his jet black hair and his soft brown puppy-dog eyes. "I get that, Ev, but it still doesn't keep him from simply shutting us out of the will. There's something else going on here, I can feel it. I just can't for the life of me figure out what it is."

Evan tried to think of something, *anything* that would explain William Tulley's paternity suit, but in the end he came up empty. Deep down inside, he knew that if Samantha Tulley couldn't figure it out, then he had less than a snowball's chance in hell of working it all out himself. The best he could hope for was to keep moving the ball forward and pray that things would become clearer over time. "Okay then, I think we at least have a plan for now. I'll give his lawyer a buzz and see what we can do to shake this out a bit, see if I can get some idea as to his end game. In the meantime, don't waste any time worrying about this, Sam. Maddie is Luke's daughter, and there really isn't anything they can do to prove otherwise."

Unless they try to pull off some kind of shenanigans to rig the end result, Sam thought to herself. *Knowing William Tulley, that sounds just like something he would do.*

21

There was nothing Sam could do at this point to derail the paternity suit, and at any rate she trusted Evan implicitly to keep the situation under control. At least until they had a better understanding about what was really going on behind the curtains. The master plan for the Meadows case had already been set in motion, so Sam was just waiting for the formal hearing to find out whether or not her trickery would pay off. Other than her everyday hearings and pleas, that left the Rollins case on the front burner. And with Cynthia Rollins still in jail, the speedy trial provisions of Texas law meant that she had a better than average chance of making it to the final trial docket in just a few short weeks. Two, to be precise.

Harry was proving to be a natural as a trial lawyer. He breezed through the mock trial with hardly any hiccups, and even Evan praised his direct examinations, despite the clear implications to Evan's hopes of ever participating in the trial. Sam thought she could also trust Harry with a cross or two of some of the minor witnesses. She made a note to point out the fact that he was a mere law student trying to get some real world experience during her voir dire. That would endear the jury to him, and any slipups would simply be chalked up to his youth and inexperience.

As soon as she entered the house, Sam noticed that the new alarm system had been triggered. For the third time that week.

Stella was still fighting a losing battle with the technology. "Stella!" she called out from the entryway.

"In here, Samantha," Stella answered. Sam headed in the direction of the sunroom, where Stella and Maddie could usually be found at this time of the day. When she rounded the corner and saw them, Maddie finishing her lunch and Stella completely apologetic, Sam melted once again.

"I'm so sorry, Samantha," Stella tried to explain. "I took Maddie out for a walk around the neighborhood, and we spent a little time working in my garden. Maddie just adores all the flowers. When we got back, I punched in the numbers like you showed me, but I guess I just wasn't fast enough. I wrote down the whole procedure on a piece of paper, and I was trying to be so careful about doing it right…"

Sam was in no mood to be angry. Or even upset. "No, no, that's okay, Stella. I understand completely. All of that even throws me a bit, and I'm pretty used to those things. To technology in general. But we still need to keep trying. I don't think anyone would actually try to pull something during the daylight hours, but it still doesn't hurt to be careful. And it does help that the security company I'm using has other ways of confirming that no one has broken in." Sam thought about the dozens of hidden cameras secreted around the property. "But practice makes perfect, and we don't want to wind up with a 'Boy Who Cries Wolf' situation, where they eventually stop paying attention to the alarms going off."

"I'll keep working on it, Samantha," Stella promised. "In the meantime, I'm glad your trial ended early. Your little girl really seems to need some quality Mommy time." Maddie had her arms up, reaching for Sam, her face completely smeared with the remains of her lunch. Sam wiped off her face with a clean white towel and pulled her up out of the chair.

"So, you had some fun in the garden with Aunt Stella today, sweet pea?"

"Mommy, I plant 'matos!" Maddie answered enthusiastically.

"Well, that is really exciting news!" Sam kissed her and gently eased her to the ground. "Whew! You are certainly getting to be a big girl, Maddie!" Her daughter looked up, beaming at the compliment.

Stella stood and started gathering her things, getting ready to leave. "I thought this might be a good time to teach her about where food comes from. So today we planted some tomatoes, peppers and eggplant. Tomorrow we're going to work on making holes in the soil with our fingers and dropping in carrot seeds."

"I think she'll really love that," Sam said, thinking back to all the time she had spent watching over the little ant farm sitting up on the dresser in her room . "Little minds expand so fast, don't they?"

"Hers especially, Samantha. I think she gets it naturally, from you and her father."

"Nature versus nurture, Stella," Sam observed. "I think she also gets a lot of it from hanging out with you. You've been a real Godsend for us. From day one."

"Well, I get a world of pleasure from her, as well. Actually, from your entire family. It really helps an old lady to have so much love and affection and activity in her life." She turned and headed toward the front door. Barley looked up for a moment, wagging his tail, then sunk back down, his nose just inches from the bone he was guarding. "What's the schedule for tomorrow?"

Sam considered it for a moment. "I have a few days off, because the trial ended early. I think I might take advantage of the opportunity and sneak Maddie and Barley off on a little adventure. Since the weather is so nice right now, maybe we could head out west to Enchanted Rock."

"And Mommy could poke her head into some of the wineries out there," Stella suggested.

"Well, Stella, I always eat poorly when I'm heading into a trial," Sam noted, laughing. "So maybe it's a good time to get caught up on my fruits and vegetables." She paused thoughtfully. "Vodka is made out of potatoes, isn't it?"

22

Evan called as she was sitting cross-legged with Maddie at the very top of Enchanted Rock. Barley was scampering around at the moment off leash, taking in the smells just as Sam was taking in the views and the warm summer air. She hesitated to pull her phone out of her shorts pocket, but was glad she did when she saw Evan's name on the caller ID.

"Hey, Ev! What's going on?"

"Same old thing, Sam. Just trying to keep the creditors at bay. What are you up to today?"

"I took some time off and drove out to Fredericksburg with Maddie and the dog. I thought we could all use a little fresh air and some new scenery for a change." Sam paused to shift the phone to her other hand. Barley seemed focused on something hiding in a crack in the Rock. "So, any news on the folks in Dallas?"

"That's exactly why I'm calling, Sam. I talked to their mouthpiece, who's a piece of work, by the way, and he wasn't very helpful. Kept insisting we get a DNA sample from Maddie that they could cross with Luke's. I still can't work out their game plan for all of this."

"Hmmm." Sam had used the peace and quiet of the hike up the rock to ponder that problem herself. "I might just have an angle on all this."

"Shoot. What do you think they're up to?"

"Well, I think we have to start with the assumption that they won't play any of this straight up," Sam suggested. "They have some kind of scam going, and they won't take any chances that the results could come back positive."

"Which you've assured me is the case."

"Believe me, Evan, unless Maddie is the second coming of Christ, she is definitely Luke's child."

"Okay, so where does that leave us? What's the game they're playing?"

"The only thing I can figure is they plan to pull the old switcharoo. Substitute someone else's DNA for Luke's. That's the only possible way they can make a credible legal claim that Maddie is someone else's daughter."

"But it still doesn't explain how that could possibly help them in any way. Unless, as you say, it's all just about the religion thing."

"Yeah, well, unless and until we figure that out, why don't we come back with an offer they just have to resist." Sam felt a surge of humor rising in her chest. "The way DNA works in these paternity cases, it's not like a DNA match in a criminal case. It's not one to one – Maddie's DNA is not a perfect match for her father's, because half of her genome is mine. So the labs actually just look for a partial match."

Evan considered that. "So whose DNA will they use? Luke's father's?"

"No, actually, I think we should insist on having an independent lab swab both Maddie and Luke's sister, Mary Ellen. She has DNA from both Luke's father and his mother, so she should be the next closest thing to being there, as the ads say."

"What if they refuse?"

"If they refuse, then we get them off our backs for good. Either way we win."

"Okay, Sam, I'll call their lawyer back right now and set this all in motion. I'll let you know what I find out."

23

The short break was just what Sam needed to recharge her batteries before gearing up for the Rollins trial. Harry was prepped to handle the cross examination of the two friends who were helping Cynthia's ex-boyfriend that night. As for the ex, Calvin Archer, Sam would handle that herself, along with the crosses of the cops and the direct examination of Cynthia herself.

She made a short trip to the Justice Center a few days before the trial to check out the audio visual equipment. Although Sam had her own computer projector, she wouldn't actually use it during trial. Instead, she'd use the DA's computer and projector, saving everyone the time and trouble of having to wait while she connected and reconnected all the wires during trial. But Sam had been warned early on that if she didn't have her own equipment sitting in the courtroom when the trial started, the prosecutor would try to screw with her by refusing to let her use his setup. It was all part of the marvelous game.

Ray Wallace wandered into the courtroom while she was testing the VGA dongle on her laptop. "Hey, Sam! What you up to?"

Sam was no fool. As the DA's tech guru, he knew exactly what she was, in fact, up to. "Just dotting the i's and crossing the t's. I have a trial starting Monday." She looked up from her laptop and checked him out. Even for a techie guy, Ray's appearance was a little….off. He was dressed in loose-fitting blue jeans and a red lumberman's style shirt, pulled out slightly in front to hide the beginnings of a paunch. His dark hair, while neatly combed, was a bit on the oily side. The smile on his face looked a little bit oily, as well.

"Well, let me know if you need any help with that. And, speaking of which, a little birdy told me you were needing some technical assistance on the Meadows videos. I'd be happy to swing by your place sometime and help you out with that."

Something in the offer seemed a little out of place to Sam. A hint of something that had nothing at all to do with computers and videos. "Well, thanks, Ray, but for now I'm in pretty good shape. We're still a ways off from going to trial on that, and I have a new intern working for me who seems to have a handle on all the technical stuff. But I'll let you know if he gets stuck on something and we need some help."

"You bet. Any time." Ray seemed to hesitate. "You know, maybe we could get together for coffee sometime…"

There it is, Sam thought. *The move he was actually planning the whole time.* "Maybe so, Ray. But I'm really pretty busy right now, so it would have to be some time in the future." *The far, far future.* "But, honestly, I thought you were dating someone right now." The rumors were that he was seeing someone who worked at the Justice Center, rumors that had spread only because the identity of this girlfriend had remained a mystery. People just naturally wanted to know what kind of woman would be attracted to a creep like Ray Wallace.

"Yeah, well, that's old news," he replied, reluctantly. "We kind of broke up recently. So I guess I'm kind of a free agent these days…"

"I'm sorry to hear that," she offered, honestly. Sorry because now he was free to go trolling for a new girlfriend, and Sam was eager to steer him clear of her waters right now. She decided to beat a quick retreat, and checked her watch. "Oh! Look at the time! Sorry, Ray, but I've got to run. I'm already late for a meeting. We'll have to catch up sometime soon. Oh, and thanks for the offer on the videos. I'll let you know if I end up needing some help on that." She quickly closed up her laptop and threw everything into her computer case.

"Sure thing, Sam."

Turning to leave, Sam could almost feel Ray Wallace's eyes on her butt as she walked out of the courtroom.

24

Sam spent the weekend before the trial huddled with Harry, organizing their trial boxes and rehearsing her voir dire and opening statement. Barley stayed with them all weekend, bolting through his doggie door periodically at full speed to scare away squirrels and other imagined intruders, while Stella kept Maddie at her house, tending the vegetable garden and mostly staying out of Mommy's way.

By Saturday night they were exhausted and decided to grab a well-deserved break. Maddie was already tucked safely into bed and the dinner dishes were cleaned and put away. Harry snagged a beer out of the refrigerator, poured a tall glass of Chardonnay for Sam and joined her in the sunroom.

"I don't know about you, boss lady, but this ol' jalopy is about out of gas," he said, handing her the glass.

Sam laughed. "You young whippersnappers are all alike. All talk, no action. Just can't keep up with the older generation."

"Older my ass," Harry shot back as he plopped into an easy chair and popped the tab on his beer. "What have you got on me? One year? Two, tops?"

"It ain't so much the distance as the gittin' there that counts, little feller." Grinning, she took a long sip from her wine glass. "Why boy, as I told you once before, by the time I was your age I was already married and had me a young'un to boot."

"Yeah, thanks in no small part to my big sister. By the way, how did all of that happen, if you don't mind dishing? Meeting Luke, that is. I asked Hailey and she just blew me off. Said it was your tale to tell."

"Me and Luke?" Sam set her glass down on the coffee table and eased into a white wicker loveseat. "What's to tell? Pretty standard stuff. Boy meets girl, boy falls in love, girl gets whisked off her feet. Happens every day."

"Sure, but how did my sister fit into all of that? Did she play Susy matchmaker? Introduce you? I mean, if it's all too private, I understand, but leaving big time litigation in Houston to wind up here? That's got to be one doozy of a story…"

Sam waved her free hand in the air. "Private? Ha! There *is* no privacy in a small town. She smiled to herself, remembering. A doozy it certainly was. "Okay, but don't say I didn't warn you." She took another sip of wine and settled back further into the cushions. "Well, Harry, I guess the fall of Rome began when I got an invitation to a birthday party…"

25

"As I recall, it was well past seven o'clock on a Friday night. I was working late, as usual. Long hours got you noticed at Truman Walker. The more you worked, the more the partners could bill their clients, and billable hours meant big money. And in those days, with the lawyering business in the dumps, Truman Walker could use all the money it could find.

"Most days I tried to make it in to the office pretty early, beating the traffic and getting a head start on the day. I liked the quiet time. Just me, my laptop and a mug of Earl Grey tea. Truly the most productive time of the day, without all the distractions of everyone bustling about in the cramped cubicle farm we first years had to share. But by the end of the day it just got depressing, being the last girl standing while everyone else was out having fun. Anyway, it was getting late, and the traffic had already died down, so even though I still had a lot of work to finish up before Monday morning, I figured I could tackle it all just as easily at home as in the office. Plus I could slip into my jammies and open up a bottle of wine..."

"Some things just never seem to change," Harry said with a wink.

"Yeah, well, everyone's entitled to a vice or two. Or twelve. Anyway, that's where your sister comes in. I was already unlocking my car when I heard her calling my name, just popping out of the elevator. I was somewhat surprised she was still there. Those days Hailey was much more focused on finding a man than on building a career. But I imagine that's old news to you… Anyway, it seems some young doctor was throwing a birthday bash for himself at a new tapas bar not far from the office, and Hailey wanted me to come along as her wing man. Or wing woman. How exactly does that work?" Harry shrugged, so she continued. "I tried to put up a fight, but Hailey was pretty persuasive.."

"I know that part from long experience," Harry noted with a laugh. "She had my dad wrapped around her little finger."

"Yeah, I'll bet that's right. It's no wonder she's doing so well in litigation these days. Now that she's decided to put her mind to it. Anyway, I caved and agreed to go along, just for a free drink or two, so we stashed our stuff in our cars and walked over. Little did I know at the time what kind of trouble I had just gotten myself into.

"As it turned out, the birthday boy was already on his third drink by the time we got to the bar, but the tab was still open, so Hailey and I each ordered a glass of wine and surveyed the crowd. She started to work the room, and I towed along in her wake. The bar was dark and pretty boisterous, and I was having problems catching the various introductions, so I finally gave up and decided to sit back and people watch. It was fairly obvious that most of the young hipsters in the bar had already gotten a head start on the alcohol, especially the guys. There were several trays of tapas spread out here and there, and I tried a few, but finally gave up. They just weren't tasty enough to justify the calories. A number of guys had quite obviously been taken in by Hailey, in particular a blonde-haired guy in a suit jacket and open-collared shirt who made it there first."

"That sounds like Dave," Harry suggested. "They've been a steady item for several years now."

"Right you are," Sam agreed. "He was her date to our wedding, as I recall." She paused for another sip of wine. "So I'm just standing there, and the two of them were all caught up in the kind of meaningful but tenuous conversation only possible between strangers in a noisy bar. After watching a little too much of this and fending off drunken advances from several of the other men, I realized I was out of wine. I checked the time and decided it was still a little early to head home, so I wandered over to the bar for one last drink.

"The bartender was busy with some frothy concoction he was pouring into a frosted glass, so I waved to get his attention. 'Is the tab still open?' I asked him. He smiled and shook his head no. 'But can I get you something anyway?' he asked. I reached down, and suddenly realized that I'd left my purse in my car back at the garage. I felt like a total idiot. I'd just have to wait until I got home for that second glass. I was turning to leave when I heard a deep voice right behind me. 'Whatever the lady wants, Jim. It's on me.' I turned back the other way and saw him for the first time up close. The birthday boy. Luke."

Harry held up his beer in a mock toast. "And so it was love at first sight…"

Sam laughed, shaking her head. "No, in fact, it was anything but. Even three sheets to the wind, Luke was a real charmer, but unlike your sister I had zero interest in guys back then. My plan was to get well settled on the partner track at Truman before I ever broke down and paid attention to boys and all that assorted nonsense. Or sordid nonsense, if you will."

"So what made all that change, Sam? How did Luke win you over?"

"Well, that was your sister's fault, for sure. Luke bought me another glass of wine, and we chatted for short while – the usual meaningless small talk – and then I made a clean escape. All he knew about me was my first name, and in a city as big as Houston that meant I was lost in the wind as far as Luke was concerned. But then Hailey ratted me out."

"How so?"

"I'm a bit surprised she didn't tell you. Hailey, that little shit, sneaked around behind my back and gave him my number and e-mail. Before I knew it he was pestering me for a date, and he didn't seem to understand the meaning of the word no. Just to shut him up more than anything else, I finally broke down and agreed to join him for a quick lunch. Which lead to dinner and a movie, then a play, and before I knew it I was head over heels in love with the slimy bastard."

"Hey, that's a great story, Sam! I just wish I had something to compare to all that, but unfortunately my love life has been more about heels and less about love. Maybe I should get my sister to help me out with that." Harry checked his beer. "Say, it's still pretty early and I'm out of suds. Care if I top off your glass and you catch me up on how you and Luke wound up out here?"

"Sure, why not?" At first, Sam hadn't been all that interested in reliving the past, particularly any of her private moments with Luke. Losing him so recently and so suddenly still left her with a gaping, raw wound deep inside. But Harry was easy to talk to, and somehow letting just a smidgen of those memories escape seemed to lessen the pain – ever so slightly.

Harry was back, handing her a fresh glass of wine and setting the half empty bottle down in front of her. "So you two got hitched, and little Maddie came along. So what brought you to Blair County?"

"Maddie was the key," Sam said, remembering. "Luke got an amazing job offer at Blair County General, which came at a perfect time for us. I had just found out I was pregnant – I hadn't even told Luke about that yet – and it made me realize that I no longer had the fire to keep up the pace at Truman. And at Truman, they had a saying, if you don't bring the fire you get fired. We talked about it, and decided that I should put my legal career on hold for a little while, until Maddie and maybe a little brother or sister were in school. So he took the job, talked me into buying this house – against my better judgment – and the rest I guess is history."

Harry nodded and took a swig from his beer. "Okay, but how did Luke's father fit into all of this? You mentioned once before that he didn't exactly approve of you two getting married."

"Saying he didn't approve would be the understatement of the century. William Tulley was violently opposed to our marriage. The problems with him started on our first Thanksgiving together. Luke and I spent the first part of the day with my parents in Fort Worth, then drove over to Dallas to spend the late afternoon and evening at his father's house. Your old family home, that is –"

Harry waved it off. "Old news, Sam. Go on. What happened when you got there?"

"Well, first off, I was completely shocked when I saw the place. I was expecting your average multi-million-dollar Highland Park cottage, but that place is a *mansion*. And opulent in a way that makes this house look downright shabby. That was the first time I ever knew Luke came from money, from one of the wealthiest families in Texas. He just never showed that side of his life to me, or to anyone else. Never. And I was totally blown away.

"So there I was, all bug-eyed, a duck completely out of her watery comfort zone, and Luke's stepmother meets us at the front door. She looks like a cross between a supermodel and a life-size Barbie doll, with a brain to match. She and Luke exchanged some frosty pleasantries, and it was clear to me immediately that she was every bit as fake as the 40 double-D's she had plastered to her chest."

"Nothing at all like Luke's real mother, based upon everything my mom has said about her," Harry offered.

"Right. No two people could possibly be less alike. So, anyway, Barbie led us into the main room. I'd call it a living room, but it looked nothing like any living room I had ever seen. The room was open all the way to the roof. There was a second story catwalk that extended along three sides of the room, and the back wall was all windows looking out onto the grounds, which appeared to be on the same monstrous scale as the house. It could have easily held an entire football field with room to spare. I was so busy taking all of it in that I didn't notice Luke's father sneaking up behind us.

"William Tulley was a massive man, with dark, close-cropped hair graying at the temples. But my first impression of him was his eyes. Cold and almost pitch black, like looking straight into the eyes of the devil himself. Luke introduced us, and the moment he mentioned my last name, Goldberg, the evening went straight to hell. Tulley was already half plastered on scotch, which didn't help, and before I knew it he was going off on a non-stop torrent of Jewish slurs that beat anything I've ever heard. Stuff about Hebrew whores, and how I was polluting their bloodlines. About how the Tulleys came over on the Mayflower…"

"Oh my God," Harry said. "What did you do?"

"Luke was pissed. He jumped in immediately to defend me, and he and his father got into this huge shouting match. Ending when Tulley threw his scotch glass at the fireplace, almost hitting Luke's sister in the process."

"What was she doing that whole time, Luke's sister? And what about his stepmother?"

"They just stood around watching it, like it was all some big game to them. Then before I knew it Luke was pushing me out the front door and we were racing back to Houston."

"Was that the last you ever saw of Luke's family?" Harry asked.

"I wish. The Tulleys showed up at Luke's funeral. They made a point of sitting well away from us at the church and – for the most part – during the graveside service. But every so often I'd catch him staring at me. No, that's not the right word. More like glaring. Angry, vicious, like he was planning to attack me or something. I tried to ignore it all, to not let him make that day any worse than it already was. And you should understand that I was already pretty devastated. Luke was my whole world. Except for Maddie, of course, but she was just a baby back then. When Luke died, I just fell apart. Literally. If I hadn't had my parents there for me, supporting and loving me, I don't think I could have even made it to the funeral. So, anyway, there I was, standing there, lost in a kind of mental fog, just trying to slosh through it all. And then suddenly I looked up and William Tulley was standing right in front of me, his eyes bulging, his face so red it looked like it was going to burst."

Harry was incredulous. "What did you do?"

"Honestly, I was so shocked I didn't really know *what* to do. I tried to back away, but he kept coming at me. My parents had moved off a little ways to take care of Maddie, who had started to cry in the middle of the service, so they weren't looking my way. And that's when he started screaming, calling Maddie and me awful names, saying it was my fault that Luke died in the car crash, that it was God's punishment for Luke's sins. For marrying a Jew and having a baby with her. People started moving toward us to intervene, but most of the crowd just seemed paralyzed, unable to believe what they were seeing. After what seemed forever, Dad finally rushed up to rescue me, quickly stepping between us. William Tulley's only response was to give Dad a rough shove backwards, then abruptly spun around and stalked off toward his limousine, his wife Olivia rushing behind in his wake. Luke's sister just stood off to one side, grinning like a fool."

"Wow. That's… crazy!" Harry leaned over to refill her glass.

"Even crazier if you were there to witness it." Sam sipped at her wine. "And that was when… I think I've mentioned a time or two that I had a little weak spell after Luke's death?"

"Yeah, but doesn't everyone, Sam? I mean, losing someone that close to you, that's gotta be devastating. And after that performance at the funeral…"

"Well, it was a little more than that in my case. My dad refers to it as my 'trip down the rabbit hole.' I pretty much went bat shit crazy myself. That confrontation with Luke's father at the funeral seemed to dislodge whatever strength I had found to carry on. When we got home, I raced into the house and went straight up to my room. For over a week I barely left the room at all, my parents bringing me meals that I hardly touched. The worst thing was, I started to neglect Maddie.

"The rest of this I don't really remember all that much. I have some vague memories of my own, but they're all intermingled with things that others told me, later on. But I guess, in the big picture, that doesn't really matter. The only thing that matters is how it all ended, how I got through it."

"You said once that your dad gave you a toy from your childhood, and that snapped you out of it." Harry finished off the rest of his beer, but decided it was a bad time to run into the kitchen for another. Sam seemed to be eager to get this off her chest, and a moment like this might never come again.

"Yeah, the ant farm. Anyway, my condition continued to worsen, and my parents were at their wit's end about how to make me better. A doctor who said he was a friend of Luke's stopped by to check me out, and left some pills for me to take, but they just seemed to make everything even worse. Mom encouraged me to hold Maddie, and feed her, but it was almost like I was holding a doll instead of my own baby. I was like a piece of wood, without any outward display of emotion. Dad says I looked like a robot.

"And he was deeply worried, because I didn't seem to be improving. I was eating again, a little, and had begun to make tiny efforts to care for my appearance, but otherwise I stayed lost in my own little world, walled off from the rest of them. And the doctor had warned my parents that the longer that continued, the harder it would be to bring me back. They worried that I might wander off into the darkest recesses of my mind, never to return. I barely remember any of that, just a sense of numbness, a sense that everything around me was just… gray. Lifeless.

"Dad tells me he had begun to pray again, using the quiet ritual as a kind of peaceful meditation, a calming of his mind. He wasn't expecting any answers from God, he was just looking for answers from himself. It was while he was praying that the memory came to him, a moment from my childhood. He says he knew instantly that he may have found a key to unlocking my mind, my lost soul. To showing me a path out of the madness.

"He drove over to Walmart and found just what he was looking for in the games section. When he got home, he wrapped it up in some kind of playful, colorful gift wrap, like something you would give a toddler on her birthday. I do remember that part, pretty clearly. The gift wrap. Anyway, Mom was off buying groceries, which gave him a perfect opportunity to be alone with me. A father daughter moment, just like the old times when I was just a little girl.

"He came upstairs and knocked on my door, calling out to me. 'Sammie, honey. It's Daddy. I have something for you.' When he eased the door open, I was sitting in an arm chair, staring blankly out the window, just like I did every day. I remember I was wearing a simple, light blue night gown. My hair had been washed, but, as usual, I hadn't bothered to brush it out.

"He grabbed another chair and dragged it over to sit beside me. 'Hey, sweetie. Look at me.' He says that when I turned toward him, slowly, my face looked completely blank. Emotionless. A look that I know must have torn him up inside. He held up his package. 'Look, angel, I brought you something. A present.'

"I looked down at the package, and he told me that for a moment he was afraid I wouldn't take it. But slowly, in what must have seemed like an eternity to him, I reached out, tracing the pictures of the teddy bears on the gift wrap with my right hand.

"Daddy says I looked up at him, and for a brief moment he thought he saw something flash in my eyes. A moment of recognition. Then it was gone. 'Open it. It's for you.' Daddy thrust the present closer toward me. Finally, tentatively, I took it from him, placing it in my lap and staring at it, toying with the folded seams at each end. 'That's right, Sammie. Tear it open. Go ahead.'

"I remember slowly tearing the wrapper off the package. When I was finally finished, I raised the box up and looked at it, confused. 'It's an ant farm, Sammie,' Daddy explained. 'Remember, you had one in your room when you were little. You used to stare at that farm for hours, watching all the little ants going about their business, building their little tunnels and rooms. I gave it to you on your sixth birthday.'

"He continued talking to me, softly. 'Then one day you ran to me bawling, screaming about how you hated our cat. How you wanted to kill him. He had jumped up and knocked the ant farm off your dresser and onto the floor. By the time you discovered it, the ants were all gone. The ant farm was destroyed.'

"I had started to slowly nod as he told the story. I remember how my eyes seemed to be glued to the picture of the ants on the box. 'You thought it couldn't be fixed. You thought the ant world you had helped to build was gone for good. That it was all over.'

"Tears were starting to drip down my face by now. I turned to look at my father. To look into his eyes for the first time in weeks. 'And do you remember what I told you that day?' I nodded. 'What was it? Can you tell me, angel?' He said that almost a minute went by while I continued to stare intently into his eyes. Finally, slowly, I felt something in me start to let go. Words started to form inside of me for the first time in weeks. Words somehow squeezed out at first, half broken. But slowly, so slowly gaining strength. 'You – y- you told me that we couldn't – we – couldn't worry about the old farm. That it was gone. That all those ants had found a new home.'

"Daddy nodded to me. 'That's right, Sam. And what else?'

"I was crying so heavily by then I could barely speak. 'Y - you said that our only option was to build a new farm. Get new dirt. New ants.'

" 'That's right, Sammie. And why was that our only option?'

" 'B-because, unless we started a new farm, w-we wouldn't have any farm at all.' I remembered his words from so long ago. 'And the cat would have won.'

"Daddy nodded again, holding me gently by my shoulders. 'So what did you decide to do about it, Sam?'

"And for the first time since the accident, Daddy saw me begin to smile. Not a big smile, only a hint of one, but a smile nonetheless. 'We – ordered some new dirt and some new ants, and you fixed the ant farm so the cat couldn't tip it over. The ants built a new farm, better than ever.'

" 'Yes. That's right. And what did you learn from that, angel?'

"I looked back at the ant farm box I was holding in my hands. The red ant farm. The brown dirt inside, ants crawling around, building tunnels and burrows. Memories. 'That you can't change the past. Only the future. And if you only focus on the past, you'll never have a future.'

"Daddy leaned forward, pressing his forehead against mine. I could smell his Old Spice cologne. Good memories. 'So, what are you going to do about all this? What are *we* going to do?'

"By then, tears were flowing freely from both of our eyes. Finally, I pulled back just enough so I could see my father's face, so I could look into his eyes again. 'I guess I don't really have any other choice, do I Daddy? I have to build another fucking ant farm.' "

Sam had gotten so wrapped up in her thoughts of all that had happened two years earlier that she was somewhat surprised to look up and see Harry's face soaking wet with tears. Seeming a bit embarrassed, he jumped up quickly to grab her empty wine glass and the almost empty bottle and headed for the kitchen.

"Oh gosh, Sam," he said, glancing back over his shoulder and making a show of checking his watch. "Look, it's getting pretty late, and we have a ton of work ahead of us tomorrow. Why don't I drop all of this off in the sink on my way out the back? I'll pop in early and make coffee for us in the morning."

"Sounds like a date," Sam promised, wiping a ring of water from the coffee table and heading toward the elevator to the third floor. "See ya in the funny papers!" But as she reached out to punch the elevator call button, she stopped and looked back toward the kitchen. Toward where she could just hear Harry locking the back door on his way to his cabin. It was nice to have a man around the house again. Even if he was just a friend.

26

Sam's plan regarding the paternity test had worked perfectly, and William Tulley's lawyer withdrew his request with no comment. She felt certain now that they had been planning all along to fake the results of the test. But she was still no closer to understanding why.

By Monday morning, Sam was stoked and itching for action. She and Harry had met with Cynthia Rollins the night before at the jail to prep her for what to expect on the first day of trial and to make sure that the clothing she had brought for her client actually fit. With women's clothing, you could never really be sure that the size on the label matched the actual size of the outfit.

The other big problem that had come up that night was the lingering issue of the gun. Cynthia continued to swear that she didn't have a gun on the night she was arrested, despite the fact that five people swore they had heard gun shots and three of them said they had seen her shoot it, identifying it as a nine millimeter semiautomatic. No gun was ever recovered at the scene, however, despite an exhaustive search by the police, and no shell casings were ever found either. That last fact was particularly peculiar, because even if Cynthia could have found a way to ditch the gun before the police arrived on the scene, there was no way she could have located two or three spent shell casings in the middle of a dark yard filled with tall grass. So Cynthia's insistence made some sense, given the missing gun and shells. But the problem, Sam carefully explained to her client, was that owning up to shooting the gun did absolutely no damage to their case, while denying it made Cynthia look like a liar. There was absolutely no way to win the case by claiming that the five witnesses were wrong about the gun – the only real option was to rely on the defense of property provisions of the Texas Penal Code, commonly known as the Castle Doctrine. Under this doctrine, a woman's home is her castle, and the law allows her to use force, even deadly force, in defense of that castle. Cynthia could have shot them dead on the spot if she had chosen to, and under the Castle Doctrine she couldn't be charged with a crime. Eventually, she caved in and reluctantly agreed that she may have fired a gun that night. Sam knew she would have her work ahead of her over the next few days to nail her client down on this crucial point.

When the jailer finally brought Cynthia into the courtroom the next morning, Sam was pleased to see that her clothing choices were dead on, and Cynthia was projecting the sweet, innocent look Sam had worked so hard to achieve. *The light gray skirt and white blouse is a far cry from prison orange*, she thought. Meanwhile, the judge was a little late, finally entering the courtroom at fifteen minutes after nine. Sam had never tried a case before Judge Naomi Starke, but she was well aware of the judge's reputation as a hanging judge. A former prosecutor herself, Starke seldom if ever granted a defense motion or objection. Trying a criminal case in front of her usually left defense attorneys feeling like they were being double teamed, with half of that team – the judge – having almost complete authority over the courtroom. The only positive side of that was Starke's record on appeal – most of her guilty verdicts wound up being bounced back by the appeals courts, often with very harsh admonitions.

The judge was a short, stout woman. Her light brown hair was thinning and poorly tinted, the gray showing prominently at the roots. "Counselors," Judge Starke announced, staring directly and sternly at Sam. "I hope we have all taken the opportunity over the weekend to think this case through, to think about what's at stake here. *Ms. Tulley.*" Sam looked up at her sharply. "If this goes poorly for your client, she could be facing ten to twenty years. And with all due respect to you, this is your first felony rodeo. She's putting her entire future, and the future of her family, in your hands. Are you *sure* you're ready for that?"

Sam stiffened in her chair and slowly rose, returning the judge's stare. "Your Honor, as we've discussed before, I'm still waiting for Mr. Kennedy to explain why this case doesn't fall under the Castle Doctrine provisions of the penal code. If he can explain that to my satisfaction, I might be willing to entertain a plea deal. Until then, however…" She paused and placed her left hand on her client's shoulder. "Until then, Defense stands ready."

"Hmmph!" Starke looked like she had just bitten down on something sour. "Well. We'll see." She turned to face Huber Kennedy, the prosecutor, her sour look quickly transforming into a slight smile. "Mr. Kennedy, are you ready as well?"

Kennedy rose just an inch or so in his seat before slumping back down. "Ready, Your Honor."

Starke nodded. "Very well, then. Let's get started. Are there any pre-trial matters we need to take up before voir dire?"

Sam stood, papers in hand. "Your Honor, we have several Motions in Limine before you that we filed last week…"

"All denied," Starke shot back, cutting Sam off before she could finish. "Anything else?" she asked, turning toward Kennedy.

He rose, looking smug. This was all old hat to him."Yes, Your Honor. The State has also filed some Motions in Limine…"

"And they look reasonable to me," Starke answered, glancing down at the State's motions that she had already checked off.

"Objection, Your Honor!" Sam rose indignantly. "Defense objects to each and every one of those motions. Mr. Kennedy is trying nothing less than to gut our case, to redact every part of the police investigation into this case that benefits the defendant, every line from the police reports that demonstrates her innocence…"

"Overruled, Ms. Tulley!" Starke spit back at her. "This Court has already ruled on these matters. If you have a problem with any of this later on during the trial, we'll take it up then. *Until* then, Ms. Tulley, you will be mindful to keep these matters to yourself."

Sam wouldn't even dignify the judge's response with a simple "Yes, Your Honor." The trial had already started off badly, and Sam was under no illusions that things would get any better. Starke had a reputation for hammering on the defense side throughout trial, trying to beat them down into accepting a plea deal mid-trial rather than facing a possible guilty verdict and the uncertainty of an appeal.

"Are there any *other* matters that I need to look at before we bring the panel in?" Starke asked, still glaring at Sam.

"No, Your Honor," muttered Sam, scribbling "bitch" on her notepad where only Harry could see. She could hear him chuckle softly to himself beside her.

"No, Your Honor," Kennedy offered brightly. "We're ready for them."

"Very well, then." Starke turned to the bailiff. "Let's get them seated."

Sam leaned over to whisper to her client. "Remember, when they file in, look up and look sweet. Smile, but not too much. And don't make eye contact if you can avoid it. Just keep sweeping your eyes slowly, back and forth, without locking on to any one juror."

"I got you, Miz Sam. Sweet and innocent, just like we practiced."

Sam nodded to Cynthia, then turned back to watch the jury pool get seated. For felony cases, twelve jurors were eventually seated, out of an original pool of sixty. Some defense attorneys had a reputation for busting the pool, getting so many potential jurors discharged due to bias that less than twelve were left to pick from in the end. For those lawyers, judges typically brought in larger jury panels, sometimes well over a hundred. But Sam wasn't at that point. Yet.

After they were all seated, the judge gave them their initial instructions. Even at this stage of the trial, before the jurors had heard a single word out of Sam's mouth, it was painfully obvious that the judge held a grudge against her. Sam thought this might play to her advantage – if the jurors picked up early on that the judge was being unfair, they would tend to stay on Sam's side throughout the trial.

Kennedy started in on his canned voir dire speech. It always amazed Sam at how little creativity went in to the state's voir dires. And how little prosecutors managed to engage the jury panel, to drag out biases and pre-sell the key issues of their case.

Sam largely ignored the actual words that flowed out of Kennedy's mouth, and focused instead on the body language that the various jurors were showing.

Finally, Kennedy's speech came to a dull conclusion and it was Sam's turn to examine the panel. Sam started with a canned but seemingly spontaneous discussion of guilt and innocence, with Powerpoint slides that explained the high burden of proof in criminal cases, beyond a reasonable doubt. That went well, other than a short sparring battle with Starke when she reached up on her tiptoes to illustrate the height of the burden of reasonable doubt.

"Ms. Tulley," the judge warned her, "I think you are misstating the rule, here."

But Sam held her ground. "With all due respect, Your Honor, since, as you know, the legislature hasn't *given* us that rule, then you aren't the judge of what that rule means, what the phrase 'beyond a reasonable doubt' actually means. This jury is. And I'll just leave it up to them to decide whether I'm explaining that phrase correctly or not." She spun away from the judge before Starke could respond and turned back to the jury. She could see that several of them were nodding.

The next phase of her voir dire was the key to her case. Sam needed to walk the jurors through the Castle Doctrine, all the while sprinkling in strong back currents of the Second Amendment. This was a deeply red, conservative county, with almost knee-jerk support for gun rights. All Sam needed was to nail down just one juror who favored the right to bear arms over any and every other right, and at the very least she had a hung jury in her back pocket. She turned back to her Powerpoint slides, and popped Section 9.42 of the Texas Penal Code up on the screen.

She turned to the jury panel. "Ladies and gentlemen, I don't know how you feel about guns, or the right to use guns. Some of you might have several dozen guns and rifles locked up in your gun safes back home, and some of you may not have any guns at all." It was time to prod the jury a bit, to test their stance on gun rights. "But that doesn't really matter, here, because this case isn't about the right to have guns, or the right to use guns. A right guaranteed to us by the Second Amendment, which says that 'Congress shall take no action to infringe on the right to keep and bear arms.' "

Several of the jurors immediately held up their hands. Sam picked one on the front row. "Ms. Erikson. Do you have a question?"

"Yes, ma'am. I just wanted to point out that the Second Amendment actually says, 'A well regulated Militia, being necessary to the security of a free State, the right of the people to keep and bear Arms, shall not be infringed.'" Sam saw that the other jurors who had raised their hands were nodding in support of Ms. Erikson's correction, as were most of the other jurors. She made a mental note of the few who weren't responding. And another mental note of the fact that Erikson had quoted the amendment spot on from memory. Whatever happened, this was one juror who had to make the final cut.

"Thank you for that, Ms. Erikson. And you're right, I did misquote that Amendment. I apologize for that, and I appreciate your stepping in and correcting me on it." Sam could see a look of satisfaction on the juror's face at the compliment. Taking a breath, she moved on to the Castle Doctrine law, projected up on the screen behind her.

"Texas Penal Code Section 9.42. The so-called Castle Doctrine," she began. "Can I see a show of hands of everyone who has heard about this law?" Immediately, almost every hand shot into the air. Sam was surprised not so much by the near unanimity, but by the speed of their response. This was a crowd that really liked their guns, she thought. She glanced over and saw Harry quickly recording which members of the panel had *not* raised their hands. People she would later fight to keep off the final jury of twelve.

"Well, good. I can see most of you have at least some understanding of what this law entails. But let's stop for a moment and take a closer look at the law, make sure we are all on the same page on this." She clicked her pointer and the phrase "A person is justified in using deadly force against another to protect land or tangible, movable property" was highlighted in yellow behind her, showing the jury panel exactly where the phrase was located in that section of the penal code. Another click and the phrase expanded to fill the middle of the screen, allowing even those with poor vision to read the words.

"There are four parts of this sentence I want you to focus on," she explained. "First, 'a person is justified.' What that means is pretty simple. It means, essentially, that a person is legally *allowed* to do something. Does that make sense? Everyone understand this part?" Sam raised her hand and nodded aggressively, a technique she had learned in law school from the nation's top expert in voir dire, Robert Hirschhorn. Hirschhorn had literally written the book on voir dire, and specialized in the use of various forms of body language to subconsciously draw out responses from jurors. Raising your hand and nodding vigorously had a remarkable effect on getting members of a jury panel to agree with you. And using that technique early on, as Sam was doing, tended to dramatically increase juror participation in voir dire. Later on, she would use the same technique in another way, to get unwanted jurors to admit to a constitutionally prohibited bias, a bias that would allow her to boot them off the jury.

"Okay," Sam continued, clicking again on her handheld pointer. Now the earlier phrase disappeared and a new phrase took its place, "in using deadly force against another." She looked back briefly to make sure she hadn't over clicked, then turned back to explain what they were reading. "Next, it says 'using deadly force against another'. Basically, this means exactly how it reads. A person can legally use deadly force, can use force up to and including *killing* another person. Not just, say, shooting them in the leg. *Killing* them."

She clicked again, and the phrase 'when and to the degree he reasonably believes the deadly force is immediately necessary' popped up.

"Okay, there are two key points here. First, 'he reasonably believes.' This is the kind of wording that can cause problems for most folk. 'Reasonably believes.' Who is to say what's reasonable? I mean, what's reasonable to one person may be unreasonable to the next person. But that's just something for you guys to work out. You guys have to look at what happened that night and decide for yourselves whether it was reasonable. Okay so far?" Again, Sam raised her hand and nodded, then moved on to the second part of the phrase. "So, now we get to 'immediately necessary.' Simply put, this just means that the person, in this case the defendant, this means that she *reasonably believed* that she had to take action immediately to stop what was happening. Notice that this doesn't say that *you* have to reasonably believe that some action was necessary that night. It doesn't say that you get to play Monday morning quarterback, to sit here in this cozy and safe courtroom and second guess her decision on that dark and dangerous night. A decision made in the heat of the moment. It simply says that *she* had to reasonably believe that, under the circumstances, she needed to act quickly and decisively to change things. With me so far?" Sam continued, nodding and clicking the pointer.

"Finally, we have the key phrase from this section of the law, 'to prevent the other's imminent commission of arson, burglary, robbery, aggravated robbery, theft during the nighttime, or criminal mischief during the nighttime.' Let's skip through most of this and just focus on the very end, 'theft during the nighttime, or criminal mischief during the nighttime.' "

She stepped up closer to the jury, resting her hands on the rail between them. "Of course, I don't think anyone's going to worry about the 'nighttime' issue in this case. It was well after ten at night on Halloween. If there's anyone here that thinks that doesn't qualify as nighttime, please raise your hand now and we'll send you on home." Sam raised her hand, nodding and laughing, causing most of the jurors to smile in return. "Okay, now that we've got *that* behind us, let's talk about theft and criminal mischief. Now, some people think theft here means that we have to *prove* that theft was actually occurring, that the other side was, in fact, stealing some of Cynthia's property. But that isn't exactly true. That whole 'reasonably believed' part applies to this part of the law, too. All it takes is for the defendant to reasonably believe at that very moment that someone is stealing her stuff, even if it turns out later she was mistaken. Simply put, the Castle Doctrine says that if you walk up to your house late at night and find some big fella walking out your front door with a television set, then you can legally pull out your nine mil and blow them away. End of story. Is there anyone here who's concerned about that? Anyone who thinks that might be a bad thing?" Sam's hand shot up again, and she walked aggressively toward the jury panel, nodding. A few hands shot up, mostly in the rear. Harry noted each of them on his jury chart, plus a few who seemed by their body language to be wavering.

Sam dove in, using a beckoning hand gesture designed to get jurors to open up more fully about their opinions. "Mr. Ambrose. Juror Number Nineteen. You have your hand up." She motioned for everyone else to drop their hands. "So, you think this law may be a bit too harsh, a bit too strong." He was nodding. "Okay, let's talk about that. What about this law bothers you?"

Ambrose hesitated before saying anything. He was nervous about speaking up in front of such a large crowd, and didn't want to sound foolish. Especially since he was clearly in the minority. "Well, I just don't think it's right to kill someone over something as unimportant as a TV set. I mean, it's just *stuff*, stuff that can pretty easily be replaced. But you can't replace a human life, even if it's the life of a bad person. Plus, what if you're mistaken, and the person with the TV set is actually innocent?" He paused. "I guess what I'm saying is that I think you need to have more at stake before you can shoot someone. Maybe to keep them from hurting someone else. Maybe if you're afraid for your own safety. But if it's just about your property? I can't really go along with that idea."

Sam was in heaven. This juror had spelled out the issue just about as well as she ever could. And it came from one of *them*, one of the jurors, and that made all the difference. Now she just needed to lock him down. "Thank you, Mr. Ambrose. I really appreciate your honesty on this. So, just so we're all sure, what you're saying is that you would have difficulties following the law in this case, you'd want to see a little more than just theft or criminal mischief before you could excuse the use of deadly violence. Is that fair?"

Ambrose was nodding, and Sam could see five other jurors doing the same. "Yes, I guess that's what I'm saying. I would need to see that there was more at stake before I could sign off on that. People shouldn't just be whipping out guns and shooting each other willy-nilly. Guns should only be used when there's really no other option."

"Thank you, Mr. Ambrose." She looked around at the entire panel, her hand again in the air. "Anyone agree with Mr. Ambrose on this? Anyone else agree that guns should only be used when there's no other option?" The five jurors she had identified earlier raised their hands. One by one, she interviewed each of them, establishing that they could not conscionably follow the law as it was written. This was a key moment in her voir dire, because it allowed her to bump them from the jury on constitutional grounds, without having to use any of her peremptory challenges. The odd thing was, Sam largely agreed with these jurors. She had some very real concerns about laws like the Castle Doctrine returning Texas to the bad old days of the Wild Wild West, with everybody packing heat and shootouts taking place in the middle of the streets at high noon. But this trial wasn't about her personal opinion, it was about establishing a firm legal defense for her client. And to do that, to save Cynthia Rollins from serving a decade or so in the state prison system, she had to pack this jury with true believers. No tree-hugging liberal peaceniks allowed. Leave your John Lennon albums at home.

With the meat of her voir dire behind her, Sam moved on to other hot button topics, in the process committing two more jurors to a constitutionally prohibited bias. Winding down, she turned to Harry for a final conference on the likely makeup of the jury. "Sam, we have a really interesting pattern here," he suggested, turning his jury chart around to face her. She saw it immediately. Harry pointed on the chart to two jurors he had starred, then pushed across another sheet of paper where he had written down the background information on each of them that he had culled from their juror questionnaires. Sam grabbed this sheet and turned back to face the jury.

"Juror Number Three. Mr. Johanson." Sam fixed him with a quizzical look. "Earlier, when the judge asked if any of us recognized each other, if you recognized the defendant or any of the attorneys, you indicated that you did not." Johanson nodded in agreement. "But now, looking at the form you filled out earlier today, I see that you're the owner of the Central Texas Pet Resort. Is that right?"

Johanson spoke up immediately. "Yes, ma'am. We board and groom dogs and cats, and sometimes more exotic animals like pet pigs."

"Usually when their owners are away on vacation," Sam added.

"That's right. Usually either vacation or some family emergency."

"And you probably see a lot of people in that business, and a lot of animals, isn't that right?" She saw out of the corner of her eye that the prosecutor was looking confused about where she was going with this line of questions.

"Yes, we've been pretty successful with the business."

Sam sprung the trap. "So, my black and brown Aussie, Barley. You don't really remember him all that well, do you?"

"Uh, no, can't say that I do," he answered.

Sam knew that she had to be very careful with her next statement, to keep it within the ethical boundaries she had set for herself. "And so, the issue of whether or not I'm one of your regular customers wouldn't have any effect on your decision in this case. You could see past all that and reach an opinion based solely on the evidence and testimony in the case, isn't that correct?" In fact, Sam had never boarded Barley at the Pet Resort – Stella always watched him whenever she needed to go out of town and couldn't take Barley along. But she hadn't actually *said* any different, even though she had definitely left the *impression* that she was a good customer of Juror Number Three.

Johanson looked confused, since for the life of him he couldn't recall ever seeing this woman. But he certainly wasn't going to insult her by saying so. "No, that wouldn't affect my judgment in any way," he promised.

"Thank you, sir," Sam told him, turning to the second name on her list. "Juror Number Eleven. Mr. Zimmerman." Zimmerman looked up, a bit surprised. "Now, Mr. Zimmerman, among other things, you teach a class at the Baylor Law School as an adjunct professor, don't you?"

Zimmerman nodded. "Yes, Federal Income Taxation."

That was the kind of class Sam had avoided like the plague during her three years at Baylor, so she had never had Zimmerman for a professor, even though she was well aware of his reputation. He was a total hard ass, and once he formed an opinion on a subject, he wouldn't waver. In Sam's opinion, a very dangerous man to leave on the jury. Now it was time to sow the seeds of distrust with the other side. Time for some misdirection. "So, Professor Zimmerman, I take it you don't recognize me right away from when I was a student at Baylor Law?"

Zimmerman took a hard look at her, but couldn't place her in any of his classes. "I can't say that I do. But then, I have a lot of students go through my classes."

Sam looked mildly disappointed at that, that she had left so little of an impression on one of her law school professors. But it was just a look. "And I guess that means that my being a student in one of your classes wouldn't affect your judgment in this case. Is that fair to say?" She hadn't actually *said* that she had ever been one of his students. The English language could be a very flexible tool, at times.

"No, ma'am. Even if you were one of my star students, my decisions in this case would be based solely on the facts as they are presented, and nothing else."

"Thank you, Mr. Zimmerman," Sam said, glancing over at the prosecution table as if she had been pleased by the juror's answer. She saw Kennedy intently marking up his juror sheet. *Now we just sit back and see if that worked,* she thought.

Sam wrapped up her voir dire very quickly after that, and both sides settled down to the process of identifying challenges for cause, followed by filling out their peremptory challenges, a list of ten jurors apiece they could boot off the jury panel for no real reason whatsoever, as long as it wasn't readily apparent that the decision was based upon some type of discrimination, like the now-prohibited practice in the Old South of dismissing all of the black jurors. This last stage presented a strategic risk for Sam, but one she knew she had to take. She used her peremptories on jurors *other* than Number Three and Number Eleven.

And when the judge read out the numbers for the final twelve jurors, she saw that the gamble had worked. Kennedy had taken the bait on Three and Eleven and struck them from the jury. As the final twelve assembled in the jury box and the rest of the panel was dismissed, Sam looked up and saw that the pattern Harry had drawn up on his jury chart was now manifested in the flesh. One male and eleven female jurors. For a case involving a single mother protecting her home at night against three male intruders. And all four of the jurors who had objected to her intentional misquotation of the Second Amendment had made it to the final twelve. At that moment, Sam knew that this case was already in the bag.

27

The next two days flew by quickly. Kennedy brought two police officers to testify about their investigation and arrest, plus the two friends who were helping the victim supposedly move out that night. None of them really damaged Sam's case in any way, and none of them provided any real surprises, given that Sam and Harry were already fully armed with the witness statements from the two friends and the official reports filed by the two officers, statements they had been pouring over for several weeks in advance of the trial. Every time witnesses tried to wiggle a little in regards to what actually happened that night, Sam and Harry would simply slam them back with their prior statements. It didn't take very long before they gave up trying.

But getting witness statements well in advance of trial was a relatively new practice in Texas, forced upon the State by the fallout from the Michael Morton case. Prior to Morton, most counties took full advantage of Rule 615 of the Texas Rules of Evidence, a rule that allowed prosecutors to withhold statements and police reports until after the witness or officer had finished testifying on direct. This had the intentional effect of severely handicapping the defense team's ability to identify significant changes or omissions in the witness's testimony. Or to develop effective trial strategies, because almost none of the State's evidence was available to them prior to the trial.

In theory, all of this should have been blunted by the United States Supreme Court's 1963 ruling in Brady v. Maryland. Brady held that prosecutors had a duty to turn over any evidence that "is material either to guilt or to punishment." But the problem with Brady was that it left the interpretation of whether certain evidence was material or could affect a jury's determination of guilt or punishment up to the prosecutors, the very individuals who historically have done everything in their power to prioritize convictions over justice. In the more progressive counties in Texas, district attorneys took this to mean that *any* attempt to hide evidence from defense attorneys was improper, even the practice of withholding witness statements until after direct examinations. These counties implemented an open file policy, giving defense counsel ample opportunity before trial to examine *all* of the evidence the State had collected in a case. Still, in many other counties, particularly those counties where the judges and prosecutors had been elected on promises to be "tough on crime," exculpatory evidence remained a shell game.

But Michael Morton changed all that. In 1986, Michael Morton was living what he called an "excruciatingly average" life as the manager of a supermarket in a small town just north of Austin. He had a wife and a three-year-old son. On August 13, 1986, the three of them celebrated his birthday at a local restaurant. The next morning, Morton left for work at around five thirty in the morning. He left behind a note for his wife expressing disappointment that she had refused to have sex with him the night before, but ended the note with three simple words: "I love you."

Later that morning, Christine Morton's body was found in bed, bludgeoned to death, her bed sheets stained with semen. When police questioned the Mortons' son, Eric, he told them that he had been present during the attack, and that the assailant had been some "monster" – and not his father. He described the attack in great detail, and assured them that "Daddy was not home" when it happened. Despite this, and despite the fact that no evidence was ever found that tied Morton to the brutal killing, the prosecutors convinced a jury that he had beaten his wife to death for refusing to have sex with him the night before, and on February 17, 1987, he was convicted of murder and sentenced to life in prison.

The day after the murder, the police discovered a bloody bandana in a construction site about three hundred feet behind the Morton house. They also took statements from neighbors describing a man driving a green van who had recently been parking directly behind the Morton house and walking off into some nearby woods. Police reports further implicated a woman who had been caught several days after the murder attempting to use one of Christine Morton's credit cards in a jewelry store in San Antonio, several hours to the south. Those reports stated that a San Antonio police officer claimed he could identify the woman who had used the card. According to Morton's defense lawyers at the time, none of this information was ever disclosed to them.

By 2005, the Morton case had finally come to the attention of the Innocence Project, a group dedicated to using DNA testing to exonerate wrongfully convicted individuals. Along with the law firm of Raley & Bowick, they filed a motion with a Texas court to force DNA testing of various items that had been recovered and stored in the case. The court agreed, but excluded the bloody bandana from testing, and the DNA tests that *were* granted were inconclusive.

For the next six years, Williamson County District Attorney John Bradley fought tooth and nail to stop the DNA testing in the Morton case, testing that would have cost the State of Texas nothing, since it was being paid for by Morton's lawyers. Finally, however, the courts relented and ordered that the bandana be tested. The blood on the bandana did not match Morton. Instead, when the Texas Department of Public Safety ran the DNA results through the national convicted-offender DNA database, the computer spit out the name Mark Norwood, a convicted felon from California who was known to have been living in Texas at the time of the murder. Even worse, a deeper look into Norwood revealed that a hair follicle from him had been found at the scene of another murder victim, Debra Masters Baker. Debra Baker, too, had been bludgeoned to death while lying in bed in her North Austin apartment, approximately two years after Christine Morton's murder. By hiding the evidence and convicting the wrong man, the Williamson County prosecutors left the real killer loose on the streets to kill again.

Two months after the DPS proved that it was Norwood who killed Christine Morton that morning, and not her husband, Michael Morton was finally released from prison. He had served twenty five years in state prison for a crime that he never committed, and for all of those twenty five years, his son had grown up believing that his father was his mother's cold-blooded killer.

Meanwhile, throughout Bradley's dogged fight to keep the bandana from being tested, he was busy advocating with other district attorneys that Texas law should be changed to prevent any such testing in the future. Shortly after the Norwood DNA match and before Morton's release, the Texas criminal justice blog *Grits for Breakfast* unearthed a series of comments Bradley had left on the Texas District and County Attorneys Association's user forum complaining that "Innocence … has proven to trump most anything." Instead, Bradley wrote, "[a] better approach might be to get a written agreement that all the evidence can be destroyed after the conviction and sentence. Then, there is nothing to test or retest." Faced with this damning disclosure, the TDCAA immediately tried to erase those comments from its website. But *Grits for Breakfast* had already made copies. And in all fairness to the voters of Williamson County, Texas, John Bradley was crushed at the ballot box when he faced reelection less than one year later, and escaped to the tiny Pacific island of Palau to lick his wounds.

While John Bradley was fighting the good fight against the pervasive cancer of actual innocence, another shadowy figure in the Morton case was struggling to remain in those shadows. Williamson County State District Judge Ken Anderson had served as the prosecutor in the Morton case twenty five years earlier, and even as Morton was in the process of being officially exonerated, evidence mounted that Anderson had intentionally hidden key evidence from Morton's lawyers, including Eric Morton's interview where he told police that his mommy had been killed by a "monster", and that his "Daddy was not home." Ultimately, Anderson was found guilty and was sentenced to ten days in jail and the loss of his law license. The *New York Times* suggested that the sentence was "insultingly short" in comparison to the nearly twenty five years that Morton spent behind bars, but noted that "because prosecutors are so rarely held accountable for their misconduct, the sentence is remarkable nonetheless."

The repercussions from the Morton case echoed across Texas and across the United States. Soon after Morton's exoneration, the Texas legislature passed a law requiring *all* of the cities and counties of Texas to establish open file policies. As a direct result, Sam and Harry were able to march into the Rollins trial with full knowledge of the evidence for and against their case. And the witnesses were now hamstrung in their pitiful attempts to change their stories on the stand. Particularly the police officers, who could still be relied upon by prosecutors to twist their interpretation of events to fit one and only one possible scenario: guilty as charged.

But the police and prosecutors weren't the only ones willing to sacrifice their integrity in the single-minded pursuit of injustice. At the beginning of the trial, Judge Starke had ruled in favor of the prosecution's redactions of various police reports, essentially erasing several critical statements the police had made that favored Sam's client. In theory, she could ask the judge to reconsider that ruling, but time and time again Starke shot her down, and none of the redacted comments had been allowed in. Sam knew that those rulings would almost certainly guarantee a win on appeal, but that would just stretch the process out another year or so before the case could be retried. A year or two that her client would spend in the county jail. Something had to change. Somehow Sam needed to thread the needle and bring some of this evidence to the attention of the jury. One statement in particular was so damning to the prosecutor's case that she knew she needed to get it before the jury despite the judge's restrictions. On Tuesday morning, with the cop in question still on the stand, she decided to go for it.

"Officer Williams," she began, "let's look again at the lapel cam video that was taken that night, the video from the camera that was attached to your uniform."

"Okay," he answered, warily.

Sam turned to face the projector screen, her clicker held ready in her right hand. "Okay, officer, I'm going to show you a few moments from that video, just to refresh our memories, and then I've got a few questions to ask you about what we're going to see. All right?"

"Sure," he replied, looking up at the blank screen.

"Super." Sam glanced over her shoulder to smile at him and then, briefly, the jury, and hit the play button. The picture was a little dark and somewhat bouncy, but after a few seconds it became apparent that the officer on the stand was talking to his partner from that night. At the exact right moment, Sam hit the mute button to turn the sound back on. Officer Williams was speaking. "All I'm saying, Jim, is why in the hell are we arresting *this* innocent woman instead of the three goons who were trying to rip her off?"

"OBJECTION!" Kennedy blasted upright from his seat. Sam hit pause. Kennedy was livid. "Your Honor, *this* section of the video was covered by my motion in limine! You've already ordered her *not* to let this be seen by the jury, and now she's gone and done it anyway!" Too late, he glanced over at the jury and realized his mistake. He should have completed his objection at the bench, where the jury couldn't hear how he and the judge had conspired to keep this important bit of information from them.

Now, not only had they heard it, but he had managed to stamp it indelibly into their minds.

Judge Starke was apoplectic. "Counselors, approach!" she ordered. Sam and Huber Kennedy stepped around their tables and marched up to the bench. Sam stole a glance at the jury on her way up and read it all clearly in their faces. Her little gambit had not only scored, it had scored *big*. Now she just had to manage the backlash from the judge.

"Ms. Tulley, I am waiting for an explanation of what I just saw in here, and it had better be good!" Starke scolded her sharply but in a quiet voice to keep the jury from hearing what was going on.

But even though they couldn't hear, Sam knew that the jurors were all watching very intently, trying to decipher from the body language and facial expressions what exactly was happening at the bench. She also knew that the judge had no way of monitoring Sam's body language from the neck down. Channeling all of the tricks she had picked up from acting in her high school plays, she tried to project a cool nonchalance, a perfect counterpoint to the tense anger emanating from the judge and prosecutor, underscoring once again to the jury that she was just a David in this courtroom fighting simultaneously against *two* Goliaths.

Sam smiled demurely. "I'm sorry, Your Honor. I had meant to play a clip from a little earlier in the evening, but I guess I must have made a small technical error. You know, I don't have the unlimited technical resources that this county provides to Mr. Kennedy, so on our side it's pretty much just me. Plus my little law school student. And since Your Honor has already ruled that I can only use the DVD provided by Mr. Kennedy's office, that I can't play clips that are copied directly off that DVD, then I guess mistakes like this are unavoidable. I simply have no way of making sure in advance that I have the machine set for the right location in the file before I push the play button…"

"Your Honor, this is *bullshit*…" Kennedy began, then quickly went silent when Starke glared at him for cursing in her court.

"Mr. Kennedy, I will handle this, if you don't mind." Starke turned back to Sam. "Young lady, this is your first and only warning. I'm going to put this down to youthful inexperience, but if anything like this happens again, and I mean *anything*, then you and I are going to have a very unpleasant discussion. Do I make myself clear on that?"

"Yes, Your Honor." Sam kept her face passive, even though inside she was laughing out loud. Getting the statement by Officer Williams that he thought her client was innocent had been huge, and there was nothing the judge could do now to unring that bell. But the real icing on the cake was the reaction by Huber Kennedy and the judge. It would take a real idiot not to realize at this point that the fix was in, that the judge and the prosecutor were conspiring together to somehow pull a rose out of the pile of cow manure that constituted the state's case against Cynthia. And while the twelve people making up this jury weren't the most sophisticated individuals in the world, they had all been around the block long enough to figure out when someone was getting screwed.

28

By the time the jury was excused for the day late Wednesday afternoon, Sam was feeling ebullient. By her count, only three witnesses were left: the so-called victim first thing the next morning, then Cynthia's oldest son, and finally Cynthia herself sometime in the afternoon. This case might actually finish up much earlier than Sam had originally planned, but she knew that some of that was because she had been blocked from cross examining the cops on the redacted statements.

She was just starting to put her trial materials away in her trial box when Judge Starke summoned her to approach. "Yes, Your Honor?" Sam had no idea what the judge was up to, but her experience told her it couldn't be good.

"Yes, Ms. Tulley." Starke had a stern look on her face. "I understand that you don't have any experience with trying felony cases, so I want to help you out a little here. We've heard almost three days of testimony already, and from what I've heard so far, it's pretty clear your girl is guilty. If not the assault with a deadly weapon charge, then at least of a lesser included charge like deadly conduct. And that means she's facing at least five years in prison at this point, and maybe as much as twenty. I would also say that probation's pretty much off the table. This jury is never going to give that to her. So she's facing real time in a state facility, and her kids are all going to be handed off to foster care."

"Your Honor, I…"

"Hold on, Ms. Tulley. Don't interrupt. Now, I know you thought you may have had a good case at first, and thought you knew how to handle yourself in a District Court. But from where I'm sitting, I'm looking at a girl barely a year into practicing criminal law, with a kid sitting beside her that just finished his second year in law school. Not very impressive. And not at all encouraging in terms of your client's future. And the future of her family." Starke paused, nodding her head in the direction of the empty prosecution table. As soon as the jury had been excused, Huber Kennedy had grabbed his things and rushed for the exit, his face dark and angry. The courtroom was now almost completely empty. "It's after five o'clock now, and we all have to clear out of here. I would *strongly* suggest that you take the opportunity before we reconvene tomorrow morning to get with Mr. Kennedy and work out a deal. And you should consider anything he offers short of five years in prison to be a gift at this point. Do I make myself clear?"

Sam was flabbergasted. Up to now, the trial had actually exceeded her wildest expectations. She took a brief moment to glance back at Harry, trying to process what the judge had just told her, to reconsider whether she was being naive, blind to the reality of what they were facing when the case finally went to the jury. But, no, she couldn't see it. At the very worst, this jury would just hand Cynthia Rollins probation. That didn't mean, though, that she shouldn't at least go through the motions. Otherwise, Kennedy would get right back to Starke and let her know that Sam had completely ignored the judge's recommendations. If it doesn't hurt to play their damned game a little, Sam decided, then just play the damned game.

"Yes, Your Honor. I'll talk to Mr. Kennedy and see what he has to offer." She paused, but couldn't help herself. "But, to be completely honest, Your Honor, at this point I'm feeling really good about my case. I think we've got this one nailed."

"Hmmph." If anything, Starke's scowl grew even deeper. "That's just your youth talking. And your ego. But, I'm warning you here. If you don't put a check on that ego and get back down to earth, your client is going to be the one to suffer. You can do what you want. I'm just trying to help you out on this one. I was once a young lady lawyer just starting off myself, you know. We girls have to stick together." With that, Starke rose and headed briskly out the door to her chambers.

29

Sam had just a few minutes to conference with Cynthia before the jailor led her client out of the courtroom and back to jail for the evening.

"Cynthia, the judge is pushing me to take a deal on this case. She says that you're going away for anything from five years to twenty if I don't. If *we* don't."

The news had driven Cynthia almost to tears. The prospect of losing her boys to foster care had left Cynthia in a perpetually fragile state, and she was leaning heavily on Sam for advice and support. "I don't know what to *do*, Miz Sam! Please tell me what I gotta *do*!"

Sam hated this part of her job, the burden of making decisions for clients that could make or break their entire lives. Even with her own elevated intelligence and extensive training, sorting through the risk versus reward calculus for a client was almost impossible. For the client herself, the emotional baggage alone made it a hopeless task.

"Look, Cynthia, I'll tell you what we'll do." Sam had her arm around her client, while her own mind was still racing, looking for the right soothing words. "We don't need to decide anything right now. I'll talk to the prosecutor tonight, and have you brought over a little earlier tomorrow morning so we can discuss our options before the trial starts up again. How does that sound?"

"Okay, Miz Sam. Whatever you say. I'll just pray on it tonight, and we can talk in the morning."

"That sounds like a great idea, Cynthia," Sam said as the jailor gently put her client back in handcuffs and led her toward the door to the secured section of the Justice Center. Sam finished gathering up her things and headed out toward the parking lot.

She made it halfway to her car when her cell phone buzzed. *Kennedy*, she noted, checking the screen. *That was quick. A little too quick.* She tapped it to answer the call. "Tulley here. What can I do for you?"

"Ms. Tulley, this is Huber Kennedy. I just wanted to touch base with you to see if your client might want to reconsider a plea deal at this point in the trial."

Sam knew it wasn't a coincidence that she was getting this call at *this* precise moment. "Sure. You know me, I'm always willing to discuss anything. So what you got for me? I'm thinking, after what we've seen so far, a dismissal wouldn't be out of the question."

There was a brief silence on the other end while Kennedy tried to decide whether she was serious or not. "Uh, actually, I can't go along with that. But I did get a chance to discuss it all with the DA, and he's pushing me to give you a real low ball offer. I think he just wants to get this over with."

"Low ball?" Sam laughed. "I like the sound of that. So what are we talking here? One year deferred?"

Again, Kennedy paused, taken aback by her seemingly flippant attitude. "No, actually, that won't work. But he *was* willing to go as low as four and a half straight up, no probation and no parole. That's one of the best offers I've ever seen for a deadly weapon assault."

Four and a half years. Just minutes after Starke suggested I should jump on any offer under five. You would think they'd be embarrassed about making their collusion so painfully obvious. "Okay, Huber, I'll take that up with my client in the morning, after they bring her over from the jail."

"You can't get me an answer before then?" Kennedy was trying to press her for a quick deal, a sure sign he was desperate.

"No," Sam replied. "You know the drill. She's being processed back in, and won't be available to meet with me for another hour or so. Meanwhile, I've got a little girl at home, and I just don't have time to hang around here any longer." She paused, fully irritated by now. "Tell you what, be in the courtroom at eight thirty tomorrow, and I'll have an answer for you then."

"You sure you can't get me an answer before then?" Kennedy insisted.

"Sure, Kennedy. You need an answer right now? I'll give you an answer." Sam and Harry exchanged a look. "You can kiss my ass. How's that for an answer?"

Cynthia Rollins was brought into the courtroom at eight the next morning, and Sam could tell right away that things were about to get complicated. The jailor uncuffed her client and led her to her seat at the defense table. Sam leaned over to check on her. "How are you doing this morning, Cynthia?"

"Oh, Miz Sam! I don't know what to do. Did you talk to him? What did he say? Am I going to go to prison? I can't go to prison, Miz Sam! I can't let them take my boys away from me!"

Oh, boy. This was going to be even tougher than Sam had imagined. "Listen, everything is going to be okay. No one is sending you to prison, and no one is taking your boys away." She paused for a second. "Look, the other side has made an offer, and I have to present it to you. I don't necessarily *like* the offer, but that isn't my decision to make. It's your life, so it's your decision. I can only give you advice as to what I think about your chances."

Cynthia looked up uncertainly. "You think it's a bad offer?"

"Let's just say I have some serious doubts as to their motivations. I think the judge and the prosecutor are playing a big game together. A game that's intended to force your hand, to make you accept an offer that isn't in your best interests."

"Then, just tell them no."

"I kind of already did, Cynthia, but I still need to run it past you, to get your buyoff on it."

"Okay, then, what is it? What are they offering? Can I stay out of jail?"

"No, and that's the big problem here, Cynthia. They're offering four and a half years in state prison, with no chance of probation or parole."

"But that means my boys –" Cynthia had started to fall apart again. Fast. Sam needed to figure out a way to pull her back together. Trial was starting up again in less than an hour. She glanced back into the visitors gallery and saw Cynthia's pastor, Ollie Moore, sitting quietly behind them as he had throughout the trial. Ollie was a rotund, exceedingly well dressed middle-aged black man with a balding head and an engaging smile. The very model of a man who had pledged his faith and his life to God. She motioned for him to join them.

"Reverend Ollie, thank you for being here for Cynthia." Sam grabbed a chair from the prosecution table so he could huddle up with the two of them.

"No way I would miss being here for Cindy," he said. "Cindy's one of my flock. She's an innocent little lamb of God that they're trying to lead to slaughter. I can't thank you enough for what you're doing for her." He turned to face Cynthia, taking her hands in his. "Listen up, now, Cindy. You gotta pay attention to your lawyer, here. I've been watching her all along, and she's a regular Perry Mason!" Sam knew the cultural reference to the old Raymond Burr television show was lost on her client, but she appreciated the compliment. "If anyone has your best interests at heart right now, it's Miz Sam. You gotta just trust her and let her see you through all this."

Cynthia was nodding now, but still not completely convinced. Sam had an idea. "Cynthia, you know the story about Saint Peter, don't you? The story of what happened right after Jesus died?" Cynthia was looking at her quizzically, not sure where she was going with this. Sam continued. "Well, Peter was holed up, afraid. The man he had been following all that time, the man he thought was his Lord and Savior, was dead. Peter was lost, and he didn't know what to do. And that's when the Roman po-pos came knocking on his door." She paused to let that sink in, the idea that Peter had been forced to deal with the police knocking on his door, too. "And the Roman po-lice, they showed Peter a picture and said, do you know this man?" It was a stretch from the real story, but Sam was reaching for understanding, not accuracy. "And when they showed him the picture of Jesus, Cynthia, what did Peter say?"

Cynthia thought about it for a second. "He said he didn't know him."

Sam nodded. "That's right. He said,' I don't know the dude.' Not just once, but three times. *Three times* he denied Christ, denied his Lord and Savior. And why did he do that?"

"Because he was afraid?"

"That's right. Peter denied even *knowing* Jesus because he was afraid of what the Roman po-lice would do to him if they knew he was one of Jesus' people. They made him so afraid, he was willing to turn his back on God in Heaven, on everything he believed in." Sam reached over to touch her client's shoulder. "And that is just exactly what they're trying to do here, what they're trying to do to you. To make you so afraid that you'll break down and take their offer, agree to go to prison and lose both of your boys. But that isn't going to happen, is it?"

"No," Cynthia replied, meekly.

Reverend Ollie jumped in. "Cindy, you know the rest of that story. Peter had to learn to put his faith and his trust in the Lord, to let the Lord shield him from harm. And that's what you have to do here. You need to let go of your fear and trust in the Lord to see you through all this."

Sam appreciated the Reverend's support, and could see that her client was finally coming around. "That's right. You need to take all your fears and give them to God. Let him guide you and protect you. And right here, in this courtroom, you need to take your trust and give it to me, so I can do God's work in saving you and saving your boys." That pledge was well outside of anything Sam had learned in law school, even at Baylor, but she knew that the only way her client could survive the next few days intact was to draw deeply from the well of her faith in the power of the Lord.

Sam watched closely as Cynthia drew two deep breaths, then turned to look up at her. "You're right, Miz Sam. They're just tryin' to scare me into losing my faith. In God. In Reverend Ollie. In you. But God's will be done. God has placed me here for a reason, and everything that happens here is part of His plan. I can see that now. I'm not going to be afraid anymore. Let's finish this trial sos I can go home and take care of my boys."

Sam glanced over at Reverend Ollie appreciatively. "Okay, Cynthia. That's just what we'll do. I'll go tell him you've rejected the offer, then let's get ready and win this one. Just one or two more days and this nightmare will be over, and we can all go home."

Sam stepped over to the prosecutor's table to give Huber Kennedy the bad news. He seemed completely astonished that his little ploy with the judge hadn't worked. Sam Tulley was proving to be a tougher egg to crack than they had thought. And at this point, he had just one last trick left to pull out of the bag.

31

Judge Starke stalked into the courtroom ten minutes early, eager to get the plea deal safely on the table and the trial closed down before it got even more out of hand. She had already decided to dispense with the Pre Sentence Investigation report and plead this one out this morning, if possible. Four and a half years was a pretty good outcome, given everything that had already happened in this case.

But as she settled into her chair at the front of the courtroom, she could tell with one glance at Huber Kennedy that something had gone very wrong with their plan. She looked over at Sam, who was sitting with a rather smug smile on her face, a smile the judge did not appreciate one bit. "Counselors!" she called out. "Do we have a deal on the table?"

Kennedy hesitated a moment, so Sam rose to address the judge. "No, Your Honor. My client has reviewed the State's offer and has decided to continue forward with trial."

Starke swiveled her eyes to stare at Cynthia Rollins. "And you agree with that, Ms. Rollins? Your lawyer has advised you that, if you lose, you could be facing twenty years in state prison?"

Cynthia didn't know that she should stand before addressing the judge, so she remained seated as she answered, "Yes, ma'am."

Starke's face had suddenly grown very dark. "And she told you that the State was offering less than a quarter of that? Just four and a half years?"

Bingo, Sam thought jubilantly. *And on the record, at that*! She rose to plunge the dagger into the judge's heart. "Your Honor, with all due respect, the specifics of the State's offer have never been brought before this court. We simply stated that they had made an offer and we rejected it. How is it now possible that you are privy to the precise details of that offer?"

Starke's eyes went wide as she realized the magnitude of her blunder. She glanced quickly at Kennedy, but he was managing to stare at something in the far corner of the courtroom. "Umm, it was just a guess –" She calmed herself. "Yes, that's it, just a guess. As I told you yesterday, I suggested you should jump on top of any offer under five years –" Once again, Starke belatedly saw the trap she had set for herself.

And Sam watched as the court reporter entered it all into the record. The judge had all but outright confessed to an illegal attempt to coerce her client into accepting the plea deal. Sam decided to twist the dagger just a little bit deeper. "But, Your Honor, your comment to my client was very precise. Four and a half years. Not four years, not four years nine months, but *four and a half years*. And, for that matter, you had no *legitimate* way of knowing that the offer wasn't *six* years. Or *seven*. So when exactly did you get with Mr. Kennedy to decide that four and a half years was the magic number?"

Starke knew that Sam had her cornered on this one, and the only possible solution was to fight her way out. "I resent that implication, Ms. Tulley. And if you think you can waltz right in here and insult this court, then you have another think coming!"

But Sam wasn't yet finished. "Your Honor, I –"

"No!" Starke snapped back. "We're done with this discussion! We're moving on. And Ms. Tulley," she continued, narrowing her eyes, "one more word out of you on this and I'll find you in contempt of court. You can plan the rest of this trial from the cold comfort of a jail cell. Do I make myself clear?"

"Abundantly, Your Honor," she responded, making a show of sweeping her eyes to stare at the court reporter. Sam knew she needed a copy of Starke's admissions before those records disappeared. She would text Evan while the jury was being brought in and get him to file an emergency subpoena to seize them before the lunch break. That record would be critical evidence in the charges she planned to file before the state bar and the Texas State Commission on Judicial Conduct. Sam also knew that she had made a lifelong and very dangerous enemy today, creating an enmity that would almost certainly be picked up by all of the other judges in the county. That would prove problematic in future cases, but she could only hope that those feelings of hostility would be offset by an even stronger fear, a fear that Sam Tulley would bring the vengeance of Shiva to bear on anyone who opposed her unfairly. That she was more than willing to go nuclear.

32

With all of the morning's drama submerged under the waves of courtroom procedure and out of sight of the jurors, the trial proceeded. Kennedy called Cynthia's ex-boyfriend, Calvin Archer. Compared to how he had looked on the police videos from the night of the arrest, Archer had cleaned up well. He had on a simple white shirt, blue jeans and bright white Converse sneakers, clearly purchased new for the trial. Kennedy's direct of Archer was very predictable, establishing his on-again, off-again relationship with Cynthia Rollins that had suddenly turned off again. He needed to break out of the relationship, but he was deathly afraid of Cynthia, who had a jealous streak that could quickly and unpredictably turn violent. To avoid this, he arranged for his friends to help him move out of the house while Cynthia was at work. His plan was to be long gone before she found out he had taken off. It was really the best way to deal with a bad situation.

Archer went on to explain what had happened when Cynthia did find out and arrived back home in an explosive rage. She drove up over the curb and onto the front yard, jumping out of the car before it had even stopped, pistol in hand. Before anyone could say anything, she started firing directly at him. He raced into the open garage and out the back, trying to escape. Once he was safe, though, he realized that he had left his buddies behind in harm's way, and so he snuck back around the side of the house to confront her and give them a chance to get away. She must have known what he was doing though, because just as he was climbing over the side fence to get to the front yard, she met him on the side of the house and fired two more shots at him, somehow missing both times as he dodged the bullets, just like he had been taught in the Army. Kennedy passed the witness.

Sam hardly knew where to start. Archer had left so much easy fruit dangling right in front of her, she just needed to pick one at random and bite in. Harry pushed his notepad over in front of her, the words "start with the shots" underlined in red.

"Mr. Archer, I want to talk to you a bit about the shots that were fired that night. Now, you said a little while ago on direct that Ms. Rollins fired three or four shots at you while you raced out the back of the garage and into the safety of the back yard. Then, when she confronted you on the side of the house, she fired another two shots at you from a foot or so away while you were hanging on top of the fence, but missed, then fired one more shot while you raced away and over the back fence into the alley. That's, what, seven shots in total?"

"Six or seven, that's right."

"Six or seven." Sam paused to fix him with a steady gaze. "And yet, the neighbors across the street heard only two or three shots in total. Your two friends – one of them said she fired two shots, the other said two, maybe three shots. But you're telling this court today that those *four* witnesses were wrong. That in fact, six or seven shots were fired?"

Archer knew it showed weakness to waver on his answers. He needed to show the jurors that he was absolutely confident about what had happened. "Like I told you, six or seven."

"Okay," Sam said. "Let's move on and talk about the bullets from those shots. You said she fired three or four shots at you while you were standing in the garage."

"Three or four, that's right. I can't be sure exactly, 'cause I was runnin' for my life at the time." Archer turned his head to smile smugly at the jury.

"Okay, Mr. Archer, whether it was three shots or four, you know that the police made a complete examination of that garage the very next day, while Ms. Rollins was in custody?"

"Don't know nothin' about that. I was long gone by then."

"Right. So you aren't aware that when the police scoured the walls, ceilings and contents of that garage, they didn't find one single bullet hole. Don't you find that a little odd?"

"Like I said, I don't know what they did or didn't do. I just know what I know, and if they didn't find any bullets then they didn't look hard enough." He glanced over again at the jury with a smile. "Guess they donuts were gettin' cold, and they had to take off early."

"Yeah, I hear that a lot, Mr. Archer. The police and their donuts." Sam paused, not looking at the jury but hearing muffled laughter coming from their direction. "Now, you said she fired three or four shots at you while you were racing for the back door of the garage, and missed. What was that, about twenty feet?"

"Twenty or thirty feet, maybe. And I was dodging the whole time, just like I was trained."

"Yes, that training. We'll get to that in a moment, sir. But first, let's talk about what happened immediately after you got through that door and into the safety of the back yard. That's when you say you stopped and realized that you had left your buddies in harm's way."

"Leave no buddy behind. That's what we always say in the Army." Archer had puffed himself up. All five foot six of a deadly wannabe Army Ranger.

"Leave no buddy behind," Sam repeated. "So, at this point, armed with nothing more than your wits and your Army training, you decide to go back and confront your crazy, gun toting – and gun firing – ex-girlfriend. Is that what I'm hearing?"

"That's right. Leave no buddy behind. I had to take her down."

"Okay, Mr. Archer, so now you go low, you're sneaking along the back side of the garage, and then down the side of the house. You crouch down to maintain a low profile for the shooter, and slowly make your way to the fence. But not too slowly. Your buddies are in danger." Sam pantomimed Archer's supposed movements as she spoke, to the great amusement of the jury. Kennedy caught what she was doing and jumped up immediately.

"Objection, Your Honor! Defense counsel is trying to use her body movements to confuse the jury!"

Sam straightened up. "Your Honor, I –"

"Sustained!" Starke interrupted. "Counselor, move on, but without the movements."

"Move on without the movement. I get you," Sam replied snarkily, but continuing her cross exam before the judge could get another word in. "So you're crouching behind the side fence, and decide to crawl over it. Do I have that right?"

"Pretty much."

"And that's when Cynthia Rollins shot you."

"I-I'm sorry. What?".

Sam waived her hand theatrically in the air. "Why, that's when she shot you." She was smiling at him, but a smile that held no warmth. "You testified earlier that, as you were stuck right there on the top of that fence, that's when the defendant pointed a gun at you from about one or two feet away and pulled the trigger. Twice. Mr. Archer, where exactly did those bullets strike you?"

"Uh, no, I testified that she missed," he explained, looking confused that she had misunderstood that point.

It was Sam's turn to look confused. "I'm sorry, Mr.Archer. Maybe I missed something. She's standing about a foot or two away from you. About this far." She held her hands roughly a foot and a half apart. "She points the gun at you. You're stuck right on top of that fence, paralyzed. She pulls the trigger. Twice." Sam turned again to face the jury, her eyes catching each of the twelve jurors as she delivered her next line. "So how exactly did she miss hitting you with a nine millimeter semiautomatic pistol at a distance of one or two feet?"

"Like I said, I used my training from the Army to dodge the bullets."

"Uh huh. Gotcha. And how exactly does that work, Mr. Archer?" She reached down inside a bag sitting on the floor beside her chair and pulled out a toy pistol that shot small foam darts. "Would you like to demonstrate those moves for us today, Mr. Archer? Would you mind stepping down from the witness box and show us how you can dodge these toy darts from a distance of eighteen inches? Standing, not even hanging on top of a fence?"

She had called his bluff, and Archer knew there was no way he could pass the test she was proposing. "Uh, you can't just do that on demand. You have to be in the *zone*."

Sam nodded, understanding. "What you're saying, Mr. Archer, is that you can only turn it on when your buddies are in danger."

"Yeah, that's right!"

Sam stared at him for several seconds to make it clear to the jury that Archer had brazenly lied about being shot at. Then, dramatically, she moved on. "Okay, my next question for you, Mr. Archer, is why crawl over it? Why crawl over the fence?"

Archer looked confused by the question. "I think that should be pretty obvious. I needed to get over it to get to the front yard and save my buddies."

"Yeah, that's what I was thinking, too, Mr. Archer. So, the only thing that confused me about that, the only thing I didn't get, was why crawl over the fence? Why didn't you just use the gate?"

Archer's brow was knotted. "What gate?" he asked, no longer arrogant.

Sam moved in for the kill. "Why, the gate right there next to the house." She picked up a copy of a police photo. "Your Honor, may I approach?" she asked, stepping briskly to the witness box.

"You may," Starke responded in a quiet voice.

"Mr. Archer, I'm showing you a photograph of the north side of the house that was taken the morning after the shooting. It has already been admitted into evidence as State's Exhibit R. You recognize this house, right?"

Archer had no way to avoid it. He couldn't say he didn't recognize the house since he had already testified that he'd lived there. "Yes," he answered simply.

Sam continued to press him. "And right there on the side of the house, right where you just testified you crept up to try to sneak back into the front yard to protect your buddies. That's a gate, isn't it?"

"Yeah, uh, yeah, I saw the gate." Archer's eyes darted sharply to the right, then to the left. "But it was locked! That's why I couldn't use it. It was locked!"

"Locked. Yes, that would explain it." Sam was standing directly in front of the witness box, where Archer had regained his smug disposition. "So what you're telling us is, there was a padlock on the latch, that little u-shaped thingy that comes down and closes the gate. A padlock the police didn't find when they arrived on the scene and walked through that gate into the back yard. Is that what you're saying?"

"Yeah, there was a padlock on it."

"And you couldn't be mistaken about that? Because the police never found any lock…"

Archer was back to his fully confident self. "I know what I saw. There was a padlock on it. She must have unlocked it and tossed it over the neighbor's fence before the police got there."

"Okay, Mr. Archer, I want you to take another good look at this picture." She handed him the photo, and then with her left hand she brought up a magnifying glass. "Here, you might need this." She handed him the glass. "Now, I want you to look very carefully at that gate. At that little u-shaped thingy. The latch. What do you see?"

It was what Archer didn't see that nailed him. There was no u-shaped thingy.

"I'm sorry, Mr. Archer. Again, can you please look closely at that gate and describe to us that u-shaped thingy? The latch for the gate?"

He paused, looking up to the judge for support and not getting it. Reluctantly, Starke had no choice but to instruct him to respond. "Mr. Archer, just answer the question." He looked back at Sam, then at the photo. Finally, he croaked out in a small voice, "It isn't there."

"Ah, yes," Sam noted, turning again to face the jury. "No u-shaped thingy. So, in fact, the gate *wasn't* locked that night. In fact, there was no way the gate *could* have been locked that night. Isn't that right, Mr. Archer?"

Archer nodded meekly. But Sam drove it home again. "I'm sorry, Mr. Archer, but the court reporter can't take down head gestures. You have to say the words. So, again, there was no way the gate *could* have been locked that night, was there?"

"No," he answered, fully deflated. "No, it wasn't locked."

Sam moved to finish him off. "The fact is, you didn't know about that gate, did you?"

"Uh, I…"

"You didn't know about that gate because you never lived at that house, isn't that right?"

"No, I…"

Sam snatched up a police report, waving it in the air. "You never lived at that house, and that's why when the police inventoried the items in the three cars, the items you and your two friends took out of Cynthia Rollin's house and stuffed into those cars, none of your clothes were on that list."

"I think I took them earlier…"

Sam turned her back on him. "Pass the witness."

33

Archer turned out to be the last of the state's witnesses, and Kennedy rested his case just before lunch. After the break, Cynthia's oldest son took the stand and told the court how he had come home that night from watching a football game against his school's top rival and caught Archer and his friends pilfering the house. Harry handled the direct perfectly. Next, Cynthia herself testified, explaining that when she arrived back home that night, she tried to stop Archer and his friends from robbing her house, but they just laughed in her face. Finally, she ran inside and grabbed a gun that she kept locked away from the children, brought it outside and fired two or three shots into the air to scare them off. Then the cops arrived, threw her to the ground, handcuffed her and, finally, arrested her and took her to jail. She vehemently denied ever firing a shot at anyone that night, especially Archer.

Sam had warned Cynthia about Kennedy's cross examination, and her warnings turned out to be prescient. In contrast to Sam's sophisticated technique of playing cat and mouse with witnesses on cross, Kennedy was a screamer, a shouter who tried to bludgeon his victims with unsupported allegations and outright threats. He laid into Cynthia early, accusing her of being a violent, drug-riddled psychopath who would rather kill her man than face rejection.

"And that gun! Who has a gun in a house with small children? You had that gun because you were actually doing dope deals on the side!"

"Objection!" For perhaps the twentieth time, Sam rose to object to Kennedy's attacks. And for the twentieth time, the result from the bench was the same. "Overruled. I think that was a fair question. The witness will answer!"

"But, Your Honor," Sam protested, "it wasn't even a question! Let alone the fact that there is not one iota of evidence to support this allegation!"

Starke glared down at her from the bench. "I said OVERRULED, Ms. Tulley. Now sit down!"

After about forty minutes of this, Sam could see that her client was starting to come apart under the attack. And worse, rather than just wither and become unresponsive, Cynthia was becoming more and more combative. Sam realized she needed to break the cycle on this, and fast, before Kennedy succeeded in turning her client's feeble attempts to hold her ground into something much worse.

"Your Honor!" Sam called out during a rare pause in Kennedy's tirade. "We've been at this already for most of the afternoon, and I think it may be time for a break. I for one would greatly benefit from a bathroom break, and I think most of the jury may be in the same boat."

The last thing Judge Starke wanted at this moment was to put a damper on Kennedy's increasingly successful efforts to crack this witness, efforts that might represent their last good chance of winning the trial. But she could tell from one glance at the jury box that Sam was right about the jury. Several were already beginning to squirm in their seats from just the suggestion of a shot at the toilet, and if she denied them now, not only would they resent her, but in their discomfort they might even miss the key points Kennedy was about to make. Reluctantly, she relented. "Fifteen minutes," she called out. "Be back here by five minutes to four!"

Sam bounced up and met her client halfway across the courtroom floor. "Join me outside the ladies bathroom on the other side of the building," she whispered. Just in case anyone was watching, Sam would duck in and out of the bathroom, then take advantage of most of the fifteen minutes to feed Cynthia instructions on how to handle the rest of Kennedy's cross.

When Sam emerged from the bathroom after splashing some water on her face to clear her mind, Cynthia was already waiting for her outside, along with Harry and Reverend Ollie. Wasting no time, she leaned in close to her client.

"Look, Cynthia, I told you this morning what to expect from Kennedy, that he would try and shake you, get you rattled. That's his only chance, now. Get you confused, then twist his questions and your answers around until before you know it, you're confessing to murder."

"Yes, Miz Sam, I know what you told me. But everything he's saying in there is a lie!"

"Of course it's a lie, Cynthia. That's just how he does it, that's his game. And the judge, who's supposed to put a stop to it, the judge is right in the middle of that game. But it's a game *you* can't win. So don't play it. Don't let them trick you into playing along."

Reverend Ollie took this opportunity to cut in. "Cindy, you need to listen to your lawyer. She's got a *plan.* I've been sitting there watching, watching the whole trial, and she's been building a jigsaw puzzle, collecting it piece by piece. But you startin' to fight him, you startin' to do your own thing, and that's messing up the puzzle, messing up the big picture she's been building. You need to settle down and stop fighting him, let *her* do your fighting, instead. Like she said before, you gotta give your fear to Jesus, and let Miz Sam take care of the rest."

Cynthia was nodding throughout his speech. "I know, I know. I just get so *angry,* and his questions made me even *angrier* —"

"And that is exactly what he is trying to do," Sam explained. "He's trying to shake you up, to get you angry enough that you stop thinking about your answers, then before you know it he's tricked you into giving him an answer that he wants, and you've lost. He'll twist a question into knots so you'll think he's asking one thing, when in fact he's asking just the opposite. And you'll say yes when you should have said no. That's the way his game works, and the judge is not just *letting* him do it, she's *helping* him do it."

"So, Miz Sam, what do we do now?" Cynthia asked plaintively.

"Okay, here's the plan." Sam checked her watch. Five minutes left. "As I told you before, during his cross, I only want three answers from you: yes, no and I don't know. And since Kennedy and Starke are double teaming you on this, since they're clearly fighting dirty, we're going to have to fight dirty, too." She paused to fish a pencil out of her bag. "When we get back in there, I want you to keep your eyes focused just to Kennedy's left, which would be to your right. I'm sitting just a few feet away from him, so you'll be able to see my right hand with no difficulty. Now, it's crucial here that you make the jury think you're looking at *him* and not me, but still make sure you can see my right hand." Sam held up the pencil. "Whenever he asks you a question, wait until he stops – completely – before you answer. Then, if I have the pencil pointed *up*, the answer is 'yes.' If I have it pointed *down* the answer is 'no.' Held in the middle, it's 'I don't know.' Can you do that?"

Cynthia nodded. "Up for yes, down for no. Got it."

"Super. Now, one last thing. If he starts to interrupt you, stop immediately, stare at him, and, when he finally stops talking, simply tell him, 'I'm sorry, but I was trying to answer you, and you interrupted me. What was your question?' Got that?"

"'I'm sorry, but I was trying to answer, and you interrupted me. What was your question?'," Cynthia repeated.

"Perfect. That will signal to the jury that he's being unfair, and that you're trying to give him an honest answer regardless." Sam checked her watch again. "Time to head back. You and Reverend Ollie go in first, and take your seat at our table. I'll come in a little behind you so it's not totally obvious that we've been powwowing on this. Remember: Yes, no, I don't know. When he realizes his strategy isn't working, he'll give up pretty quickly. And by all means, *don't make it obvious that you are watching my right hand.* Okay?"

"Okay, Miz Sam. And thank you, again. You've fought so hard for me, and I don't want to mess it all up."

"You're doing fine," Sam assured her. "Now scoot!"

34

The rest of Kennedy's cross examination of Cynthia Rollins went by relatively smoothly, if unsuccessfully for him. Once again, he tried to bludgeon her with heated accusations, but this time her responses were short and calm, effectively sucking all the energy out of his attacks. Then he switched gears and started prodding her with highly contorted questions, questions that appeared to mean one thing but in fact meant entirely the opposite. But, somehow, amazingly to him, Cynthia managed to perfectly parse any question he threw at her and return with the proper answer. Or, at least, the proper answer from her perspective. And she deftly dodged his blatant attempts to throw her off by interrupting her mid-answer. Finally, completely frustrated by his inability to draw blood, he passed the witness.

Sam stood immediately, glancing briefly at Harry to see him shake his head and point down to where he had written "Nothing more" on his notepad. "No more questions, Your Honor."

Judge Starke could read the tea leaves in this case. So far, Tulley had put on a remarkable defense, and the trial was lost for the State unless something dramatic happened, and happened soon. "Ms. Tulley, call your next witness."

"No more witnesses, Your Honor. The defense rests." Sam smiled sweetly at the jury and sat down.

Starke turned to Huber Kennedy. "Mr. Kennedy, any rebuttal witnesses?"

Kennedy rose, smiling wickedly at the defense table. "Yes, Your Honor. The State calls Detective Ira Rather."

Sam shot to her feet. "Your Honor, Detective Rather is not on the State's witness list. We would therefore object to the State tendering him as a witness."

Kennedy waved his right hand theatrically. "Your Honor, Detective Rather is a *rebuttal* witness. He is being brought to rebut evidence presented during Ms. Tulley's case in chief. Since we had no way of knowing in advance what evidence or testimony she was going to offer, we couldn't anticipate what witness or witnesses we would need to address the dishonesty of that testimony –"

Starke looked bored. "Overruled. Bring him in, Mr. Kennedy."

Detective Rather entered the courtroom and strode directly toward the witness box. He was an average-sized man, with the exception of a huge beer gut that threatened the integrity of the buttons holding the front of his tan uniform together. Completely bald, he sported a short goatee, brownish but starting to show streaks of gray.

Once sworn in, Rather turned to face Huber Kennedy, an arrogant sneer showing on his face. "Detective Rather," Kennedy began, "can you please identify yourself to the jury?"

"My name is Detective Ira Rather. I'm with the Briar County Sheriff's Department."

"And how long have you been with that department, Detective Rather?"

"Almost twenty five years, now. And thirty five years total in law enforcement."

"Thank you, detective. Now, do you happen to recognize the defendant, here, Cynthia Rollins?" Kennedy turned toward the defense table with a cat-ate-the-canary look, obviously relishing the surprise he was about to spring on his opponent.

Sam bent over to converse quietly with her client. "Who *is* this guy? Why is he here?"

"He handled my rape," Cynthia answered, with a slight quiver to her voice.

"*Rape*? *What* rape? How does that fit into this case?" Sam was suddenly alarmed. What new game were they playing here?

"I was raped two years before all of this happened. A guy I knew broke in to my bedroom while the boys were asleep. I reported it to this detective and pressed charges. Then the guy who raped me called and told me to look on the Internet, where he had posted a video he took of the rape on a revenge website. He said he would leave it up there unless I dropped the charges."

"And so what happened? Did you do that? Did you drop the charges?" Sam was aghast. This was *horrible*! And what in God's name did it have to do with this trial?

"Yes, I told the detective what was going on, and he downloaded the video."

"What happened then? Did he go after the guy?"

"No, he advised me to just drop the charges and move on. So that's what I did. Then I bought the gun. To make sure it never happened again."

Sam was speechless. At the rape, at the detective's callousness four years before, at Kennedy's decision to make it an issue in this trial.

Rather was just explaining his connection to the defendant. "Yeah, she came to us about four years ago, complaining of a so-called rape..."

"Objection!" Sam jumped to her feet, rage clearly showing on her face. "Your Honor, may we approach?"

"Counselors." Starke gestured for them to approach the bench.

Arriving at the front of the courtroom, Sam lowered her voice to a whisper, still managing to maintain an edge to her voice. "Your Honor, I object to this witness and to this line of questioning. Evidently, Detective Rather handled a rape investigation about four years ago, when someone my client knew broke into her home and assaulted her while her boys were sleeping. The assailant, the rapist, evidently videotaped the rape, then threatened to make it a public spectacle unless she dropped the charges." She paused. "The thing is, Your Honor, as tragic as all that is, it has *zero* relevance to this case, and none of this testimony should be allowed under the Texas Rules of Evidence."

Starke turned to Huber Kennedy. "And what do you have to say about this, Mr. Kennedy? What is the relevance?"

Kennedy drew himself up with a smirk. "Your Honor, this testimony is relevant because it goes to Cynthia Rollin's credibility, in particular her record of dishonesty in her dealings with the police. The defendant made a false accusation to the police four years ago about being raped, then had to recant that accusation. That shows she's a liar, that she has a history of lying to the police. That's the relevance, Your Honor."

Sam started to object. "Your Honor, I –"

"That's enough, Ms. Tulley," Starke interrupted. "I would agree, Mr. Kennedy. This testimony is directly relevant to the issues in this trial. Overruled."

"Your Honor," Sam responded, exasperated. "This is outrageous! This testimony –"

"As I said, Ms. Tulley, that's enough from you." Starke leaned in dangerously. "I told you on Wednesday what your client needs to do to end this trial. You want to stop this testimony, just say the word. Otherwise, we're moving forward."

Sam considered carefully what to say next, then out of the corner of her eye she suddenly noticed that the court reporter was busily typing away. The judge's warning had been captured in full on the official trial transcript. *This isn't over, Your Honor,* she promised herself. She spun around without a response and stalked back to her table, feeling Starke staring knives into her back the entire time. Finally, with both lawyers back in place, Starke nodded to Kennedy. "Proceed, counselor."

Huber Kennedy could barely contain his glee. "Go on, Detective Rather. You were saying that you first met the defendant when she falsely reported being raped."

Sam thought about objecting again, but a quick glance at the jury told her it wasn't necessary. This line of questioning wasn't going quite the way Kennedy thought it was.

Rather smiled back at Kennedy, his hands spread generously across his belly. "That's right. She came to us, claiming that she had been raped by a guy she knew."

"Did she have any proof of the rape?" Kennedy asked.

"Nope. Not at first. It was just a he said, she said. We get those all the time."

"You said 'not at first.' Did things change?" Kennedy was grinning viciously.

"Yeah. A few days after she first came to us, she told me there was a sex video of the whole thing that was posted up on the Internet."

Kennedy nodded. "And did you get a chance to view that sex video?"

"Yeah, I saw it. I watched that movie three times. Everybody in the office watched that movie." Rather looked very pleased at his answer.

Kennedy was ready to zero in on the kill. "And in your professional opinion, after watching that sex video, was that a rape?"

Rather puffed himself up on the stand. "Ah, hell no! That wasn't no rape! It wasn't *forcible*, and if it ain't forcible rape, then it ain't *real* rape. Our office only prosecutes *real* rapes!"

Sam was completely outraged by Rather's testimony, and thought briefly about objecting. But then she swept her eyes across the jury again and changed her mind. The twelve of them had reacted exactly the same way she had. Including the one man.

Kennedy, on the other hand, was apparently oblivious to the impact Rather's testimony was having on the jury. He seemed about ready to wrap up his direct examination. But he still had one more little surprise to pull out of his bag of tricks. He smiled slyly at Detective Rather. "Now, detective, did you happen to make a copy of that sex video?"

"Why, yes, of course," Rather answered. "In fact, I've got it right here."

Sam was instantly on full alert. He wouldn't dare –

But apparently he would. Kennedy licked his lips in anticipation of what was about to happen next. "Your Honor," he began, turning slightly to face Judge Starke. "The People offer the sex video, marked State's Exhibit U, into evidence."

"OBJECTION!" Sam couldn't believe what she was seeing. This was so outside the bounds of propriety that she hadn't seen it coming. Not even in her wildest dreams had she imagined that something like this could happen in a court of law.

"Counselors, approach!" Starke ordered, now openly smirking herself. When Sam and Huber Kennedy arrived at the bench, Starke leaned in close. "What is the nature of your objection, Ms. Tulley?" she asked, sarcasm coating every word.

"Your Honor, there is absolutely no way this video can come into evidence in this trial. Even if it was relevant – which of course it is not – under Texas Rules of Evidence 901, a video cannot be admitted unless it is authenticated by the videographer or some other third party who can testify as to the authenticity of the recording. And neither of those two witnesses are available here."

Starke looked thoughtful. "Hmmm. I'm not sure I would agree with that, Ms. Tulley. I am disposed to allowing Mr. Kennedy to show the video, and let the jury decide for themselves whether it is relevant or authentic." She paused, looking down at her notes.

But Sam wouldn't be deterred. "Your Honor, this is outrageous! It's nothing short of *degenerate*! There is absolutely no legal justification for allowing this in!"

Starke looked up, spearing Sam with a searing stare. "Counselor, I have already warned you. If your client doesn't want this to come in, then you know what she needs to do. The offer is still on the table."

"What you're proposing is nothing less than blatant, illegal coercion!" Sam insisted vehemently.

"That may be so, Ms. Tulley, but it's a choice your client needs to –" At that moment, Starke glanced over at the jury, and what she saw in their eyes stopped her cold. She looked back at Kennedy, who seemed to be basking in his new-found victory. Starke looked back at the jury, and again saw no escape from the hole she and Kennedy had dug for themselves. Finally, in a low voice, her eyes sinking, she turned back to Huber Kennedy. "Objection sustained."

The change in plans was so unexpected that it took Kennedy several seconds to realize what had just happened. "Wha-what?" he sputtered. "Your Honor, I think you've got that backwards. Don't you mean 'objection overruled' "?

"No, Mr. Kennedy," Starke answered in a voice suddenly loud enough to carry to the jury. "Ms. Tulley is right. Unless you can bring the person who filmed that video, or a third party who was in the room at the time and can authenticate it as valid, I am going to have to rule against its admission. Do you have any more witnesses at this time?"

"Uh, no, Your Honor." Kennedy was floored. This had all been sketched out so well, using the video to pressure Rollins into taking the plea deal. What had happened in those few seconds in front of the bench that had caused the judge to back out of their plan?

Starke nodded at Detective Rather. "And I think we're finished with this witness, as well. Detective Rather, you may step down."

"Your Honor!" Sam objected. "I have the right – I have an *obligation* under the Constitution to cross examine this witness."

"Not today," answered the judge in a voice so low she could barely be heard. "No, we're finished, here." She turned to the bailiff. "I think it might be a good time to let the jury take a break while we prepare the jury charge and counselors prepare for final arguments. It's a little early, but why don't we give everyone a long lunch. Ladies and gentlemen, you have until one thirty. Be back here and ready to proceed at that time."

The bailiff saw the jurors out of the courtroom, while Sam and Huber Kennedy stood staring at each other in the well of the courtroom, completely stunned by Judge Starke's sudden U-turn.

In Texas criminal courts, the prosecution goes first during closing arguments, followed by the defense, and then, finally, by a prosecution rebuttal of the defense arguments. Sam thought Huber Kennedy's closing argument was absolutely masterful in managing to confuse most of the facts she had uncovered during the trial, while still bolstering the few points that had emerged in his favor. In conclusion, he hammered home the idea that Cynthia Rollins had not called 9-1-1 that night because she wasn't really trying to stop a robbery. She had caught her boyfriend red handed trying to leave her and decided to kill him rather than lose him to another woman. "You saw her in the back seat of the police cruiser after she was arrested!" he shouted to the jury. "She was hysterical! And a hysterical woman will do anything to keep her man! Even kill him if she has to!"

Once again, Sam read the faces of the eleven female jurors, and knew that every one of them had, at one time or another, been accused by some man of acting hysterically. Kennedy was so caught up with the brilliance of his argument that he failed to take into account the way that argument would be received by those eleven crucial members of his audience.

Then it was Sam's turn. "Ladies and gentleman of the Jury," she began. "Mr. Kennedy has just explained to you that the Second Amendment says you can *own* your guns, but you better not try to *use* those guns. Especially not when you are all alone on a dark night, outnumbered by thugs who have broken into your home and are robbing you blind. And robbing your children blind. No, ladies and gentleman, Mr. Kennedy says you better keep those guns locked away, and pick up your phone, instead, and dial 9-1-1. Because when seconds matter, the police are just hours away." She let that thought soak in and was rewarded by affirmative nods from all twelve jurors. "But we'll get back to that in a moment. First, I want to briefly cover what we've learned during this trial. I want to talk about all the things we've heard this week that Mr. Kennedy has apparently forgotten all about, since he went to such painful steps a moment ago to ignore them. Each and every one of them."

Slowly, carefully, Sam began to walk through all of the evidence and testimony from the trial, using a blue marker to write important points on a white flip-chart she set up in front of the jury. Rushing through the testimony of the two friends, she then focused on how Calvin Archer's testimony contrasted sharply with his buddies' testimony, and with the police investigation. "He said she fired six or seven shots at him. He was *sure* of that – six or seven shots. But everyone else that night heard only two or three."

Stepping up directly in front of one of the Second Amendment jurors, she held her right hand out like a gun, extended approximately eighteen inches from the juror's chest. "And there he was, he tells us, perched right up there on top of that fence, with the broken gate right next to him, and he says Cynthia Rollins stood at point-blank range, pointed her pistol right at him, and fired. BLAM!" The juror in front of her flinched, as did most of the other jurors. "She fired once, then fired again! BLAM!" Her targeted juror looked down at her chest, Sam's message clearly and indelibly delivered. If Cynthia Rollins had fired at Archer from that distance, there was no way she could have missed. Calvin Archer had lied.

Since Sam had unveiled Officer William's confession that he thought Rollins was innocent by flagrantly violating the judge's pretrial orders, she couldn't directly bring it up during her close. But she did manage to dance around the issue, effectively reminding the jurors of what they had heard. Finally, she returned to the issue of 9-1-1 and gun rights, using her Powerpoint presentation to show, first, the Second Amendment and, second, the Castle Doctrine law. "Ladies and gentleman, do you see those three little numbers anywhere at all in those laws? Do you see anywhere where it says a person must first attempt to call nine one one? That using your gun is just a last and final option?" She paused, shaking her head slowly. "No. It's not there. Mr. Kennedy wants you to think it's there, wants you to *believe* it's there. But it's not."

She paused a brief moment, building suspense for her next statement. "But the fact of the matter is, Cynthia Rollins *did* call 9-1-1 that night."

The jurors looked confused. Did someone mention that and they somehow missed it? Sam smiled and continued. "Yes, ladies and gentleman. Cynthia Rollins *did* call 9-1-1 that night. Because, back before we all had cell phones, back before 9-1-1 even existed, firing a gun in the air *was* 9-1-1. You fire a gun in the air, and help comes a'running! When Cynthia Rollins arrived home that night to catch those folks robbing her home, her castle, when she couldn't get them to stop any other way, why, she fired her gun in the air and they *left*! Hightailed it out of there! And you heard the police, they were there in just minutes. You know how fast the police normally respond. Hours, usually. Sometimes even *days*. But when Cynthia Rollins fired those shots into the air, they were there in *minutes*. Yes, ladies and gentleman, Cynthia Rollins *did* call 9-1-1 that night. She called nine *millimeter* one one."

36

In his rebuttal, Kennedy doubled down on his twin themes of hysteria and 911 calls. Once again, he showed the police car video of Cynthia Rollin's emotional collapse after her arrest, oblivious to the real impact her cries of "My babies! Who's gonna take care of my babies?" had on the eleven woman jurors. And oblivious to the dark stares he got from the four Second Amendment jurors when he claimed that citizens had no right to self defense, that they should just keep their guns locked up and leave the guns and policing to the cops. As his rebuttal stumbled to an inconclusive conclusion, Sam couldn't see any other outcome for the case than a two word verdict. Not guilty.

The judge issued final instructions to the jury, then sent them back to the jury room to pick a foreperson and deliberate on a verdict. Sam had barely made it in and out of the bathroom down the hall when her phone buzzed. The jury was coming back. They had reached a decision.

As Sam and Harry made it back to the courtroom, the other side was already packed with prosecutors and staff members from the DA's office, as well as the cops from the case and any other cops who happened to be in the building. They were all high-fiving, hugging and handshaking, exuberant that the jurors had managed to see through all of Sam Tulley's manipulations of the truth and the evidence in the case to reach the only possible conclusion: guilty. Even Judge Starke seemed to have snapped out of her brief funk, and was smiling as broadly as any of them.

Sam understood the reason for their celebration. Quick verdicts almost never favored the defense. While jurors might walk back into the jury room and take a quick vote for guilty, not guilty verdicts almost always required long-winded discussions regarding reasonable doubt and conflicting evidence and testimony. This verdict was one of the quickest Sam had ever seen, and it did not look good for her client. She leaned in close to Cynthia. "Look, however this turns out, don't panic. Even if we lose this round, the appeals court will almost certainly reverse it and send it back for a new trial. And next time we might get a more favorable judge."

"You mean you think we've *lost*, Miz Sam?" Rollins was on the verge of tears.

"No, no," Sam told her. "This could go either way at this point. I just want you to know that if we *do* lose, it isn't over. We'll get another shot."

Just then, the door to the jury room opened and the jurors all filed in. None of them looked in Cynthia's direction, which Sam took to be a bad sign.

Once they were all seated, Starke addressed the jury. "Has the jury picked a foreman?"

"We have, Your Honor," said the one male juror, rising to his feet. Sam was amazed. Eleven women, and they still pick the *one man* to be foreman.

"And have you reached a verdict in this case?" Starke asked.

The foreman nodded and handed her a slip of paper. "We have, Your Honor."

Starke was grinning as she opened the verdict to read it aloud to the courtroom. Glancing to her right, Sam could see that the prosecution side was all smiles, as well. They could read the not so subtle signs in the jury's body language as well as she could. Starke started to read the verdict. "We, the jury find the defendant…" Suddenly her face went ashen, her grin evaporating like drops of water on a hot skillet. She could barely get the next two words out of her mouth. "Not guilty."

"THANK YOU JESUS! THANK YOU MIZ SAM!" shouted Cynthia Rollins, throwing her arms high in the air. "THANK YOU JESUS! THANK YOU MIZ SAM!" Reverend Ollie raced up from behind them to congratulate Sam, Harry and her client, as the prosecution side sat in stunned silence.

37

Harry's sister, Hailey, had come up from Houston for the last day of trial, and as soon as Sam and Harry could gather up their papers and stuff it all into their trial boxes, the five of them left the courtroom together and headed for the exits. Even as confident as Sam had been about the likely outcome of the trial, the result had left her somewhat stunned. She had poured so much of her own soul into fighting for Cynthia Rollins that it almost felt like it had been her future that had just been redeemed.

As they stood outside the Justice Center recounting the week's events to each other, suddenly the twelve jurors poured out of the courthouse and mobbed them, the ladies all hugging and kissing Cynthia, Sam and each other. Harry was literally jumping for joy as several of the jurors started shouting "God bless you, Ms. Tulley!" As the melee slowly died down, one of the jurors, Ms. Erikson, the one who had corrected Sam when she misquoted the Second Amendment during voir dire, stepped up and grasped her hand. "Miz Tulley, I just want you to know that, when Mr. Kennedy and that fat cop started going on and on about the rape and that movie, I was just glad I didn't have Miz Rollin's gun, 'cause I would have shot them dead right there on the spot!"

"Amen to that!" shouted another juror, setting off another round of celebration.

Amidst all of the commotion, Sam noticed that Reverend Ollie had moved off to one side, and there was clearly something eating away at him. She freed herself and walked over to speak with him. "Reverend Ollie, is everything okay?" she asked.

"Yeah, Miz Sam. I just want to thank God for sending you to help my little lamb. I don't know if I have ever seen a better example of Satan doing his work than I saw in that judge and prosecutor, and you just beat them back. Everything they threw at you, and you just swatted them away like they was flies." He grasped her hand, sharing a deep and heartfelt smile.

But Sam could tell there was something else troubling him. "It was my pleasure, Reverend. And I'm like you. I don't know that I've ever seen such a blatant attempt to subvert justice, to turn truth into lies and lies into truth. But thank the Lord, this jury saw it, too." She paused, looking into his eyes. "But there's something more you need to tell me, isn't there? Something else you need to get off your chest."

He nodded. "I don't have any right to ask this of you, Miz Sam, after all you've done for Cindy. But I have another member of my flock that needs you, too. They're trying to do the same thing to him, sell him down the river. He has a trial coming up in just two weeks, and his lawyer hasn't seen him but once. Won't return any of our calls or letters offering to testify. And he's completely innocent, Miz Sam. I know the boy, I've known him almost all his life, and he didn't do it."

Sam didn't know how to respond. "Two weeks? Wow. That's pretty short notice…"

"Yes ma'am, I know it is. But seein' what you did for Cindy, seein' how the Lord works in you, I know you can save him."

"Okay," Sam agreed. "I'll take a look at the case. But no promises. Let me see if there's anything there to work with. Who's the client?"

"I think you've probably heard of him. His name is Curtis Jordan."

"The guy who killed his entire family? *That* Curtis Jordan?" Sam was incredulous.

Reverend Ollie spread his hands wide. "You see, Miz Sam? They've even got you convinced, and you don't believe anything they *ever* say is true! You think they're all liars, but even you are willing to believe they're right about Curtis. But I'm telling you, I know the boy. I know him like he's my own son. I knew the whole family, every Wednesday and Sunday at the church, like clockwork. And I'm telling you he didn't do it. They had some problems, him and Katie, but they were working them out, and my understanding was he was about to move back home with them, just before it all happened."

"But Reverend, even if I wanted to take on the case, that's a capital murder case! That's *way* out of my league! And in just two weeks –"

"Just promise me you'll look at it, Miz Sam. That's all I ask. Just look at it, talk to him. Then you'll have spent as much time on the case as the lawyer they gave him, Charlie Bower."

Charlie Bower. Rock the Boat. It was all coming back to her now. Judge McDaniel had subverted the appointment wheel to put Rock the Boat in charge of ushering the case through the system. It was capital murder, and the DA wasn't willing to budge on the death penalty, not with an election coming up. So that meant no plea deal, it had to go to trial. And Bower would coordinate with the DA to make sure the trial went smoothly, that nothing would happen during trial that could support an appeal. By law, since it was a capital case, an appeal would have to be filed, but the only major argument left to appeal would be ineffective assistance of counsel. In the case of Bower, that should be a no brainer, but unfortunately the system didn't work that way. Jordan would see the needle in record time.

"Okay, Reverend. No promises, but I'll take a look at it. If I can get hold of Bower over the weekend, I'll see if I can get a peek at the file. Otherwise, it'll be Monday or Tuesday at the earliest, cutting my preparation time even tighter. And there's no guarantee that the judge will let me sub in this late, even if I *do* decide to take the case."

"I couldn't ask for any more than that, Miz Sam." The Reverend pulled her into a bear hug. "You are truly an angel sent down to us from God!"

"I don't know about that," Sam said when she finally broke free. "But if half the things I've heard about the case are true, then we are definitely going to need a heavenly miracle to save his life. So I'd suggest you start praying for that miracle right away. Curtis Jordan is going to need every one he can get, because at this point, I'd say he doesn't *have* a prayer of winning."

"We've got a special church service set for tonight, to celebrate Cindy's victory, to welcome her back home. We'll start those prayers right then. We're going to lift you up on the wings of angels, Miz Sam!"

And God help me, indeed, Sam thought, if I actually make the mistake of a lifetime and take this case on.

38

Sam went by Charlie Bower's office on the way home and found it sealed up tighter than a tick. So taking a look at the file would have to wait for Monday at the earliest. Over the weekend, she and Harry met with Curtis Jordan at the jail. She had hoped to be able to get a copy of the police reports from him, but Bower hadn't shared anything from the file with his client, and Jordan knew even less about his own case than she did.

One bright spot for the weekend was a small envelope in the Friday mail. It was from the Texas Parole Board, and Sam ripped it open eagerly. She knew what the letter *should* have to say about her client, but the past year had taught her that being legally *right* about something didn't necessarily carry any weight with the powers that be. This time, however, she was in luck. Everything had checked out, and in slightly less than one week she could execute her plan. Sam could already feel some of the sexy attraction of playing dirty, of being the bad girl for a change. She just needed to constantly remind herself that evil should only be used to combat other evil, and even then only when no other strategy would work.

As Monday morning rolled around, Sam headed back to Bower's office right after breakfast. If she hadn't peeked in the window on Friday evening and seen that the office was completely empty, Sam could swear that Solitaire hadn't moved an inch since their last encounter, and her stringy hair was even oilier than before. If that was possible.

"Bower ain't here," Solitaire managed to wheeze out between plays.

Sam decided to stay in the doorway as long as possible to avoid the heavy haze of cigarette smoke. "Do you have any idea when he'll be back?" she asked.

Solitaire looked annoyed by the interruption of her card game. "Well, he's had all weekend to get polluted. So could be today, could be tomorrow. Who knows, and who cares?"

"I just need to take a gander at one of his files. Do you think he'd mind if I checked to see if he's got it in his office?"

"Well, I sure don't care, sugar. But you go digging around in what he calls a filing system in there, and you'll likely be here all week." Solitaire dug out a new cigarette and lit it with a green Bic lighter. "Better off waiting 'til he shows up."

Sam checked her watch and considered the prospect of waiting for hours on the hard wooden bench outside. "Look, why don't I just leave him a note. He can call me when he gets in."

"Suit yerself, sugar. Just drop it here on the desk and I'll make sure he sees it when and if he shows."

Sam slipped outside and scribbled off a short note, then ducked back inside and tossed it on the desk. "Thanks. 'Preciate it!" she muttered to Solitaire without inhaling.

Escaping outside once again, Sam headed for the Justice Center to negotiate some pleas for two of her newest court-appointed clients, a routine family violence case and a case involving a mother charged with illegal possession of a dangerous drug. The mom had repackaged her son's Ritalin into individual doses that she sealed in small baggies she bought at Walgreens. A police officer who pulled her over for a malfunctioning taillight spotted one of the baggies lying on the passenger seat and arrested her on the spot. There was no question that her son had a legitimate prescription for the Ritalin, but the police insisted – wrongly – that it was illegal to separate the drug from its original pill bottle. Sam was certain the case would end in a dismissal, but only after her client had spent a night in jail and three hundred dollars in non-refundable bail money for the crime of closely monitoring her son's health.

Flashing her county bar association badge, Sam barely made it through security when her phone buzzed. Pulling it out of her purse, she checked the caller ID, hoping that Bower had made it into his office early after all. But it was a number she didn't recognize. The area code and prefix suggested the caller was from inside the courthouse, so she answered the call.

"Sam Tulley here. How may I help you?"

"Yes. Ms. Tulley. This is Diane, down in Judge McDaniel's office. He wants to see you in his chambers right away."

McDaniel? Sam knew that the timing of this call meant that the judge had somehow gotten wind of her potential substitution in the Jordan case. And for him to jump her even before she filed the motion to sub was a very bad sign. "I just walked into the Justice Center. Tell him I can be there in just a few moments. How do I get back to his office?"

"He has a deputy waiting in his courtroom to see you back here."

"Fine. I'm headed there now." Sam ended the call and doglegged right toward McDaniel's courtroom. As promised, a deputy sheriff was waiting to buzz her through the locked door at the rear and point her down the hall toward McDaniel's office. Diane was seated at the front desk and waved her into the judge's chambers.

"Your Honor," Sam greeted him as she entered. "To what do I owe the pleasure this morning?"

McDaniel was a grizzled old man who had already served on the court well past his prime. But he was a fixture in the county's Republican party, just as his father and grandfather had been fixtures in the old Democratic party before everyone flipped sides, so the voters kept sending him back to the bench each and every election cycle, blissfully ignorant of his disqualifications as a judge. He eyed her over the top of a set of black-rimmed bifocals. "Sit down," he commanded, pointing to the seat closest to the door. Sam complied. "I got word from the jail that you've been poking around in a case of mine."

"Oh," Sam responded, injecting a sweet lilt into her voice. "I wasn't aware that you were still practicing criminal law. Isn't that a bit of a conflict, since you're also sitting on the bench?"

"Don't get smart with me, young lady!" McDaniel growled. "You know exactly what I mean. You went to visit that murderer over the weekend."

"If you mean the *defendant*, Curtis Jordan, then yes I did. But I would think you of all people should be aware that Mr. Jordan is presumed innocent until the state proves otherwise." If McDaniel wanted to play games with her, Sam was more than willing to try some moves of her own.

"Hmmph. Well, that's all just a matter of time, I'd say." McDaniel drew himself up and leaned threateningly across his desk. "The point is, we've got a trial scheduled in that case, and a damned fine attorney has been appointed to represent him. I'm not going to sit by and let some wet-behind-the-ears upshot just stroll in and upset all that."

"I see," Sam said. "Well, I haven't decided yet whether or not I'm going to take the case, but I might suggest that the question of whether or not I do isn't really up to you, Your Honor. It's my decision to make, and my client's."

McDaniel stood up, towering over her and thumping his desk with a meaty left fist. "Listen up, little lady. That dog won't hunt with me. This is *my* court we're talking about, and in *my* court we play by *my* rules! There's no way in *hell* I'm going to sign off on your taking over that case! That's my final word on the subject!"

Sam refused to be intimidated by the old judge. She rose to her feet and faced him eye to eye. "Well, let me just explain a few things to *you*, Judge. Up until this meeting I had pretty much decided to stay clear of this one. It's a big, bloody mess, and I'm not too thrilled about getting any of that blood on my hands. But now, thanks to you, I've changed my mind." She paused to reach down and grab her briefcase and purse, then straightened up again, her face now barely six inches from his. "This afternoon I'll be holding a press conference announcing that I've agreed to take on Curtis Jordan as my client. I'll explain to the reporters that, in my professional opinion, Mr. Jordan is being railroaded by this court and by his appointed counsel. A lawyer who up to now has only met with his client once, and who has never once discussed the evidence in the case or even his trial strategy with Mr. Jordan. I will then file a Motion to Substitute, which you will quickly and freely grant."

"Like *hell* I will!" McDaniel roared.

Sam was livid. "You *will* grant it, Judge McDaniel. Because if you don't, I'll make sure Curtis Jordan's story becomes the lead news item from Dallas to Houston to Austin. And I'll petition the appeals court to remove you and Bower from the case and move it to a more neutral setting. I already have enough on Bower to make that happen, and I really don't think you want to crawl into that dirty bathwater with him, do you?"

McDaniel didn't know what to say, so he just glared at her for most of a minute. Finally, reluctantly, he caved. "Just so you know, I'm not moving the trial date. And you can expect no favors out of my court when the trial commences."

"I would expect nothing more, Your Honor. And if there *is* nothing more, I'll bid you adieu." Sam spun quickly toward the door and made her exit. She had a lot of work ahead of her before the press conference. And a lot of time to regret what her temper had just gotten her into. *So I guess I'm taking on Jordan's case after all.*

39

The presser went well, the single biggest question she had to answer being "Why?" Why was she taking on this loser of a case, particularly since she had so little time to prepare for it? Her only answer was simply to point out that, as unprepared as she might be to provide her client with adequate legal representation, it was far better than what he had received so far from his court-appointed lawyer, Charlie Bower. Which, to date, was zero.

Sam knew that putting the news spotlight on Bower would make him a lifelong enemy, and make it impossible to get him to cooperate with turning over the Jordan file. Since she had no use for any notes Bower might have scribbled on the file regarding trial strategy and evidence issues, she just marched into the DA's office and demanded a fresh copy. After all of the expected protests and complaints, they finally promised her a copy of the file by early the next morning. Sam reminded them sternly that tardiness would not be an option – any delays in getting the file would make the lead story for the evening news and morning papers.

Despite all of McDaniel's attempts to keep a lid on things, Sam was ready to turn this murder trial into the three ring circus it needed to be. In the end, that was the only way she knew to prevent a repeat of the near lynching that she had just lived through in the Rollins trial. In addition to Bower, Judge McDaniel was now an enemy, but while the press could be relied upon to play up the almost certain guilt of her client, they could also be relied upon to report any obvious foul play by the judge and prosecutor.

While she waited for the official file on the case, Sam filled her time by collecting whatever she could from the news stories that had piled up over the past half year. In the old days, she would have had to bury herself in the morgues, the files of old newspapers and film clips kept by the various news organizations. Nowadays, though, she just had to do a little Internet surfing. She already had a subscription to the local newspapers, so online access to their old stories was a snap. Televised news stories about the case were also easily available, but Sam couldn't find anything new or remarkable from that source. Television news was largely just a shallow recap of what the newspapers had already covered in depth anyway.

By the time she was finished, Sam had run through several reams of paper printing off all the newspaper stories, not a few of them headlined with some variation on an OJ Simpson theme. Black man stabs his white ex-wife to death in a jealous rage. Picking an impartial jury in a small town in Texas was already tough enough, but this case promised to make that task almost impossible.

Sam arrived at the DA's office early Tuesday morning, and was surprised to find that the file was ready on time for once. She headed back to her office to pour over the contents of the file with Harry and start hashing out some semblance of a defense.

What she found in the file was alarming. The DA's office and police had done a great job of keeping a lid on any leaks about the evidence they had collected in the case. Other than the fact that they had found the murder weapon hidden in a dumpster just outside of Curtis Jordan's apartment, so far none of the other evidence had made it into the papers. And it was all very damning. Sam guessed that the plan was to wait and reveal it all during the trial in order to build drama, to make the eventual guilty verdict look inevitable and just.

Much of the evidence was fairly circumstantial, especially given the fact that Jordan had not been a stranger to the house, but in fact had come by on a regular basis to visit his kids. Fingerprints, shoe prints, all of that could be explained away pretty easily. But what had him nailed to the wall was the evidence that couldn't be explained: that the murderer had apparently used a key to enter the front door of the house and lock it back up as he left. Even worse, a Microsoft Word file had been found on Jordan's computer – deleted, but later restored by the county's forensic expert – outlining in great detail the plan to murder his wife and two children. A file that also established the motive for the murders: Curtis Jordan's discovery that his wife had been unfaithful to him during their separation.

But most disturbing of all was a report from the coroner's office that they had discovered blood inside Katie Jordan's vagina. Her blood – blood that had evidently been deposited inside of her postmortem. Whoever killed her had returned to have sex with the cooling and bloody body. Even more than the gruesome nature of the murders of his wife and children, that fact alone painted Curtis Jordan as a sick degenerate, a man unworthy of continued life among the righteous. Even Sam was now uncertain as to how she could face a man who had committed such a horrendous deed, let alone fight for his acquittal.

She decided it was best to put the file down for a bit and focus on something else. Clear her mind of an image that stubbornly refused to fade away.

"Harry, what say we take a short walk, then come back and polish off our arguments for next Friday? We can go check out what Stella and Maddie have been up to in the garden."

"Sure, Sam." Harry hadn't yet reached the coroner's report in the file, but he was very disturbed by the discovery of the Word file – the smoking gun. Combined with the murder weapon found just outside of Jordan's front door and the fact that only someone with a key to the house could have possibly committed the crime, it was becoming increasingly obvious that his boss was about to experience her first loss as a criminal lawyer. And that Jordan was almost certainly destined for a date with the needle.

<h1 style="text-align:center">40</h1>

Sam and Harry spent most of the rest of the week fruitlessly trying to work out some angle on the Jordan trial short of an insanity defense. The deadline had already passed for that, but Sam filed it anyway. An appeals court down the line might take a hard look at the evidence in the case, and in particular the postmortem sex act, and decide that Jordan needed another shot at a trial. Certainly no rational human being could have ever treated his wife and children the way Jordan apparently had.

When Friday morning rolled around, Sam was well past being ready for a change of pace. The courtroom was packed with the usual pleas and routine hearings, and she and Harry had to wait their turn before the judge took up contested issues. Like her motion. She checked the jail sheets and was pleased to see that Tanja had already been brought over and was waiting for the hearing in the secure area next to the courtroom.

Judge Jack Reynolds had a reputation for being fairer minded than the other district judges in the county, and that was a good omen for what Sam was trying to pull off that morning. He tended to play it by the book, and Sam and Harry had put together some solid arguments and case law that should work to win him over. Particularly since, apparently, there was no real down side to granting her a minor victory.

Finally, Tanja's case was called, and she was brought in, handcuffed, to take her seat at the defense table next to Harry. Judge Reynolds looked down at the case file in front of him. "The court now takes up Cause Number 17-0923, The State of Texas versus Tanja Meadows. The Defense has filed a Motion to Dismiss in this case. Is the State ready?"

John Dubcek rose from his seat. "Ready, Your Honor."

"The Defense stands ready, as well, Your Honor." Sam glanced over at Dubcek to try and get a read on his disposition. This was the first time she had seen him in person since the Andrea Owens case.

"Very well." Reynolds flicked a hand in Sam's direction. "Your motion, counselor. Proceed."

"Yes, Your Honor." Sam arranged her notes in front of her. "In addition to our motion, Your Honor, you should have in front of you a copy of the brief we filed in support."

"Yes, I have it right here. Give me just a second while I look it over." Over the next few minutes, Reynolds flipped through the twenty pages of the brief, stopping occasionally to take notes. "Okay, I got it." He looked over at the prosecutor's table. "Mr. Dubcek, I don't see a reply brief from you. Am I missing something?"

"No, Your Honor," Dubcek replied. "We didn't think the motion merited any extended effort on our part."

"I see…" Reynolds appeared put out by Dubcek's answer. "Okay, Ms. Tulley, I've had a look at your brief. Can you boil it all down for me a little? Why should I grant this motion today?"

"Yes, Your Honor." Sam took a deep, calming breath. Even after all this time, she still felt a little nervous starting oral arguments before a judge. Particularly when so much was at stake, as it was here. Tanja Meadow's entire future rested on the power of her arguments over the next few minutes.

"The indictment in this case charges the defendant, Tanja Meadows, with 'Intentionally, Knowingly and Recklessly' assaulting a police officer with a deadly weapon, specifically by striking him with a car. The problem with this indictment, however, is that the language regarding 'Recklessly' does not meet the legal requirements imposed upon it by Section 21.15 of the Texas Code of Criminal Procedure. Specifically, 21.15 requires the indictment to specify which acts by the defendant were, in fact, reckless. It's not enough to rely upon the offensive act itself, to simply say that striking an officer with a car is in itself reckless. You have to actually spell out something else that *made* the conduct reckless."

She picked up a case law file. "I believe our brief does an exhaustive job of covering the analysis of Professors Dix and

Dawson regarding the parsing of 21.15 and its implications to charging instruments, so I won't go into any of that. I would, however, like to point you to what the Texas Court of Criminal Appeals said about this subject. In Gengnagel, the court overturned a conviction for indecent exposure because, and I quote, his 'indictment did not allege any act or circumstances which would show that this exposition was done in a reckless manner, as required by Article 21.15.' The indictment alleged that Gengnagel exposed his genitals to an undercover police officer. The problem with this, the court explained, was that the information alleged only 'exposition of his genitals by the defendant to the complainant.' Although constituting part of the forbidden conduct, this 'act' was not something from which a trier of fact could infer recklessness, because exposing one's genitals is not by itself reckless."

She stopped for a moment to set the file on the table, then looked back up at the judge. "Here, as in Gengnagel, the indictment alleges that Ms. Meadows struck the police officer with a car, but it fails to specify what part of that conduct was reckless. There are a number of ways that an officer could be struck by a car that do not involve recklessness on the part of the driver. For example, the policeman could step into the path of a car without warning. Or the car could experience some malfunction, such as a blown tire, that causes it to veer out of control. So, since the indictment before us fails to meet that requirement as specified under 21.15, it must be quashed as a matter of law."

Reynolds turned his attention to Dubcek, who was standing impatiently, shaking his head throughout Sam's speech. "The State's response, Mr. Dubcek?"

Dubcek looked put out by having to give any response at all to the defense motion. "Your Honor, I fail to see where this is getting us. Even if this indictment is quashed, we'll just run it in front of another grand jury and get it fixed. Why don't we all just agree to amend the indictment as it stands and avoid all that nonsense?"

"Your Honor," Sam explained, "we don't agree that this indictment can simply be amended. Under 21.15, it is clearly and fatally defective, and the Code of Criminal Procedure tells us what we have to do with a fatally flawed indictment. Quash it, Your Honor. And that is exactly what we are asking for this morning. Quash the flawed indictment."

"Look, Your Honor." Dubcek waved his hand dismissively at Sam. "Let's just dispense with all this nonsense. Ms. Tulley's client is stuck in jail on a blue warrant, and she isn't going anywhere. Meanwhile, I have a flight to catch this afternoon to take my kids out to Florida to see Mickey Mouse. So if defense counsel wants to stand firm on her little Mickey Mouse motion, so be it. Go ahead and quash it, and as soon as I get back from

Florida I'll push another indictment through the grand jury. We've wasted enough time on this already."

For Judge Reynolds, the State's capitulation on the issue made his decision a no-brainer, particularly since it had no real effect on anything. The defendant would remain in jail on the blue warrant and the indictment would get fixed. Reynolds looked over at Sam and shook his head. "Well, then, I guess everyone finally agrees. Motion granted," he ruled, striking his gavel for added emphasis.

41

After the hearing, Sam finally had some time to kill. She couldn't move on the remainder of the plan until Dubcek was safely in the air and out of touch. "Harry, that was some brilliant work you put in on that brief."

Harry smiled, embarrassed. "Well, thanks, but it was really just some routine research, and most of the brief was just a matter of copying and pasting from the court rulings and the legal analysis by Dix and Dawson. To be honest, their take on the issue kind of had my head spinning for a while there, all that talk about how an 'act' couldn't constitute by itself a mens rea of recklessness."

"Okay, as long as we're being honest, I *still* don't really get it. That's why I decided to gloss over all that during my argument. But I hope you got a good look at the difference between being prepared and trying to just hoof it during a hearing. Dubcek looked like an idiot for not filing a reply brief. And, faced with twenty pages of precedent with nothing to offset it from the state, very few judges are going to issue a ruling and risk getting their knuckles rapped by a higher court."

"Actually, Sam, I'm thinking right now that I'm a pretty darn lucky boy. I get to learn from the master, and get paid to boot." Sam waved off the compliment, but Harry wouldn't have it.

"No, seriously, I'm amazed at what you manage to pull off around here. You take these cases that everybody else has written off, and somehow turn them into slam-dunk wins."

"Whatever, Harry. Anyway, we've still got one more win to put in our column today, and then we need to figure out what to do about the Jordan case. You know, one of the reasons I've been so successful up to now is that my clients are innocent. I just have to sell that to the jury, or, in cases like Tanja Meadows, find another solution. But Curtis Jordan… I'm afraid at this point, even I can't see it. And all that postmortem stuff really gives me the creeps."

"I hear ya, Boss. But why don't we put all that on hold and go grab some lunch, and by then Dubcek will be on his way to Disneyworld. Then we can work our special magic and pull our little rabbit out of the hat."

42

Sam was fighting a battle with her waistline, but after the big win that morning she decided to throw caution to the wind and order up a big cheeseburger with unlimited, greasy french fries. She and Harry exchanged mostly small talk over lunch, and she was starting to appreciate the fact that Harry seemed to have a special flair for keeping up with all the gossip flying around town.

Sam was also starting to regret that the summer was quickly coming to a close, meaning Harry would have to head back to Waco to start the fall semester. Having spent almost a year and a half in a solo practice, she had grown to appreciate having him around to plot and scheme with. Plus, she had to admit that Harry was awfully cute. Physically he *was* on the attractive side of average in that regard, with piercing blue-gray eyes and a wicked little smile. But mainly, he was cute on the *inside*, and that was starting to stir things inside *her* that were best left unstirred. So maybe it was a good thing that summer was coming to a close.

In the middle of their meal, Sam got an unexpected call from Evan Murphy. "Yo, Murf, what's new with you?"

"Hey, Sam. Just wanted to give you a head's up on the Jordan trial. Looks like they just swapped prosecutors on you. Kennedy's off the case."

"Really? That's interesting. Why would they do that?" It was pretty late in the game to still be moving pieces around on the board. And Sam of all people understood just how tough it was to gear up for a trial with little or no warning.

"My guess is that they got spooked with how well you handled Kennedy in that last trial. And he was just going to be reading from the script they had worked out with Rock the Boat, anyway. So now that the trial script is in the trash, they're sending their top dog after you. Ariel Morrow."

"Is she any good?" Sam had heard of her, but barely.

"The best. She's almost as smart as you, and, given her experience, she may just have the jump on you in the courtroom. She's a tricky piece of work. I just thought you'd want to get the news sooner rather than later."

"Hey, thanks, Evan. I'll owe you one. Wanna try grabbing lunch sometime next week? My treat?"

"Sounds like a great idea, Sam. I'll touch base with you on Monday and we can see how our schedules look. Meanwhile, have a great weekend. Looks like good weather for a change."

"Back at you, Evan. Talk to you Monday."

Sam hung up the phone, then caught Harry up on the news. After lunch, they headed back to the Justice Center to grab a copy of Judge Murphy's order, then straight over to the jail. It took a little over an hour to get the paperwork processed, but by mid-afternoon Tanja Meadows walked out of jail a free woman.

"I can't say I understand how you got me out of there, but I can't tell you how thankful I am. It sure is nice to see the outside again. It's been a long time."

"I'm sorry that it's taken this long, Tanja," Harry answered, "but until we got that blue warrant off your back, you weren't going anywhere."

"So how did you pull that off?"

"We didn't really do much at all," Sam explained. "We just noticed that all the time you had spent in jail on *this* charge had soaked up the remaining time on your *old* charge, so the blue warrant expired a couple of weeks ago. Then we sat on that information a bit so Dubcek wouldn't find out, and finally got it vacated a week ago."

"And the parole board wouldn't let him know?"

"No," Harry replied. "There just isn't any kind of mechanism in place to communicate that to him. Just as the jail doesn't have a way of telling him that you got released today. So unless Dubcek for some reason looks it up on the county's online jail records, he won't have a clue."

"Okay, I'm starting to get it, now. The hearing today was about getting rid of the current charge, so until they indict me again, I'm a free girl!"

"Exactly," Sam agreed. "And the truly beautiful thing about today's hearing was that I'm pretty sure Dubcek and the judge thought I was an idiot for filing that motion."

"Why's that?"

"Because it fixed a fatal mistake that the DA's office made when they originally pushed the indictment past the grand jury," Harry explained. "A mistake that might have forced any guilty verdict to be overturned on appeal and sent back to the court for retrial."

Tanja laughed out loud at the way her lawyers had hoodwinked the other side. "Boy, they're probably going to be royally pissed off when they find out what you did."

"Yeah," Sam acknowledged. "But that only matters if they don't have a way to fix it, to put you back in the slammer. What are your ideas on that?"

Tanja looked introspective. "Well, I'm not sure I want to run from this one. I mean, I've made some mistakes in the past, and I have the record to show for it. But this time I'm completely innocent. If they hadn't shot me with that Taser, none of this would have happened."

Sam nodded. "I can appreciate that, Tanja, but here's the deal. If we take this to trial, the prosecution's gonna hammer you about hurting that cop. Our defense is that the cops brought it all on themselves by shooting you with the Taser, then failing to get away from the car and continuing to run alongside it as the car zoomed backward. It's a great defense, and it has the added benefit of also being true. But my gut tells me the jury is gonna want to see some blood for that cop getting injured, and regardless of how innocent you are, they're going to take it out on you."

Harry piped in. "We did some mock trials on this, Tanja, brought in some strangers from around the county to try out our case. And every one of them ended up the same. A unanimous verdict of guilty. And it didn't take them long to get there, either."

"So what you're saying is, I haven't got a chance at all of winning if we go to trial on this. Not even a slim chance."

"I think that's the tall and the short of it, Tanja," Sam answered ruefully.

"Okay, so I guess my choice is already made," Tanja agreed, but then had a second thought. "Wait. Should we even be talking about this? I don't want to get you two in trouble for aiding and abetting, or whatever it is they call helping someone escape."

"No, that's not a problem," Harry explained. "Technically, you're not a fugitive right now. Your case has been lawfully dismissed, and until they reindict it, you're every bit as free to do whatever you want to do as anyone else. I might point out that Mexico is very pretty this time of year…"

"Actually, Harry, it's pretty damn hot down there at the moment," Sam pointed out. "But if you hang around much longer, Tanja, it's fixing to get even hotter for you right here. You need to make hay while Dubcek's sun is still shining down in Florida."

"I got you," Tanja said. "Look, you know my momma passed away last month and left me some money, enough to help me get lost for a while. I owe the two of you my life. Literally. So I'll run down to Houston and pull all that money out of the bank, then send you guys a check to thank you for all your help."

"There's no need to worry about us," Sam answered. "In fact, getting money from you might prove to be a problem for us. The judge is very likely to take a hard look at us when he finds out you're gone, and I don't want anything popping up that suggests what we did was improper."

"Which it wasn't," Harry added with a laugh. "Everything we did was perfectly legal and aboveboard. A little on the sketchy side, perhaps, but still perfectly legal."

Tanja shared a brief look of concern. "Well, I hope all of this doesn't get the two of you into hot water."

"Don't worry, Tanja," Sam assured her. "Harry and I, we're big boys and girls. If they try to turn up the heat on us, they're the ones who are going to wind up getting burned."

43

Tanja was long gone to destinations unknown by the next Monday. Sam tried to finish off a few pleas that morning, but none of her clients showed up, forcing her to once again beg the county attorney's office to sign off on continuances. Done with that, and with no money to show for her efforts, she cleared her calendar for the rest of the week to focus on the upcoming Jordan trial, now just a week away. And for her promised payback lunch with Evan Murphy.

Pulling up to her house just before lunch, she pressed the Homelink button on her visor, then waited impatiently as the large metal gate swung slowly inward. She started to drive forward, but suddenly noticed Barley lying on the ground asleep, dead in the middle of the drive. She honked, then honked again, but the dog wouldn't stir.

Cursing under her breath, Sam climbed out of the car and stalked irritatedly over to the dog. She was already frustrated with her day, and this wasn't helping. But as she got nearer to him she started to worry about why Barley was so sleepy in the middle of the day that he didn't hear her honking.

She sensed it even before she saw it. The small puddle of blood. "Barley!" she yelled, and immediately began to run. As she got to him, screaming out his name as she ran, she thought she noticed a small flicker of movement in his left eyelid. Sam dropped to her knees, tenderly examining him, desperately looking for any sign that Barley was going to live. Then she saw it, the ragged hole in his left chest, just behind his front leg. Barley had been shot. She looked around wildly, desperately searching for someone to help. Anyone. Then she noticed it. The front door was hanging wide open. *Oh my God! Maddie!*

44

She sprinted to the house, screaming frantically for her daughter. Dashing through the front door, she noticed at a glance that the silent alarm had been triggered. Tearing into the living room, she saw that the elevator was parked on one of the upper floors, so she raced up the steps, kicking off her shoes and taking them two at a time. On the second floor landing, she turned right, down the hallway and up the last set of stairs at the end.

Breathless, Sam threw open the door to the nursery. Empty. She spun around and darted into her bedroom, but it was empty, too. *Oh my God! They took my baby! They took Maddie!* And then she heard a noise, coming from downstairs.

45

Sam took the stairs down to the second floor landing in her bare feet, trying not to make any sound that would alert the intruders. She was carefully peeking through the wrought iron stair rail into the living room when a voice called out from below.

"Sam! It's Randy! I can see you upstairs on the security video from the hallway cam. Come on down. Everything is okay."

Suddenly realizing how much all of the fear-filled running had drained her, she stood up uneasily and grabbed the stairway railing to catch her breath. "I'll be right there, Randy," she called out, then slowly headed down the stairs, picking up speed as she neared the bottom.

Randy met her at the foot of the stairs, reassuring Sam before she even reached him. "Stella and Maddie are safe at her house. They went over earlier this morning to work in the garden. I have a guard on them already."

"Oh, thank God!" Sam exclaimed. Then she remembered. "Barley?"

"He's on his way to the vet now." Randy wrapped an arm around her protectively. "He's lost quite a bit of blood, but I think it looked worse than it really is. We'll know for sure very shortly. Doc Brown said she would call me as soon as she has something."

Sam was lost. "Who could have done this, Randy? What were they after?"

"I'll need to get with my security people and check the tapes, then maybe we'll have some answers. But right now I need to get you, Maddie and Stella to someplace safe. Is there anyone else around here I need to worry about?"

Sam caught her breath and tried to think. "Harry Crawford. He's the summer intern who's been helping me with my cases. But he's back in Waco doing some research at Baylor for a trial that's coming up."

"Okay, we'll track him down and put someone on him. I also have a team headed over to your father's clinic in Fort Worth. I think your parents are off the radar, but you can never be too sure." Randy looked off into the distance. "As a matter of fact, all of this caught us completely off guard. Attacking your house in broad daylight? It just doesn't make any sense."

Just at that moment his phone rang, and he answered it, talking tersely to whoever it was on the other end. After about a minute, most of it spent listening, he hung up. "Look, Sam, I'm going to have to call in the big dogs on this one. We just can't trust the locals, for obvious reasons. That was a guy I know at the FBI who worked with me on the Tyler Andrews case. He's got a safe house not too far away, and some of his folks are already en route to pick up the three of you and get you to safety."

"Do you really think that's necessary?" Sam's voice was quavering.

"Yeah, I have good reason to believe it is. But give me an hour or so to dig into what happened a little better. Then you and I can sit down with the FBI and figure out what we're going to do next."

"Wait." Sam looked back upstairs. "Don't we need to pack some bags or something? Particularly for Maddie?"

"We'll take care of that later. Right now your safety is all I care about." Just then his phone buzzed again. It was Doc Brown. "Yes, Doc, what's the news on Barley?" Sam could see relief wash across his face. "Good, good. Yeah, let's plan on leaving him with you for the next few days, then if he's doing better we can bring him home." Randy paused to give Sam a thumbs up. "Oh, and Doc? Thanks. That little guy is a trooper. He took on all of the bad guys single-handedly. He's coming home to a hero's welcome just as soon as you can get him back on his paws again." He hung up and turned back to Sam.

"He's going to be all right?" she asked expectantly.

"Yeah, Doc says he got lucky. A bullet hit him in the upper left leg, shattering the bone and ricocheting against his chest. She's got an IV in him and is starting to pump blood. It's all still pretty early, but she thinks he'll be okay."

"Oh, thank goodness for that!" Sam sighed with relief. Then everything started to finally sink in. "Oh, my God! You got here right behind me! And you already have so much set in motion! I was so panicked when I realized Maddie was gone… what would I have done if you hadn't gotten here when you did?"

"Well, Sam, that's why I insisted on all the security gear and cameras." Randy looked up at one of the hidden cameras in the ceiling. "Evidently, they cut the lines to your regular alarm, but didn't realize you had the backup system in place. Still, these guys are *good*. *Too* good. Something just doesn't add up here…" He gave Sam a curious look. "Did something happen recently that I don't know about? Did you manage to piss off any more of the judges and prosecutors since we talked last?"

Sam looked a little sheepish. "Well, it does seem to be a talent of mine, lately. I won a case against Huber Kennedy a little over a week ago that left him a little bent out of shape. And I think Judge Starke would have locked me away if she could. Then I pulled a fast one over on John Dubcek and Judge Reynolds on Friday and got a felon released into the wind when they weren't looking –"

"And that's all, Sam? That sounds like a lifetime achievement for stirring up old hornets nests around here…"

But Sam wasn't finished. "Oh, one other thing. I ticked Judge McDaniel off by subbing in on that big murder trial he has coming up in a week, the one where the father is accused of killing his wife and two children. They had Rock the Boat propped up to help them put on a big show, but I got him bumped off the case, and I kinda had to threaten McDaniel with major media nightmares if he tried to stop me. And now I just heard that they replaced Kennedy as the prosecutor for some lady named Ariel Morrow –"

"Oh, crap!" Suddenly, Randy looked very worried. "McDaniel and Morrow are the odd couple who tag-teamed Tyler, sent him to prison after he went upside of them on a few cases. That might be it, Sam! Now they're coming after you. And it sounds like they have the whole courthouse behind them to take you down." He whipped out his phone again. A few rings later and someone answered on the other end. "Gavin? It's me, Randy. This is some serious shit, bro. Looks like we're going to have to reassemble the old posse."

46

FBI Special Agent Gavin Larson hauled his chair in close. He knew Sam was a criminal defense attorney, so he didn't need to pull any punches. He'd give it to her straight.

"Ms. Tulley, Randy and I have been over the video feeds from your house, and I'll have to tell you, what we saw was some pretty scary stuff."

"What do you mean, scary?" Sam asked, still stoked with adrenalin from the events earlier that day. She stole a glance over at Maddie, blissfully asleep in Stellas's arms, and fought back a selfish urge to hold her baby herself. *Plenty of time for that later. Maddie's safety is all that matters right now.* Stella waved to her as she took the baby down the hall to one of the back bedrooms.

Larson cleared his throat and pointed toward the front door. "Well, the outside cameras show two individuals, and possibly a third, pull up in a van in front of your house and activate your gate –"

"But how could they do that?" Sam was confused. "That's supposed to be a scrambled-frequency gate opener –"

"Right," Larson acknowledged. "But it really isn't very secure at all. It'll keep the good guys out, but not the bad guys. All they needed to do was send someone inside the fence in the middle of the night to pop the cover off the gate mechanism and hit the learn button. Then they just used the Homelink device in their van, or a portable radio keypad, and stored the code for when they needed to use it to get inside."

"Great. Now they can come and go whenever they want."

Randy leaned in. "Not exactly, Sam. That was something we should have looked at when we installed the security system. But I have some guys over there now patching in something much more sophisticated. You'll have to live with a handheld transmitter for a while until all this blows over, but at least you'll still have the first line of defense intact against these goons."

"Okay, I can deal with that," Sam said. "What else did you find out?"

Larson continued, frowning. "Okay, so they pull into the driveway and two guys jump out. Your dog must have heard them because he tore around the side of the house at full throttle, barking furiously. One of the guys pulled a pistol with a silencer on the end and fired twice. We think it was the second shot that hit the dog, because he fell down at that point and didn't move again."

"Barley has a doggie door on the side of the house, and he'll blast through the door anytime he hears a strange noise outside."

"Right," Larson said. "Anyway, now the shooter goes to the side of the house and deactivates the regular alarm system. That shows a pretty advanced knowledge of both the alarm system and the layout of your house. So we're not talking amateurs here."

"And that raises some other concerns," Randy added. "But we'll get to that in a second…"

Larson nodded, returning to the story. "Now that the alarm was off, the other man opened the front door, evidently with a key —"

"Where did he get that?" Sam asked, concerned again about the failure of some very fundamental security measures.

"It isn't all that complicated to crib a key off standard door locks, if you know what you're doing."

"Again, professionals," Randy reminded her.

"The next few minutes flew by very quickly," Larson continued. "Both men entered the house and, after casing the downstairs, climbed the stairs and headed straight to the nursery. They looked inside and, finding it empty, scurried back down the stairs and out the front door, leaving it open. In seconds they were back in the van and gone. You showed up on the video just a few minutes later."

"Just missed them Sam," Randy pointed out. "I hate to think what would have happened if you had gotten home just a few minutes earlier…"

"So what you're saying is, someone was after Maddie." Sam was stunned. How could this be happening to them, given everything that they had already been through after Luke's death? "They broke in to kidnap her, but didn't realize she was down the street at Stella's playing in the garden."

"That's what it looked like, Ms. Tulley. Thank God they had a breakdown in their intelligence and didn't think to cover the other house." Larson sat back now, a look of deep concern on his face.

Sam tried to think it through, but very little of what had happened made any sense to her. "So, the big question is still why? Why would anyone try to kidnap Maddie? What could they possibly hope to accomplish?"

"That's why I called the FBI in on this, Sam," Randy answered. "Gavin here headed up a task force that was assigned to investigate the systemic corruption here in Briar County. In particular, an unholy alliance that had popped up between the judges, prosecutors and police."

"The big test case was the takedown of Tyler Andrews," Larson added. "Absolutely nothing about that case smelled right. And I think we got really close to cracking it, to taking down

Judge McDaniel and a bunch of his thugs. But we fell just short of enough evidence to take it to a federal judge for a warrant."

"And one of McDaniel's 'thugs' was a prosecutor named Ariel Morrow," Sam observed, finally catching on to Gavin Larson's bigger role in all of this.

"Dead spot on," Larson said. "Now you can see why we're so interested in what happened to you today. To your family. We think they're back to their old tricks."

"But this seems to be a major elevation in tactics for them, doesn't it?" Sam asked. "I mean, to go from planting drugs to kidnapping a little child?"

"I'm with you on that one," Larson agreed. "And that's what has us really worried. If they're willing to go this far to knock you down, to teach you a lesson about rocking the boat, then what's next? I'd have to agree with Randy here. You have really pissed off a lot of people in a very short period of time. It may be a good time for you to back off for a little while and let things cool down."

Sam thought about that. "The problem is, I've got a trial coming up next week. A trial, by the way, with McDaniel and Morrow." Larson and Randy exchanged a knowing and worried look. "I could see about putting it off, but that would only stretch all of this out even further. But, of course, none of this matters at all if Maddie's safety is as stake. Or Stella's, for that matter."

Randy spoke up. "Sam, doesn't Maddie have a grandmother somewhere off in Europe she could visit? That would get her out of the local area for a while, and let you finish up your trial. Then, after the trial you could take a break and skip town as well."

She thought about that. "Well, it's not a bad idea. I know Margaret would love a visit from Maddie. But how would I get her there? We'd have to apply for some type of travel permit... and I can't take the time at the moment to fly all the way to Italy and back..."

Larson considered that. "Travel papers are not a problem. The FBI whisks people across borders all the time with fake papers. And I'm pretty sure I could arrange seats on a private jet, maybe one of the State Department or CIA flights." He paused to work through all of the complications. "Do you think your daughter's nanny would like to go along as well? That would work wonders to keep them both safe, and make it a lot easier on Maddie at the same time. She wouldn't be suddenly thrust into the arms of a whole bunch of strangers..."

"I think Stella would jump at the chance for an adventure," Sam answered. "Why don't we ask her?"

47

With Maddie and Stella safely on their way to Italy, Sam eventually returned home. As an added safeguard, the FBI assigned two agents to guard the house, including a female agent they dressed up to resemble Stella. The idea was to trick any would-be attackers into thinking Maddie was still at home, adding an extra layer of misdirection to keep anyone from looking for her in Italy.

Harry returned from Waco late in the week, and he and Sam turned the dining room into a war room for the trial. They had a mock trial scheduled for Saturday morning, with Evan Murphy serving as the prosecutor and several of Harry's law school buddies acting as witnesses. Sam threw a barbeque for all of them on Friday night, with the FBI watching uncomfortably from the sidelines.

The mock trial went pretty much the way Sam expected. She had almost no evidence to work with, and her client didn't even have an alibi – he was at home that night feasting on a frozen pizza and watching television. The one good piece of evidence she *did* have working for her – a bloody partial boot print found in the kitchen that didn't match any of the shoes recovered from Curtis Jordan's apartment – could be explained away pretty easily. Jordan had simply ditched the shoes when he discovered they were covered in his wife's blood. At this point, if the state was willing to offer a plea deal for life without parole as an alternative to the death penalty, Sam would have urged him to snap it up. But Morrow could read the tea leaves in this case as well as she could, and they both knew that Curtis Jordan didn't have a prayer of winning an acquittal.

By far the most damning piece of evidence was the smoking gun, the Microsoft Word file that had been recovered from Jordan's computer. In it, Jordan railed on and on about his belief that Katie was seeing another man, and how it disgusted him to think about someone else having sex with her. How there was only one sure way of stopping that. And the detailed description of his plan to kill Katie and the kids with a box cutter while they lay asleep in their beds fit the rest of the evidence in the case to a T. That document alone was enough to guarantee Curtis Jordan a quick ride to death row.

Monday morning rolled around too quickly, and as Sam glanced around the packed courtroom, she knew her case was hopeless. She didn't even have a plan for how she was going to handle voir dire, usually one of her key strengths during trials. When Curtis Jordan was ushered in by the jailor, she just reached over and shook his hand quietly. Sam didn't have any words of comfort left to give him. She glanced back and saw Reverend Ollie near the back row, his head bent in silent prayer. Sam wondered if even divine intervention could save her client now.

Judge McDaniel cleared the visitor's gallery temporarily to make room for jury selection. Morrow breezed through her voir dire, and Sam noticed she seemed far more adept than her colleagues at drawing out responses from the panel. None of that really mattered at this point, though. This trial would turn on the evidence, and that evidence was very bad for Curtis Jordan.

When it was finally Sam's turn to address the jury panel, she managed to put even more emphasis than usual on the burden of proof and the presumption of innocence, with a special focus on the reliability of circumstantial evidence. In the end, she was able to strike seven jurors for cause, along with her ten peremptory strikes. But again, none of that really mattered.

Ariel Morrow's opening statement was masterful, pounding away at the defendant's depravity, at her disgust at even having to share the courtroom with such a monster. She painted Jordan as a rabid dog that had to be put down before it bit again. But Sam noted that Morrow failed to mention anything about the blood that was found in Katie Jordan's vagina. She was obviously saving that little tidbit for later. For now she had enough to ensure that every pair of eyes in the courtroom were turned toward Curtis Jordan with an unbridled loathing.

When Morrow was finished, Sam made a decision she had been bouncing back and forth on all weekend. She had nothing to offer the jury at this point in the trial, so any opening statement she could give would be pointless. Knowing that she couldn't afford to waste a single opportunity in this trial, she decided to reserve her statement until the State had rested its case.

After a short break, Morrow started bringing her witnesses. With the victims dead, the State's witnesses were police officers, investigators, the coroner and, finally, Ray Wallace. Over the next few days, one-by-one they paraded to the witness box to recount the evidence they had collected from Jordan's apartment after the box cutter had been found in the trash bin outside of his front door. Most of the testimony was duplicative, drawing quick and repeated objections from Sam, but Judge McDaniel simply waved her off. Under Sam's intense cross examination, the police officers agreed that almost all of the evidence could be explained away by Curtis Jordan's routine appearances at the house to visit his children. But the box cutter was a major problem for the defense, as was the fact that the assailant had evidently used a key to gain entrance to the front door. And, of course, the Microsoft Word file, which would serve as a final bullet to the head of any defense Sam could muster.

On Thursday, the coroner finally took the stand. Morrow had saved this witness until the end of her case, just before Ray Wallace, to refresh the horror that the jury had experienced at the outset of the trial when the first policeman authenticated the crime scene pictures of Katie and her two children. Now the coroner walked through pictures from the autopsy that, if anything, were even more gruesome. At one point, Judge McDaniel was forced to order a break to let several of the jurors race to the bathroom. When everyone returned, Morrow decided to move on. She had already made her point in spades.

But one more little detail still remained to be ferreted from this witness. Morrow tapped her pencil on the table in front of her briefly, building suspense for what was yet to come. Finally, she addressed the coroner in a soft, almost apologetic voice. "Dr. Cartwright, I want to direct your attention back to your examination of Katie Jordan. Now, we've already covered the wound she suffered, and the cause of death, exsanguination…"

"Yes," Cartwright responded. "She bled out onto the bed and floor."

"Yes, thank you." Morrow was moving cautiously, theatrically. "Now, did you happen to examine the other portions of Katie's body. In particular, did you examine her vagina…"

The courtroom let out a collective gasp.

"Yes, I did, Ms. Morrow," Cartwright answered quietly.

Morrow turned slowly to face the jury, making eye contact with each and every one of them as she drew out her next question. "And, Dr. Cartwright, what, if anything, did you discover when you examined Katie Jordan's vagina?"

Cartwright sat up a little straighter before he answered. Every eye in the courtroom was now on him. "I discovered blood that had been deposited there. It was her blood, Katie Jordan's."

Morrow turned and gave him a long look. "And could you determine how the blood got there?"

"First of all, it wasn't caused by internal injuries – so the blood had to come from outside of her body, from the wound to her throat. And, I can't really be certain here, but judging by the depth of the deposits, the blood was in too deep within the vagina for it to have been placed there by somebody's fingers. If I had to hazard a guess, I'd say that the blood in her vagina was actually a side effect of the repeated penetration of her vagina by something approximating the size of a male penis."

"You mean he had sex with her, after he cut her throat." Morrow was looking at Cartwright, but out of the corner of her eye she could see several members of the jury visibly react to this news, their hands automatically flying up to cover their mouths.

"Yes, that is correct," Cartwright answered, nodding.

Morrow drew her voice low, almost to a whisper as she asked her final question. "Dr. Cartwright, was that before or after she died?"

Cartwright shook his head sorrowfully. "According to the results of the autopsy, it was postmortem. Katie Jordan's killer slashed her throat, then waited until she was dead before he raped her."

Dr. Cartwright's testimony had rocked the courtroom, and Judge McDaniel decided it might be a good time to break for the day, to leave that image indelibly stamped into each of the juror's minds all night long and into the morning.

On the way home, Sam and Harry picked up some pizzas for a quick and easy dinner, adding a couple extra for their two FBI bodyguards. Settling back in to the dining/war room, they chewed on the pizzas and considered their limited trial options. Morrow had choreographed the coroner's testimony masterfully, and Sam knew that the jury was already on board for a guilty verdict, even considering that all of the testimony and evidence they had seen so far was almost totally circumstantial. But tomorrow would be the final nail in Curtis Jordan's coffin. The Microsoft Word file would establish conclusively, with no doubt left whatsoever, that Jordan had killed his children and murdered and raped his dead wife.

"Harry, we need to pour over that document one more time. Surely there's something in that letter that doesn't make sense, that stirs up some tiny bit of uncertainty…"

Harry shook his head, looking down at the printout of the file he was holding in his hand. "Sam, I've been over it and over it. There's just nothing here."

"Well, how about the digital copy of the letter?" Sam was desperate by now. "I mean, Ray Wallace recovered it from the hard drive after it was deleted. Maybe there's something else hanging on to the end of the file, some extra data from the deleted file block that can tell us something."

Suddenly a light came on in Harry's head. "Sam, you mean to tell me you have a *digital* copy of the letter?"

"Yeah, we got a DVD with all that on it. It's sitting in my laptop right now. Why?"

"And you're *sure* Curtis Jordan didn't write that letter?"

Her brow wrinkled as she considered the question. "Well, no. Truth be told, I'm pretty sure he did. But the thing is, if he did write it then he's the killer. No one else could have known about all those little details. So that's what it comes down to. Unless we can prove that the letter's a fake, then we don't have a ghost of a chance. Curtis Jordan is going to die." She was sitting at her desk, tapping a pencil in frustration, but when she looked up she saw a smile starting to creep across Harry's face. "What? You've thought of something, haven't you? What is it?"

Harry ran over to where her laptop was sitting, his fingers whirring across the keyboard. "I just remembered something I learned in a class I took on cyber security. It's a long shot, but maybe..." The DVD was taking its time spinning up, but finally the folder popped up on the screen. "Okay, here's the digital copy.

Let's just open it up in Word…" A quick click on the mousepad, and he was in. "Now, let's see what's behind the curtain…"

There it was. The smoking gun had one more bullet left in its chamber.

49

As she pushed through the door to the courtroom to start the final day of testimony, elbowing the door open while struggling with her trial box and a handful of briefs, Sam spied Reverend Ollie sitting patiently on a bench seat just outside cooling his heels, as he had throughout the week. At the beginning of the trial, Sam had invoked the Rule, which kept any potential witnesses from hearing testimony from other witnesses and adjusting their own statements to fit. She had planned to call the Reverend later as a witness to establish that Curtis and Katie's marriage had been on the mend at the time of her murder, so he had little reason to want to murder his wife. But now the game plan had changed, so Ollie was no longer her last and only weapon to ward off a certain guilty plea.

"Hey, Reverend, great to see you this morning!"

Reverend Ollie jumped up to take command of her trial box. "Morning, Miz Sam. You gonna need me in there today? Cause I'm ready to do whatever it takes."

Sam smiled at him warmly. "Actually, Reverend, I don't think we'll need you to testify after all. We came up with some ideas last night that might just work. So that means you can join us inside this morning, if you want to."

"Oh, golly yes!" he said, smiling broadly. "I've been prayin' on this, Miz Sam. We had a special prayer meetin' at the church last night, askin' God to lift you up today. Sounds like it may have worked."

"Well, we could certainly use God's help today, and I think Curtis would appreciate you being behind us, as well. And I mean physically – I know you've been there supporting us this whole time."

"Yes, ma'am." They had moved through the bar gate and up to the defense table, and Ollie leaned over to set the trial box down in the middle. "Now, I knows you have a lot to get ready for, so I won't takes up any more of your time. I'll just grab me a good seat back by the door where I can see. You just let me know if I can help."

"I'll do that, Reverend." Sam reached out to give him a small squeeze on his right shoulder. "And I can't promise anything, but I think you'll like today's show a little better than what you've seen so far." She heard a noise and glanced to her left. The jailer was bringing Curtis in from the secured area. The day's drama was just about to get underway. Sam crossed her fingers and said her own little prayer.

50

Ray Wallace was on the stand, and Ariel Morrow was carefully directing him through a simplified yet technically accurate explanation of how he had discovered the deleted file. Sam noted that Morrow had managed to clean him up pretty well from his usual slovenly appearance. He was even wearing a tie.

"First of all," Wallace was saying, "you need to understand how files are stored on a computer's hard drive. He clicked a pointer, and a stylized picture of a hard drive appeared on the courtroom's flat-screen display. Another click and the outside casing of the drive disappeared, leaving an image of the disc buried inside the hard drive. Wallace continued his explanation. "When you format a drive, the computer lays down little blocks of digitally blank space called clusters. You can think of them like the squares on a checkerboard, except they aren't square, and the board is more of a circle. Each cluster is essentially the same size as any other cluster, so they all hold the same amount of data." He clicked again, and a pattern of clusters appeared on the disc. "Now, when you create a file on a hard disk, it may only take up part of a cluster, or it may take up more than one cluster. That all depends upon how big the file is."

"I see," said Morrow, pretending that she hadn't already been through this presentation a dozen times already. "So how does the computer keep track of all of these – what did you call them? Clusters?"

"Yeah, clusters." Wallace pointed toward the screen. "Well, the clusters are where the data on a computer is actually stored. If you create a Microsoft Word file, for example, the actual contents of the document are stored in one or more clusters. But the operating system also simultaneously creates an entry for the file in what's called the FAT, the File Allocation Table. The FAT entry is what tells you the name of the file and where it sits in the directory structure. The FAT also records where each cluster is located and the sequential order of those clusters. When you open up a file, the operating system reassembles the file from the various clusters where all of the actual data is stored."

"Whew!" Morrow noted, wiping her forehead theatrically. "That all sounds very complicated!"

"Well, it's really not all that much more complicated than the way the old phone books worked," Wallace explained. "You look up a person by their last name, then scroll down to find their first name, and the phone book tells your their address and phone number."

"Okay," Morrow said. "That makes sense. But, tell me, what does any of that have to do with recovering files that are deleted?"

Wallace was enjoying his time in the spotlight, but now they had to get down to the nitty gritty. "Right. Well, generally speaking, when you delete a file on a computer, you don't really delete anything. Instead, that file's entry in the File Allocation Table is marked as empty, allowing it to be used for another file in the future. The actual data that made up the file is still lying there on the disk in its clusters, and it stays there untouched until the computer reuses one or more of the clusters in the future."

Morrow was nodding, following along. "So what you're saying is, if someone deletes a file today, and you come along and look at that hard drive a few days from now, the file will most likely still be there, completely intact."

"Actually, depending upon how much you use the computer, it could still be there for months. Maybe even years."

"I see," Morrow said, waving her hand in a let's-move-along gesture. "So tell us about Curtis Jordan's computer. When did you first get access to it?"

"The investigators brought it to my office the morning after they executed the search warrant on his apartment."

"And did you search right away for any deleted files?"

"No. First I made a duplicate of the drive, a copy that was read-only so I couldn't accidentally change any of the data on the drive. Then I started to examine every non-deleted file on the drive, one file at a time."

"And how long did that take you?"

"Several days, actually. There was a lot on that computer."

"Wow. That sounds like a lot of work. So after that is when you did the search for the deleted files. How did you accomplish that?"

"Well, you can do it the hard way, by using a program that examines the FAT and the hard drive cluster by cluster. But, if I did it that way, I might still be at it. So I just used an off-the-shelf program, UndeletePro. It handles all of that automatically. It can even recover files if you've reformatted the entire drive." Wallace glanced over at the jury, who were visibly impressed with his technical knowledge.

Sam noted that Morrow had her pointer in hand, ready to show the damning file from Jordan's computer. Just a few more questions. "And when you ran UndeletePro, what did you find?"

"Oh, a lot of the usual stuff. Mostly YouTube downloads and stuff like that. But I found one file that caught my eye right away."

"And why was that?" Morrow asked, her brow furrowed.

"Because it had been deleted just one day before the murders. I knew instantly that there was something in that file that Jordan didn't want anyone to see."

"Do you happen to have a copy of that file with you today, Mr. Wallace?"

He whipped a DVD out of his jacket pocket. "I sure do. I have it right here."

Morrow went through the standard motions of authenticating and entering the DVD into evidence. Sam could have objected at any point to all of this, but she was having way too much fun watching Morrow dig her own, deep grave. Finally, the contents of the Word file were projected up on the screen and Morrow went through it line by line. At this point, everyone in the courtroom knew that, for all intents and purposes, the trial was over. Curtis Jordan was stone cold guilty.

Finally, Morrow was finished, and with another theatrical flourish, she passed the witness. Now it was Sam's turn to ask questions of Ray Wallace, technical guru for the Blair County District Attorney's office. But before she started, she turned and waved to Randy Martinez, who was lingering in the back of the courtroom, a fat manila folder in his hand. During Morrow's direct examination of Wallace, Randy had texted Sam the results of the raid and the complete contents of the folder he was now handing her. She turned back to her desk, pulling out the files and laying them out in a neat arc before her. She looked over to her client and gave him a hidden and conspiratorial wink. Now it was time to have some fun.

<h1 align="center">51</h1>

"Mr. Wallace, my name is Samantha Tulley. But then, you and I already know each other, don't we? By that, I mean, we're on friendly terms, aren't we?" Sam had decided to launch this attack on Wallace with a velvet glove instead of a hammer. The hammer would come later.

"Wh-why, yes," Wallace stammered, wondering what she was up to by starting her cross in such a friendly fashion. "I think I even offered to buy you a cup of coffee a few weeks ago."

"And I'll be sure to take you up on that offer, Mr. Wallace, after we're finished here. But first, I have some questions I need to ask you about that file you discovered…"

"Go right ahead, Ms. Tulley. Fire away!"

"Okay, now, all this talk about clusters and FATs, that's all pretty advanced stuff, pretty confusing. You sure you didn't have someone else helping out with all that?" Sam gave him a disarming smile.

"Uh, no, I handled all of that myself. In fact, I don't think there's anyone else in the area who even really understands all that. I'm pretty much at the top of the food chain in Blair County when it comes to technology."

But Sam persisted. "So you're *sure* no one else had access to that computer once the investigators dropped it into your hands?"

"Nope," he answered. "Just me. And I kept it safely locked up any time I wasn't around."

"Okay, okay. Just you. I get it. Well, let's drop that computer thing for the moment and focus on some other things." She looked down at a sheet of paper she had picked up from the table. "Now, Mr. Wallace, is your current address 1347 Peachtree Lane?"

Morrow shot up so fast she bumped her thigh hard on the bottom of the prosecution table. "Ouch! Objection, Your Honor! What relevance does Mr. Wallace's address have to this case?"

Judge McDaniel peered down the top of his glasses at Sam. "Counselor? What is the relevance?"

Sam held up the sheet of paper, unfazed. "Your Honor, I will establish the relevance immediately after Mr. Wallace answers the question."

"Very well," McDaniel relented, glancing briefly at the reporters scattered throughout the visitor's gallery. "I'll allow it for now. But I'm expecting to see that relevance *immediately* after he answers you. Not an hour from now. Not ten minutes from now. Immediately. Do you understand, Ms. Tulley?"

"Yes, Your Honor," she replied, turning back toward the witness box and Ray Wallace. "Mr. Wallace, I'll repeat, is your current address 1347 Peachtree Lane?"

Wallace looked visibly confused. He had no idea where she was going with this. Nor, apparently, did anyone else in the courtroom, save the three people seated at the defense table. "Well, yes, that's my address, all right. What about it?"

"Your Honor, may I approach?" Sam asked, walking straight to the witness box and dropping a sheet of paper in front of Ariel Morrow as she swept by. Judge McDaniel muttered his blessing, as confused about what Sam was up to as everyone else in the courtroom.

Sam stopped in front of Wallace and handed him a copy of what she had already shared with the prosecutor. "Mr. Wallace, I am showing you a copy of a search warrant that was issued late last night and executed this very morning as you were being sworn in as a witness." She paused and caught his eyes. "Can you please read the address listed on that search warrant to this court?"

He looked down, and his hands started shaking. After a moment, he was able to force it out. "1347 Peachtree Lane."

Sam nodded pointedly. "The very same address where you just testified you live? Your home?"

"Yes," he answered, weakly.

Morrow was back on her feet. "Your Honor, this is all very peculiar. It still isn't at all clear what any of this has to do with this case."

Sam was ready for that, handing the judge a copy of the warrant. "Your Honor, as you can see, this warrant was signed by a justice of the Court of Criminal Appeals out of Austin just last night. And the probable cause to support the warrant is spelled out in plain black and white. It was to seize evidence related to the murder of one Katie Jordan. Which is, of course, the very purpose of this trial. I can't see how that can be anything *but* relevant to this case."

Judge McDaniel knew he had very little wiggle room here. No less than a justice of the state's top criminal court was watching over everything he did. "Overruled."

Sam turned her attention back to Wallace. "Okay, then, Mr. Wallace, let's talk about what the police found when they searched your home this morning. First of all…" She glanced at the jury. "How well did you know Katie Jordan prior to her death?"

"Katie Jordan? I-I don't know. She worked at the Justice Center, same as me. Maybe we had coffee together once or twice. Like you and me. Just friends."

"Just friends," Sam repeated. "Are you sure there wasn't something else going on? Something a little more… *romantic* between the two of you?"

"No, no. Nothing like that!" Wallace threw his hands in the air like he was surrendering. "I just knew her from the office!"

"The truth is, Mr. Wallace, the truth is you were madly in love with Katie Jordan, weren't you? Head over *heels* in love with her."

"No, that isn't so!"

Sam bored down on him. "And you stayed after her even though you knew she was married. You stayed after her until, finally, you convinced her to leave her husband and take up with you."

Morrow was back on her feet. "Objection, Your Honor! This is pure speculation on Ms. Tulley's part. There is absolutely no evidence to support these lies!"

"You want evidence, Ms. Morrow? I'll *give* you *evidence*." Sam reached down and grabbed a folder off her desk, flipping it open and spreading an array of pictures out in front of her. "How is *this* for evidence? Pictures that were found in a box hidden under the sink in Ray Wallace's house. Pictures of him and Katie Jordan together. And not in the office. No! On the couch. On the beach. In *bed* together! That's how he got his hands on the *key*. She *gave* him a key!"

Morrow was stunned into silence, uncertain of what she could possibly do to stop this. Sam turned back toward Wallace in full fury. "And what *else* did they find, Mr. Wallace? How about flyers for the Aryan Brotherhood. For a *white supremacist group*! That was why you did it, wasn't it? You found out that Katie Jordan, *white* Katie Jordan, was planning on going back to her *black* husband, Curtis. She dumped you for a *black* man, didn't she? And you couldn't have that. You had to kill her. And not just her. Kill all her *half black* children, too. And even then you weren't finished. You had to make sure that the last man she ever had sex with was you! *Isn't that right*, Mr. Wallace?"

Wallace was looking wild in the witness box. McDaniel was pounding hard with his gavel, trying to restore order. But Sam wasn't finished. "Guess what else they found in your cozy little house, Mr. Wallace? A boot! That's right, I said a *boot*. A boot that perfectly matched the boot that left the bloody footprint in the kitchen the night of the murder. And when we test that boot, you know what we're going to find, don't you? Her DNA! Katie Jordan's DNA!"

McDaniel was yelling now. "Order in the court! Order in the court! Ms. Tulley, you're out of order!"

But Wallace had finally found his voice. "Sure, I knew her. Katie and I even dated a few times, after she got rid of her shiftless husband. But I didn't kill her, I swear! The file I found on her husband's computer proves that *he's* the one who killed her!"

"Yes, Mr. Wallace. The file that *you* found on his computer." Sam had moved and was now standing in front of the keyboard of the computer that held Wallace's copy of the deleted file. "So let's just look at that file, Mr. Wallace. Let's take a closer look at the file you say came from Curtis Jordan's computer." She turned slightly and pinned Wallace with a dangerous stare. "Do you know what meta data is, Mr. Wallace?"

"Meta data? Sure, but what does that have to do with –"

Sam smiled widely, flashing her canines. "Microsoft Office programs like Word all contain meta data, information that is hidden within each file. Behind the curtains, so to speak." She spun back to the keyboard, grabbing the mouse and making a few quick clicks to open the meta data screen on the file Wallace said he had recovered from Curtis Jordan's computer. Just before the final click, she glanced back at the witness box, meeting Wallace's gaze with a hard glare. "And, as the county's foremost forensic evidence guru, you would know that the meta data for a Word document tells you just when the file was originally created. And who the original author was." *Click.*

Right there, in black and white, it listed the original author of the file: Ray Wallace. The predatory smile Sam was showing held no warmth, no humor. "So Curtis Jordan hadn't written the step-by-step plan for the murder of his wife and children, after all.

It had all been a clever plant by the real killer. *You*, Mr. Wallace! *You* killed Katie Jordan!"

The courtroom exploded into chaos at the shocking revelation. Looking around in panic, Wallace realized that he had just one last chance to escape before they grabbed him and charged him for the murder. He jumped over the front of the witness box and bolted past Ariel Morrow before she could even move. In just a few short strides he was already at the back of the courtroom. The guard who was normally stationed at the rear doors had previously stepped up to the front of the courtroom to confer with the bailiff, and was desperately trying to draw his gun. Everything was happening so fast he couldn't even think to shout "Stop!" Wallace turned his body slightly, ready to blast through the doors right shoulder first, as he had when he had starred at running back for the Blairton High School Eagles. So he never saw the Reverend Ollie suddenly rise up in front of him, a well-placed round house from the Reverend's right fist connecting solidly with his chin and laying him out cold.

52

After the courtroom finally calmed down and Ray Wallace was led away in handcuffs, Judge McDaniel had no option but to declare a directed verdict of not guilty in favor of the defendant, Curtis Jordan. Now a free man, Jordan alternated his attention between Harry, Sam and the handful of supporters from his church who had stood by him throughout the ordeal. Reverend Ollie was all smiles, even as he carefully rubbed his swollen hand. "You got the good Lawd inside you, Miz Sam! You got the good Lawd inside you, doin' his work!" Ariel Morrow sat stunned in her seat at the prosecution table, overwhelmed by the fact that she had almost helped to send an innocent man to death row, her case built largely upon the clever machinations of the real killer. Her employee. Her key witness. Meanwhile, the jurors poured out of the box and surrounded Curtis Jordan and his defense team, shouting out praises and hallelujahs for the suddenly and unexpectedly free man.

Sam managed to squeeze away from all of them for a moment to locate Randy Martinez, still standing quietly in the back of the courtroom, a small satisfied smile on his face. "Randy, great work! You really moved mountains for me last night."

Randy waved off the thanks. "Just glad I could help. But I think the real miracle workers in all of this were you and Harry. Up until last night I thought Curtis Jordan was guilty as sin. But

310

you guys stood by him to the very end. This verdict is nothing less than a testament to your faith.”

“Well, we didn’t have much choice, did we? Once we accepted him as our client, we had to keep fighting for him all the way to the end. And thank God Harry figured out all that stuff about the meta data. Up until last night I’d never even heard about that. And I’m still not quite sure I understand it even now!” Sam was laughing, the nervous kind of laughter that comes after you’ve been rescued from the edge of a precipice and finally realize just how close you had come to falling.

Randy nodded. It was all Greek to him, as well. “So what’s the plan, now, Sam?”

She glanced over at Harry, who was talking to his twin sister, Hailey, and three guys she didn’t know, probably some of his buddies from Baylor Law. Hailey had planned to boycott the event, not wanting to see her brother go down in flames in such a notorious trial. But Harry got in touch with her the night before and shared his big discovery with her. And evidently called some of his friends, too. That was great for him. He would go back to school in about a week as a conquering hero, his friends sharing overblown accounts of all his daring exploits in turning around what had been until last night an unwinnable case. And, as she thought about it, the publicity from this case would almost certainly sweep across the state, if not the country, and Harry’s stock with the major law firms would soar. Just when she had begun to think the law firm of Crawford Tulley had a nice ring to it…

Suddenly she realized that Randy had asked her a question. "What? I'm sorry, Randy, I was daydreaming a bit. What was your question?"

"I just wanted to know if you had any plans for the rest of the day. I think some form of celebration may be in order."

"Yes. Of course." Sam paused a second to return to the present. "I was able to get in touch with a caterer just before we got started this morning, and they should be putting something together back at the house well before we get there. We'll have some adult drinks, of course – God, do I need one right about now – and some sweet tea for the reverend and the folks from the church. If you don't have anything else pressing, I'd appreciate it if you joined us."

"I wouldn't miss it," Randy assured her. "But look, I've got something I have to take care of right now, so I may be a little late, but rest assured I'll be there."

"Thanks, Randy." She squeezed his upper arm tenderly. "And once again, you're my knight in shining armor!"

"No, Sam. You're my Lady Guinevere, leaving yourself completely exposed as usual, just so you can take care of the common folk. All I'm good for is to give you some cover, to keep you out of harm's way." Randy glanced over at Curtis Jordan, now completely surrounded by his church folk. "You did good, today. Real good. And it just makes me proud to say I had even a little bit to do with any of it. You keep changing the world, Sam Tulley, you keep taking on the bad guys, and I'll be there behind you making sure the bad guys don't lay a finger on you in return."

53

The light bothered her long before the smoke, which was still gathering well above her head thanks to the high ceilings. Sam had gone to bed early after downing three full glasses of wine, largely because she hadn't slept a wink the night before, geared up in anticipation of the next day's events. The victory party had petered off pretty quickly once the food was gone, and Harry and his sister and friends had wandered off to carry on their own private celebration.

Sam shook the cobwebs from her mind. But the light was still there. And the smoke. And the fire.

FIRE! The room was surrounded by fire. The doorway to the hall was still clear, but that could change quickly. Sam turned to the windows, but they were fully engulfed in flames. The only escape was into the hall. She grabbed a half-full glass of water off the night stand beside the bed and soaked a pillow case with it. Holding the wet pillow case against her mouth, she stumbled through the doorway. To her left, the entire hallway was now a sheet of fire. To her right, flames were licking up the stairwell leading to the downstairs. There was no way out. She was trapped.

Then she noticed the dumbwaiter. A dumbwaiter that led down to the kitchen, and so far it was clear of the fire. Sam thought of the warnings about using an elevator in an emergency, and the fact that the machinery for the dumbwaiter was easily as old as the house, but this time she had no choice. It was either that, or burn to death up here in the hall. She flicked open the dumbwaiter's door and checked for smoke, but so far the shaft leading down to the kitchen had remained clear of the inferno. But the flames were getting closer, and she could feel the heat starting to scorch her nightgown, so she climbed quickly into the small opening, folding herself tightly to fit into the tiny space. Reaching awkwardly back through the opening into the hallway, she punched the button to send the dumbwaiter *down*. Slowly, glacially, it began its descent. As she left the third floor, the top of the dumbwaiter compartment sealed off the smoke that had begun to pour into the shaft, smoke that was making it increasingly hard for her to see or breathe. At the second floor landing, though, the smoke poured in again, even thicker, forcing her to cover her entire face with the moistened pillow case. Finally, excruciatingly, she reached the bottom, and flung herself out onto the kitchen floor. Sam was surrounded by fire, and a wall of flames stood between her and the door to the outside. With no other option, she steeled herself and raced through the fire, grasping blindly for the searing door handle and throwing herself through the doorway to the outside. Her nightgown on fire, she fell to the ground, rolling to put out the flames, finally coming to a stop against the trunk of an oak tree not twenty feet from the house.

54

Sam was still on her back, gasping from the pain stabbing through her burned hands and feet, when the fire trucks finally came screaming down the street. The firefighters missed her at first in the dark, focused on training their hoses on the house in a fruitless effort to contain the blaze. Finally someone thought to canvass the area with flashlights, and they quickly came upon her, curled into a fetal position against the tree, her heart pounding in her ears, her breathing ragged with smoke damage and fear.

"Ma'am! Are you okay?"

Sam could barely respond. The EMS workers checked her quickly for injuries, and determined that any burns she had received from her nightgown were not life threatening. One of the firemen, seeing that she was now almost completely exposed, thought to cover her with his jacket.

A voice cut through the haze. "Sam! Oh my God! Are you okay?" It was Randy, her knight in shining armor, here to rescue her from the castle. A castle that was quickly turning into a smoking ruin. One of the EMS workers tried to shoo him away, but he flashed a badge that the FBI had given him, and they reluctantly moved aside to give him access.

"It hurts," Sam admitted, "but otherwise, I'm alive." As her thoughts cleared and her concerns for her own personal safety became less immediate, she suddenly thought about everybody else who might have been in peril, stuck inside the house when the fire broke out. "Barley!" she screamed in panic, and, almost on cue, the Australian Shepherd emerged from the chaos and smoke surrounding her, limping noticeably, but still alive.

"He was with me all night, Sam," Randy explained. "Once I realized this afternoon that you were in no shape to look after him, considering all of the drama that had taken place over the last few days, I loaded him up in my truck and we shared a couple of cheeseburgers together. Perfect reward for all of his bravery earlier in the week." Randy looked back over his shoulder at the house as the third floor finally collapsed in a big whoosh. "Good thing, too, because I don't think he could have gotten to the doggie door in his current condition."

Barley staggered up to her, licking her face energetically, some of the grease from his earlier cheeseburger still stuck to his whiskers. And that was when she finally noticed the other fire. The guest house. With Harry's truck parked right in front of it. A familiar, stabbing pain clutched her heart. There was no way anyone could have escaped that –

Suddenly, a familiar voice punctuated the night. "Well, I guess I sure picked a great night to get stinkin' drunk!"

Sam spun around. "Harry! You're alive!" Without thinking, she flung herself into his arms, wincing sharply at the sudden pain shooting up her arms from her scorched hands.

"Hey, Sam, I was thinking the same thing about you! Coming up on all this, I didn't see how you could have escaped from the third floor in time." Sam was holding on tightly, and Harry was suddenly becoming uncomfortably aware that, underneath the fireman's jacket, she had next to nothing on. He pushed her lightly away before something happened that he would have trouble explaining later on. "Are you okay?" he asked, brushing her hair back to check for injuries. For the first time, he noticed tiny flecks of gold in her green eyes. *Probably just reflections from the fire*, he thought.

"Harry!" she stuttered, trying to shake off the pain in her hands. "I-I saw your truck, and it was so late, so I thought…"

"That I was asleep inside," he finished for her. "Well, normally that would have been the case, but Hailey and my law school buddies plowed through my small stash of beer pretty early, so we moved over to Rattler's to finish celebrating the win. Kind of lost track of the time, and they were just tossing us out into the street when all the fire trucks whizzed by down Main Street." He gestured at the burning house behind him. "There's only one house like that in the whole county, so there wasn't much doubt what was on fire, even from that distance. None of us were in any condition to drive, so I had to flag down a speeding patrol car, and then convince them to give me a ride over here instead of tossing me in the drunk tank. I think that was the longest three or four minutes of my life, imagining what I was going to find when I got here…" His voiced choked up, and for a moment Sam found it harder to breathe than when she had been running through the upstairs hall, surrounded by smoke and fire.

"Well, it's all over now, Harry. We're both here. Safe." Her whisper had a hint of smokiness, as well. *Just temporary lung damage*, she convinced herself.

One of the EMS workers butted in, hooking his right thumb back toward the waiting ambulance. "Ma'am, I hate to break up the reunion, but we really should get you over to the hospital and get those injuries looked at before they begin to scar over –"

Harry grinned. "Yep, I agree, Sam. It's time you traded in that tacky fireman's cape for something a little more swanky. Like a backless hospital gown."

Randy was busy talking on his phone, so Sam waved to get his attention. After a moment, he hung up. "I've already got a security detail on its way to meet you there, Sam, and we'll have a police cruiser accompany the ambulance, just to make sure there are no more… *developments* tonight."

Sam had completely forgotten about the FBI agents that had been assigned to guard her house. She looked around but didn't see them anywhere. "Randy, what happened to Vivienne and Tomas? I thought they were supposed to be on duty tonight?"

Randy had a guarded look in his eyes. "Yes, well… that's a complicated issue." He nodded his head in the direction of the ambulance. "Look, we've got a lot to catch up on, but right now you have a date with the doctors. I'll wrap things up here, then Harry and Barley can grab a ride with me to look in on you at the hospital. That'll also give us a chance to get things sorted out with Harry's sister and his friends."

The EMS tech had finally lost patience with all the delays and was now firmly guiding Sam to the back of the ambulance. Barley seemed determined not to leave her side again, somehow sensing her injuries and, likely, her fear. She stroked his head as she paused for one last look at the inferno. Something had been lost forever that night, something big. But maybe something had been found, as well.

55

Randy and Harry had to wait outside her room while the doctor finished his examination. Once Sam was decent again, though, he opened the door to let them in. Along with her newly crowned service dog, Barley, courtesy of Randy Martinez's FBI badge.

The doctor handed Sam several sheets of paper. "Here are some instructions on how to take care of your burns over the next few days. You'll need to apply the Silvadene cream to the burn sites three to four times a day, depending upon how active you are. That will speed up the healing and minimize any scarring. But I need to warn you, you should be very careful about any sun exposure to the Silvadene treated skin. The silver in the ointment can be activated by strong sunlight and will etch into the skin, leaving permanent gray spots. I've seen some of those, and believe me, you'd be better off with burn scars than living with ugly gray streaks on your skin."

"Thanks, doc," Sam said. "I'm not much of a sun worshipper, anyway, so I'll keep everything well covered up until the burns are fully healed." She gestured toward the bed. "So, is there any medical reason why I need to stay here any longer, or am I free to leave?"

Randy spoke up. "I think that falls into *my* bailiwick, Sam. Medically, there's no reason for you to stay here." He glanced over at her doctor, who nodded his agreement. "But after what happened tonight, I'm going to insist you spend the next few days in lock down, where no one knows where you are and no one can possibly have access to you. Gavin has offered a safe house in Katy, just outside of Houston. That will give us a window to hunt down whoever did this, without having to worry about whether they'll try it again."

Sam looked over at Harry. "What about…"

"Harry can come along. And Barley, of course." Hearing his name, Barley looked up at Randy expectantly, and was rewarded with a pat on his head. "And we're only talking about a few days. Three or four at the max. Gavin has a lead on the most likely suspects for tonight's attack. As professionals, they all have their own signatures, their own particular ways of setting the fires. He thinks he can track that back to ground zero, the actual person who ordered and paid for the hit, by following the money trail. But we need you tucked in safely while we follow that trail, because we can't afford another fuck up like we had tonight."

Sam thought about what Randy had said earlier. "Vivienne and Tomas?"

Randy watched her for a moment, slow to respond. Finally, he decided that he couldn't hold back the truth any longer. "Yes, Vivienne and Tomas."

"What happened to them, Randy?" Sam asked quietly.

Randy shook his head. Both of the FBI agents had been close friends, ever since the Tyler Andrews task force had first been assembled. "Vivienne is still missing. Assumed trapped inside the house. Tomas is in surgery. The outcome on him is… guarded. He took a sniper round to the right side of his head."

Sam was devastated. "All this just to protect *me*?"

Randy gave her a long, hard look. "No, Sam, this was never just about you. Vivienne and Tomas put their lives on the line for the very same reason you did, ever since the first day I met you. But they weren't there to protect *you*. They were there to protect the *law*. There are forces out there that fight day after day to whittle down our most basic protections, to strip from each and every one of us our most basic rights, to steal from us nothing less than our humanity. At some point, we have to draw the line. I've seen you do that, over and over again. Draw the line, regardless of what it costs you. And that's exactly what Vivienne and Tomas did tonight."

56

Sam slept in late the next morning, and Harry was already sitting in the kitchen nursing a cup of coffee when she finally ventured downstairs. The safe house came complete with a set of blue men's pajamas, and although they were a little baggy on her, Sam wasn't going to complain.

Harry smiled at her as she stifled a yawn. "Morning, Sleeping Beauty. You look like you could use a cup." He jumped up and pulled down a large brown mug from the cupboard above the coffee maker. "Black as usual?"

"No, how about some cream and sweetener, if we have it. And real sugar, not the yellow stuff. After last night I think I've earned it." She pulled up a chair across from him at the kitchen table and watched as he fished a pint of half-and-half out of the refrigerator and measured a teaspoon of sugar into her cup. "A little more, please," she begged in her best Dickensonian manner. "I need some *energy* this morning…"

Harry set the mug down on the table in front of her. With both of Sam's hands still wrapped in gauze, he didn't feel it was safe to just hand the steaming cup straight to her. "Here you go, boss lady."

Sam experimented with grabbing the mug with both hands, finally succeeding in raising it to her lips for a quick sip of morning courage. "Aaahh. Perfect. Thanks, I needed this. Man, I feel like I've been through hell these last few days."

"Well, Sam, as they say, if you're going through Hell, don't stop."

"I wish we *could* stop at this point, but until we find out who's behind the fire and the attempted kidnapping, hell looks to be items one through ten on our daily agenda for a while." She held the mug up gingerly with her fingertips, trying to avoid her burns. "By the way, if this is supposed to be coffee, I think I might need to pay for you to take a few lessons."

"Give me a break, Sam! These G-men only care about the caffeine, not the quality. All I had to work with was a dried up can of Folgers for God's sake."

"Okay, you're forgiven. Just make sure we put something more drinkable on our shopping list for breakfast tomorrow morning. Along with something else to wear to bed tonight." She looked down at her borrowed nightclothes. "These are a little scandalous for an old widow woman to be here playing house with some hunkin' college kid. What will people say?"

"I think they'd say it was a huge upgrade from what you had on last night. Although I might make a fortune back at Baylor selling calendars with you on the cover, decked out in nothing but a fireman's jacket."

"Boy, I'm sure that would really go over well at Baylor," she teased him back. "But hey, watch it with the flirting. You might just get a response back you're not expecting." Sam saw a quick flash of alarm sweep across his eyes, and knew immediately that she'd crossed a line and needed to cross it back. She made a show of checking out the room. "Oh boy! We partied so hard last night we burned down the house, and now here we are, shacked up in a posh, all-expense-paid federal resort in beautiful downtown Katy, Texas. We're living the dream! What's for breakfast?"

Harry couldn't help but break out in a smile over Sam's resilience in the face of disaster. He felt completely devastated by the fire, and it wasn't even his house. "About what you'd expect from federal agents. They dropped off a box of donuts a little earlier this morning. But at least they threw in some sausage and jalapeno kolaches."

"Oooh! Dibs on the kolaches!" Sam held up her bandaged hands. "But first, these need to come off, or they'll just wind up getting coated with grease and sugar glaze. Would you happen to know where a girl could find a pair of scissors in a place like this?"

"Well, Miz Sam, I do believe I might just have the answer for that." Harry stepped across the room and dug into one of the drawers next to the refrigerator. "Voilà!" He raised a pair of kitchen shears above his head triumphantly. "Now ze doctor must do ze delicate operation. Var is ze patient?"

"Get over here, you knucklehead." Sam still felt pretty edgy from the night before, but Harry already had her in a much happier mood. She held out her hands and watched as he cut carefully through the gauze. He took his time, making sure he didn't scrape the back of the scissors across her blistered hands. In two long minutes she was finally free.

Harry stared at her hands with barely concealed horror. "Ugh. That looks like it really hurts."

"I have a cream the doctor gave me for the pain, in addition to the Silvadene. But the pain medicine appears to be wearing off now, so it's starting to itch like the devil." Sam pointed to the box of donuts and kolaches still resting on the counter. "Let's dig into those while it's still just an itch, and I can get cleaned up and reapply the medicine afterwards."

"Sounds like a plan. Speaking of which, what *are* our plans for today? I take it the Fibbies don't want us strolling around town just yet, dodging bullets and related chaos from whoever is behind all this."

"No, I think Randy might have a cow if we tried that, so my suggestion is we binge watch Netflix, assuming they have it here. I've been wanting to get into the *House of Cards* for quite some time, but never had the free time to devote to it. Now might be a great excuse." She checked the clock on the oven. "But before we dive into that, I need to make another attempt to reach Margaret in Italy and check on Stella and Maddie. I called the house just before I came downstairs, but nobody answered. It's getting close to six in the evening now in Siena, and I can't imagine their managing to keep Maddie out and about much longer than that."

"Couldn't you reach her on her cell phone?"

"No. Margaret has one of those new-fangled phones that only makes calls, doesn't receive them, and Stella still hasn't picked up an Italian SIM card for her phone."

Harry was confused. "How does that work? A phone that can't receive calls?"

"Easy. Every time Margaret finishes a call, she turns the phone off. I think it's an older generation thing. She doesn't want anyone bothering her while she's out having fun." Sam picked up one of the kolaches from the box. "Hmmm. Cold kolaches. If I weren't starving already I might bother to nuke it. Maybe the second one…"

Harry helped himself to a chocolate glazed donut. Normally he would feel guilty digging into a donut like this, what his sister called a sugar-coated fat bomb, but under the circumstances he figured it was a forgivable sin. A delicious forgivable sin.

57

Margaret finally picked up on the tenth ring, just as Sam was about to hang up. Margaret liked answering machines about as much as she liked cell phones, and unless one of the staff managed to answer the house phone, it was as likely to go unanswered as not. "*Pronto, mi chiamo Margaret…*"

"*Ciao Margaret, sono Sam.* How are you three girls doing tonight?"

"Samantha! *Meraviglioso per sentire la vostra voce*! But I am very angry with you, *la mia dolce figlia.* You did not tell me Maddie had become *così bello,* so beautiful! And so very intelligent. You must not keep her from me so long next time!"

Sam struggled to keep up with Margaret's Italian. She had studied French in high school and college, and even then she still spoke French *comme une vache espagnole,* as the French would say. Like a Spanish cow. Luckily, however, Margaret usually made the switchover from Italian to English pretty quickly, and with Stella and Maddie around every day now, Sam hoped Margaret could remember to stick to English full time. "Little Maddie is free to visit her grandmother any time you want her. But I must warn you, be careful what you wish for. She's become quite a handful lately."

"Yes, I see that. It is always *perché*, *perché*, *perché* with her. Why, why, why. But it is such a delightful problem to have. So much like her father, always into things. And it is wonderful to finally meet Stella. Such a grand lady. But I have a question for you. Why did you send them to me on the government plane? So *terribile*. How do you say? Such a dreadful way to fly!"

"Well, a commercial flight wasn't really possible, given the security issues and the fact that we didn't have a passport for either Maddie or Stella. So that was our only real option at the time. And it couldn't have been all *that* bad…"

"The passport I don't know about, but any time you or Maddie need to travel somewhere, why don't you take her plane? It's just sitting there most of the time at the airport, anyway, rusting away."

"What do you mean, take *her* plane? Maddie doesn't have a plane. She's just a child." Sam wondered if she was simply misunderstanding what Margaret was trying to say, if the language issues were getting in the way.

"Well, of course she's a child, but *Mio Dio*, you're her mother, so you have full use of the trust assets as part of your allowance. Didn't anyone explain that to you?"

"Whoa, whoa, hold on a second Margaret. What trust? What allowance? What in the world are you talking about?"

"The Ricciardelli Family Trust, of course. The money Maddie inherited when Luke died. The same trust that pays your allowance every year."

"Margaret, honest to God, this is the first I've heard about any of this. Maddie inherited a trust? And I'm supposed to get an allowance? Where did all this come from?"

"Oh, Samantha, I'm so sorry. I just assumed you knew, that being a lawyer you would have known all about Luke's financial affairs."

"Well, Luke was never the one to talk about money. Unlike his father, he thought it was just showing off, a sign of poor upbringing…"

"*Sì*, that was the Ricciardelli in him. Old money never has to advertise. Just like his grandfather. But surely you would have heard about the trust when Luke died, when you were busy wrapping up his affairs."

"No, actually, if you recall I had some… health issues at the time, and I never really got involved in the legal work for his estate. I left all that to his family's lawyers…" Yes, the *Tulley* family lawyers. Suddenly it was becoming very clear to Sam. It wasn't the Tulley money they were worried about after all. It was the Trust. Maddie had apparently inherited a large estate when her father died, and the Tulleys had managed to whisk it away right under their noses, while Sam was lost in never-never land. But that was a secret they couldn't keep hidden forever. At least not as long as Sam and Maddie were still alive, and the truth was just one conversation with Margaret away. A conversation the Tulleys quite literally couldn't afford.

"Okay, Margaret, I think we both need to grab a glass of wine and start over again from scratch. I need to know everything you can tell me about the trust. And, even more important, about William Tulley…"

58

"Okay, Sam, time to dish. What did you find out from Margaret about what's going on?" Harry had waited impatiently throughout the long phone call. He knew whatever they were discussing was pretty serious, because Sam went through two glasses of wine during the call. And this was the first time he had *ever* seen her day drinking, even on vacation.

Sam hesitated, wondering how much she should share with Harry. But then she remembered all that William Tulley had done to Harry's family, and everything they had risked together over the past few weeks, and she knew in her heart that he deserved the whole story. "Just a quick question, Harry. Does the name 'Ricciardelli' mean anything to you?"

"No, other than it sounds a lot like a chocolate bar. And I think you told me once that Ricciardelli was Margaret's maiden name, a name she reclaimed after she divorced Luke's father. Why? Does it hold some special significance in all this?"

"It does indeed. In fact, it's the key to everything. You see, according to Margaret, William Tulley has been pulling a fast one on everyone regarding his family's roots. He doesn't come from old money after all. In fact, his father was a coal miner from Eastern Kentucky, who died early on from lung disease he developed after too many years in the mines. William Tulley wanted a better life than that, so at an early age he chose to put on airs and hang out with a moneyed crowd, a crowd he hoped could open up opportunities for him in the future. One summer he happened upon the opportunity of a lifetime. Margaret Ricciardelli."

Sam took a last sip of wine and continued the story. "Margaret was an exchange student from Siena, Italy, and was staying with a wealthy family in Georgetown, Virginia. Tulley met her at a party and, sensing a lingering insecurity in her, a vulnerability, he moved in for the kill. Before anyone really knew what was happening, he whisked her off her feet and straight in front of a judge. They were secretly married, a marriage he managed to *keep* secret until she was safely pregnant. With Luke. So when her father finally found out, it was already too late to have the marriage annulled. He had to live with the new, scheming son-in-law, and learn to cherish his upcoming grandson."

"And Luke never told you anything about this, the real truth about his family?"

"Luke probably didn't have a clue. His mother is *still* deeply embarrassed about what happened, all those years ago. And she certainly didn't want to burden her son with the fact that he was the ultimate reason she stayed with her husband for so long. She loved Luke too much to hang that kind of guilt on him."

Harry considered what he had just learned. "So, Luke is born, and a few years later Mary Ellen. What happened then? How did William Tulley make his fortune? Why did Margaret leave him?"

"Margaret's father couldn't stand by and watch while his daughter and grandchildren lived in poverty, so he gave William Tulley several million dollars as seed money to help start a commercial construction business. That may seem like a lot, but Margaret assured me it was just pennies to her father. Anyway, Tulley chose to settle that company in Dallas, for two reasons. First, the town was booming, so there was a great deal of money to be made in construction. Second, he found a partner, your father, a man who had amassed a small fortune of his own building up his own company from scratch, Crawford Construction."

"So that's where we fit in to all of this."

"That's right. Evidently your father was a brilliant engineer and a natural salesman, but he had one weakness – he was far too trusting for his own good. While your dad focused on building and managing the business, Tulley handled the legal and financial affairs of the firm. And I think you have an inkling of what happened next. Right about the time Mary Ellen was born, Tulley pulled a scam on his partner and cheated him out of not just the business, but also the home he had built for his young family in Highland Park. Kicked all of you out on the street with barely a suitcase of clothing each, and then moved right in to your old house with Margaret, Luke and the baby."

"So there never was a rich family legacy for the Tulleys?"

Sam shook her head. "No. In fact, when I visited the house that one Thanksgiving before Luke and I got married, Tulley made a point of toasting a large painting hanging over the fireplace, suggesting that it was a Tulley ancestor. But that was just a big lie. According to Margaret, that picture came with the house."

"Yeah," Harry responded. "I know exactly what you're talking about. That was my grandfather. That bastard Tulley wasn't just content to steal our home and our money. It sounds like he was trying to steal our family identity, too. Down to the paintings we had hanging on the wall."

They both paused for a moment to reflect on that. It was Harry who finally broke the silence. "So, what happened next? Why did Margaret decide to divorce him?"

"You have to understand that Margaret wasn't living in a vacuum. She had become close friends with your family, and in particular your mother, and when she found out what her husband had done to you, it wound up being the last straw for her. She packed up the kids and her things and headed back to Italy. Her father made sure the divorce came through very soon after that. She got the kids, and Tulley got to keep the money he treasured so deeply." Sam thought back on all the crazy stories her husband had shared with her during the good times before his death. "Luke often told me about how he'd spent so much of his childhood roaming around Europe. I just assumed that was how the rich vacationed. I never dreamed that he actually grew up there, living with his mother in Italy, and only occasionally coming back to the States to visit his dad."

"So how did he wind up back in Dallas for college? Why not just stay in Italy, or go to one of the universities in England?"

"I had the same question, Harry. Apparently, the answer was quite simple. He was slated to start school at Oxford when he met a girl in Dallas the summer before and fell in love. She had already been accepted to SMU, so using the Tulley money and influence, he snagged a last minute admission to the school so he could be with her. That love affair lasted about three years, but when she found out that he was planning on going to med school instead of taking his rightful spot at the top of Tulley Crawford, she dumped him. Being a doctor's wife just wasn't lucrative enough for her Highland Park tastes."

"But that doesn't make any sense, Sam. From what you're saying, Luke was already filthy rich. The doctor money was just a hobby."

"Right. But Luke didn't tell her about the real money, any more than he told me. It wasn't that he was trying to hide it, he just didn't think it was particularly important. It was just money, after all, and money was never something Luke really cared about. It didn't define him — saving sick babies was what drove his soul."

"So what kind of money are we talking about? And how is it that Maddie wound up inheriting everything instead of you?"

"From what Margaret told me, and you have to keep in mind that she was evidently pretty detached from the family business, the Ricciardelli Family Trust represents one of the largest remaining private fortunes in Europe. It would be hard to throw a rock anywhere in Europe without hitting something that was either owned or controlled by the trust."

"Holy smokes. I get it, now. That's a serious chunk of change. So now that money is Maddie's?"

"Okay, bear with me a little here, because my focus in law school was never wills and trusts. I was more of a civil litigation kind of gal." Sam leaned forward again. They were about to get to the real meat of the story. "From what I've been told, Luke's grandfather put together a generation-skipping trust before he died. He didn't want William Tulley to get his hands on the real money in the family, so he set it up to go directly to Luke, his grandson. When the grandfather died, Luke had sole possession of the entire empire, with the exception of a small yearly allowance for his mother and sister."

"Small? How small?"

"It works out to a little less than a million dollars a year, plus or minus depending upon the Euro exchange rate. Also free use of the family jets, yachts and about a dozen houses scattered throughout Europe."

Harry whistled, incredulous. "So Luke was able to manage all that and you never once had a clue?"

"No. Not even a hint. I imagine almost all of it was run by professional managers. I mean, I knew that he would leave town for meetings every now and then, headed to places like Vegas or New York, but I just assumed they were medical meetings or something related to his research. In retrospect, those were most likely board meetings, or rendezvous with some of his managers." Sam looked down at her blistered hands, which were already crying out for medical attention. "It's a little disturbing, to tell the truth. To find out that the man I thought I knew so well was, in fact, someone quite different. That he kept so many secrets from me, his closest and most intimate friend. I suppose it was all just a natural protective response to the kind of wealth he controlled, putting up walls to keep people from trying to take advantage of him. God knows the world is full of people who would cozy up to him and feign affection just to get their hands on some of his money. Like his college girlfriend. I can only hope that he would have learned to trust me more at some point. Ha, there you go. The irony. Trust me enough to tell me about the trust."

Harry let that thought hang for a moment between them. Sam obviously had some serious personal issues to work through, issues he didn't feel he could help her with at this point. For several reasons. But one crucial legal question still remained. "So, putting all that aside for the moment, how did the trust wind up in Maddie's hands? And where exactly does that leave you? If any of that is too personal, you don't have to share it. I understand. I'm just trying to figure out how all of this fits into the attacks."

"No, that's all right. In fact, Maddie's connection to the trust is very much germane to what has been happening over the past week or so. And to what we can expect in the near future." Sam glanced at her notes from the phone conversation with Margaret, more out of habit than from any need to refresh her memory of the story. "According to Margaret, after Luke's death the trust should have transferred directly to Maddie, leaving me with a life estate similar to hers and Mary Ellen's. But, and this is critical, if something happened to Maddie before she bore any children, ownership of the trust would have rolled back upstream to William, and then to Margaret's sole surviving child, Mary Ellen."

The pieces finally fell into place for Harry. "Right. So as long as Luke was alive, William Tulley was content to just squeeze him out of his paternal inheritance and save that money for his daughter. But then came the accident, and everything changed. At first he probably thought he could seize control of the

Ricciardelli trust just by keeping you in the dark, particularly given the unique opportunity that arose when you had – issues – following the funeral. But then he realized that Luke's mother would start asking questions, particularly once Maddie came of age to take over the estate. So he had no choice but to tie up all the loose ends and make sure his control of the trust couldn't be challenged."

"Yep. And every single one of those loose ends converged in Maddie. She had to be killed so Tulley could legally take over the reins of the Ricciardelli trust. And I had to die to wrap up any remaining loose ends, any final investigation into Maddie's death."

Harry studied his soda. "It all makes perfect sense. There's no way the local yokels in Blair County could have pulled off what happened last night, and even less chance they could have scraped together enough money to pay for the professionals to do it. So that leaves only William Tulley. He had the money, the means and the motive. As criminal lawyers, we know what that adds up to. Guilty as charged."

Sam had to agree. You just couldn't argue with the cold hard facts.

59

Randy pushed the button on his steering wheel to answer the phone almost before it rang, his voice thick with concern. "Sam, I didn't expect to hear from you so soon. Is everything okay?"

"Everything's just peachy, Randy. No reason to worry. But listen, I just got off the phone with Margaret Ricciardelli back in Italy, and she told me some things you really need to hear. Things that make everything that has happened over the last week suddenly crystal clear."

"Really? Well, that is certainly welcome news. Hold on a sec." He quickly pulled off to the side of the road and switched the call off speakerphone. He also double-checked to make sure the call was being recorded, so he could play it back later if necessary. "What sort of things did she tell you?"

Sam carefully repeated everything she had learned that morning, including her conclusion that only William Tulley could have possibly masterminded the attacks.

"Boy, Sam, it all seems so obvious now. And I feel like a complete fool. I just can't believe we didn't put all this together before now. The attacks were way too professional to have been masterminded by that gang at the Justice Center. And the attempted kidnapping never made any sense at all. But, if the

Ricciardelli fortune is as big as you say, paying someone to murder you and Maddie would be the least of Tulley's concerns."

"Plus there's the religious thing," Sam pointed out. "A little Jewish girl getting her hands on all that money –"

"Had to get under his craw, that's for sure." Randy stopped for a second to think. "Look, Sam, I need to run this by Gavin and the rest of the FBI team, get them jumping on it. They already have some folks from Treasury trying to chase down the payoff money for the hit men. Now that we know where to look, it should be pretty easy to tie that back directly to Tulley's bank accounts. I think you may have broken this thing wide open."

"Glad to help, Randy. But one thing I'm still concerned about. Now that we know what's at stake, this safe house doesn't seem all that safe anymore. And it won't take Tulley long to put two and two together and send someone to check out what's going on in Italy."

"I'm way ahead of you on that. I'm sure he's got the inside scoop on anywhere his ex wife might try to hide away on her own, so that won't work. We'll need to call in some more favors and lock Stella and Maddie down tight. Maybe even get them out of Italy for now."

"And remind Margaret not to use the family jet. If Tulley has control of the trust, it's almost certain he has someone monitoring her trips and reporting back to him. If they travel anywhere, they're going to need to go incognito."

"Yeah, Sam, good thinking on that. Okay, just sit tight for now and I'll get back to you as soon as I can put some things in motion. In the meantime, is there anything you need?"

"No, the FBI agents here are taking pretty good care of us. They're even trying to get us hooked up with Netflix, so we don't die of boredom just sitting around waiting."

"Dying of boredom is certainly a much better alternative than what William Tulley has in mind for you. But don't worry, Sam. Even if this case didn't revolve around an enormous European fortune, we've got an FBI agent to bury later this week. And that's a pretty big deal. The President has made finding the person responsible for Vivienne's death a top national priority, and every agency of the government has been ordered to give the search their full and undivided attention. William Tulley has just made the mistake of his life. He reached out and poked the bear. And it turns out this bear is not very happy about being poked."

60

The next morning, Randy showed up with Gavin Larson at the safe house in Katy. Sam ushered them into the living room and settled them into two overstuffed easy chairs, across a low coffee table from the brown leather couch where she and Harry sat facing them. She gestured toward the kitchen. "Can I get you some coffee? Or maybe a soda? I think we still have some Dr Peppers in the refrigerator…"

Gavin Larson shook his head. "No thanks, Sam. We just had breakfast with the investigative team, catching up on overnight developments. I'm pretty coffeed out at the moment."

Randy also waved off the offer. "Grab something for you and Harry if you want, but I'd just as soon get down to business. We've made a lot of progress in the case since you dropped that bombshell in our laps yesterday, and we need to get you up to speed."

Gavin butted in. "Before we dive into the details, Sam, the really good news is that I think we've identified the hit men in all of this, the group that tried to kill you and Maddie. We have some teams in place that should have them all in custody within the next few hours. And that means you should be able to jump on a plane to Europe sometime tomorrow or the next day to see your daughter."

Sam and Harry were suddenly all ears. "You located them *already*? Who was it? How did you find them?" Sam leaned forward expectantly, her bandaged hands gingerly clutching the edge of the coffee table in front of her.

Gavin smiled. "Well, I'd like to say it was all because of the wonderful men and women at the FBI, with their training and assets committed to the pursuit of justice, but actually our big break came from the NSA, the National Security Agency, with some help from Treasury. As we said before, it was clear from the git-go that this was a professional job, especially after the last attack."

"All that had to have cost a fortune," Sam pointed out. "Especially for two separate attacks, back to back."

"Right on, Ms. Tulley. That lead us to check out several groups we've been keeping a close watch on, and compare the two attacks on you to their signatures, the methods they've used in the past. It didn't take long before we narrowed it down to one organization, a group of assassins based out of Sardinia. Which makes some sense, given your family's connections to Italy."

"That's when NSA and Treasury gave us a hand," Randy explained. "We were able to get a look at their cash flows over the last few months, since they obviously weren't doing this for free. They expected to get paid, and paid in a big way, with large amounts of untraceable cash. Half up front, half on completion."

Harry looked confused. "But if the money is untraceable, how could you figure out where it was coming from and where it was going?"

"Good question," Gavin noted. "When we say untraceable, we mean it is almost impossible to figure out exactly what *specific* accounts the money comes out of and ends up in, and who owns those accounts. But unless it's all an internal transfer within one bank, the money still has to flow through the international banking system. And that means we can track which bank originates the transfer, and where the money ultimately winds up."

Randy jumped in. "And since we already knew which banks the Tulleys used, and NSA gave us the bank and even some account numbers for the Sardinians, it was just a simple matter of looking for large cash flows between those banks at or around the time of the attacks."

"It took less than an hour for Treasury and the NSA to make the connection," Gavin explained. "Then we lined up a federal judge for a warrant to search the bank records for the Tulley family. By early this morning we had everything we needed to prove who actually paid to have you killed."

Sam was amazed at how much the government could accomplish when it actually tried. And how fast they could get it done. "So all that led you straight to William Tulley," she said, thinking out loud.

"That's a very good guess, Ms. Tulley," Gavin observed. "William Tulley had more than enough money, so he wouldn't even sneeze at the two or three hundred grand it cost to pull this off. Plus, he had a long history of unbridled animosity toward you and Maddie. So he was the very first person we looked at. But, no, as it turned out, it wasn't Luke's father." He paused, shaking his head. "It was his sister, Mary Ellen."

61

"His *sister*?" Sam couldn't believe what she had just heard. "But why *her*? I mean, I don't even *know* her, and I haven't even *met* her, other than one time from across the room that first Thanksgiving at the Tulleys. And at the funeral. Why in God's name would she ever want to hurt my *daughter*?"

Gavin nodded. "All very good questions. None of it made sense to us, either. But when Treasury pulled a trace on all of the bank accounts associated with the Tulley family, they found several wire transfers to the Sardinians' offshore accounts that originated from accounts *she* controlled, not William Tulley. Big dollar amounts, nice round numbers, all of them destined for untraceable bank accounts in the Caymans. And all of them clustered around the two attacks on your house."

Sam was shaking her head, trying to sort it all out. "Luke once said that she was very close to her father, that she was willing to embrace his crazy religious ideas in order to gain access to his money. Was that it? Was she just trying to be a proxy for her father? To get rid of Maddie and me as a favor to him?"

"No, Sam," Randy answered. "It wasn't anything as twisted as that. Mary Ellen's motivation was really very simple. It wasn't religion, or personal loyalty. It was money."

"Money?" Sam was, if anything, even more confused. Then she finally got it. When her mother-in-law told her the day before that the trust would roll back to William and Margaret's sole surviving child if Maddie died, in her blind anger toward Luke's father she had completely misinterpreted what that actually meant. She had assumed that meant it went first to William Tulley, and then, at his death, to his daughter. But Luke's grandfather would never have constructed the trust in a way that allowed even the remotest possibility that William Tulley could get his hands on the Ricciardelli fortune. It would have to skip William once again and go straight to his sole surviving child, Mary Ellen.

Gavin could see the light coming on in Sam's eyes. "So when your husband died, and Mary Ellen discovered that you were in no condition to handle the legal side of closing out his estate, she saw the perfect opportunity to swoop in and snatch it up from right under your nose."

"And the lawyers handling all of that at the time were the Tulley family lawyers," Sam pointed out. "There's no possible way they could have switched control over the trust by mistake. So that means they were all in on it the whole time. Hiding Luke's inheritance from me, leaving us with just the insurance money and the contents of Luke's personal bank account. Here I was worried about running out of money before Maddie got old enough for college, and all the time they were robbing us blind."

"That's right." Gavin checked his watch. "And in case you're wondering, the lawyers and accountants involved in this are probably all sitting in the back of a police cruiser right now, handcuffed and heading toward a date with federal prison. Given the fact that they are about to be charged as accessories in the murder of a federal agent, I expect they'll become extremely cooperative with us in the not so distant future."

"Couldn't happen to a nicer group of people." Sam thought back on everything that had happened over the past four years, from that very first Thanksgiving with Luke, to their wedding, to Luke's death and funeral. It all seemed so surreal to her now. And, with their house just a pile of smoldering ashes, with everything they had shared together literally now up in smoke, all she really had left of her time with Luke were the memories. And Maddie.

Harry suddenly had an idea. "Wait! Are we even sure your husband is dead? I mean, you told me once it was a closed casket funeral. Is there any way they could have faked it all?"

Sam shook her head. "No, Dad had to identify the body at the morgue. It was Luke." *But...* "You know, though, after the funeral, when I was having problems, a doctor came to see us out of the blue. He gave my parents some pills to give me, and after I started taking them I got worse, not better. A lot worse. I wonder if that wasn't part of their plan, as well. Send a doctor to knock me out, keep me completely out of the loop while they moved everything around. While they stole Maddie's inheritance."

"That makes a lot of sense, Sam," Gavin said, standing up and getting ready to leave. It was still pretty early in the day, and he had a ton of work ahead of him. "I'll have someone check into that, assuming we can figure out at this late date who it was." He checked his watch. "Well, that's pretty much the whole shooting match, Sam. So now you see why several hundred thousand dollars in hit money was a pretty solid investment for Mary Ellen. Maddie's death would nail down a fortune for her, a fortune that made her father look like a pauper." He paused. "Speaking of which, just because Luke's sister was the ringleader of this whole enterprise, that doesn't mean William Tulley is completely off the hook. First of all, it's hard to believe she could manage to pull all this off behind his back. He had to have known what was going on. And at the very least, the FBI and Treasury have been tracking some mysterious payments to several hate groups, hate groups that have direct connections to recent attacks on synagogues and abortion centers around the country. Now that we have unlimited access to all of the Tulley family finances, I'll bet you dollars to donuts that at least some of that money can be traced back to the father."

"Well, as Maddie's guardian, I'll authorize your guys to look into anything having to do with the trust, so that part of it won't be a problem. Go get 'em tiger." Sam looked around the room. "The next big question is, where do we go from here? Now that Mary Ellen and her henchmen are in custody, I guess the danger to us is pretty much over. As soon as I can get a replacement for my passport that burned up in the fire, I'll need to catch that flight to Italy to see Maddie and Stella."

"We can get you a passport overnight, and we might even be able to squeeze you in on a private flight to Siena," Gavin offered. "But I would prefer it if you and Harry would sit tight for at least another day or two. There could still be one last contract on your life sitting out there that Mary Ellen is in no position to cancel, so I'd rather keep you under wraps a little longer."

Randy looked up. "Oh, one last item. This whole thing with the FBI started because we thought the good old boy network at the courthouse was behind the first attack, the attempted kidnapping. So Gavin here got permission to reassemble the old team from the Tyler Andrews case, to see if we could finally get enough evidence to put an end to the corruption at the Justice Center. And hopefully even get Tyler freed from prison." He nodded to his partner. "I gave Gavin the transcript Evan Murphy seized from the Rollins trial, and he thinks that might be enough to pull Starke and Kennedy in on federal charges. They're going to press the RICO angle, the Racketeer Influenced and Corrupt Organizations Act, which could mean a sentence of life in prison. At the very least, Starke would be facing twenty years, which at her age is effectively a life sentence, anyway. And that should be more than enough to get her singing like a canary. So maybe at the end of the day, some good will come out of this whole mess. It won't make up for Vivienne Newsome's death in the fire, but my guess is she'll be smiling down on us from heaven if Tyler Andrews can walk out of prison a free man."

"That sounds like a great plan," Sam agreed. "And it needs to be done, even though it probably means I'm toast in this town, at least as far as criminal law goes." Sam paused a moment to work through all of the details that still needed to be wrapped up before she took off for Italy. And one of those details wasn't optional. "Gavin… can I put off the trip to see Maddie for a few more days? I think I owe it to Vivienne to see her off at the funeral."

"I'd like to be there, too," Harry added.

Gavin nodded. "I think she would appreciate that, Sam. And as for your security at the funeral, someone would have to be a complete lunatic to try to pull something with at least a thousand police officers and Fibbies in attendance. I think even the Vice President is planning to be there." He smiled. "It *is* an election year, after all…"

62

"What do you mean, *she's gone?*" Gavin Larson was livid, and the poor agent who had to deliver the news was taking the brunt of his fury.

"I don't know any more than what I just told you, sir. When we pulled in the net on her this morning, it came up empty. Mary Ellen Tulley seems to have just… disappeared. And her father, as well. Someone must have tipped them off, probably someone at the bank."

"How in the *hell* could you people be so *incompetent!*" Gavin literally spat the words out. "We're gonna bury a federal agent in two days, another agent is clinging to his life at Bethesda, and you somehow let the woman responsible for all that *slip through your hands?*"

"Yes sir. I don't really know what to say. We had trackers on all of their cars, and none of them left the garages. They couldn't have caught a flight – their names were flagged at both Bush and Hobby airports as terror suspects. And there's no activity on any of their credit cards. So there's no way they could have gotten far…"

Airport. Gavin suddenly knew exactly how they planned to escape the FBI dragnet.

<h1 style="text-align:center">63</h1>

"It appears they took off very early this morning, right after their jet got refueled." The counter agent for Million Air FBO looked apologetic, but there was nothing he could do. The FBI had failed to distribute the terror alert to the private aviation terminals, so to him the early morning flight was simply routine, one of a dozen or so departures scheduled – or, more typically, unscheduled – that day.

"Do you have a copy of their flight plan? Any idea of their destination?" Gavin knew he was grasping at straws, but straws were all he had at the moment. And the FBI Director wanted answers. Now.

"No sir, they went VFR, and I can't find anyone who overheard where they were headed. Not that we would ask. The folks who own those private jets don't take kindly to people snooping into their private affairs." VFR meant Visual Flight Rules. Once they left Houston Class Bravo airspace, their flight plans were anyone's guess. Especially if they veered out over the Gulf of Mexico, where they could drop out of radar coverage in minutes.

"God *dammit!*" Gavin already had agents checking with Houston Departure in a final, desperate effort to locate the jet's last known location, but with a range of 7,500 nautical miles and a top speed of almost seven hundred miles per hour, Tulley's Gulfstream G650ER could be almost anywhere by now. And from what he already knew about the Tulleys, this wasn't just a last minute gamble to avoid capture. They probably had an escape plan in the works from the very moment they first hatched their scheme to grab the Ricciardelli fortune. As long as Maddie lived, the risk of discovery loomed over them like a dark cloud, so they needed an infallible rainy day plan, a safe house of their own they could run to if the feds came knocking. Which is exactly what happened. And with the kind of resources William and Mary Ellen Tulley had at their disposal, once they disappeared there was next to no chance they would ever be found. Gavin was pretty sure they had money stashed away in secret bank accounts all over the world. And while money can buy you attention, it can just as easily buy you anonymity.

He would give his agents another hour, to make doubly sure the Tulleys hadn't slipped up somehow and left a few crumbs along their trail. Then the really unpleasant part of his day would begin.

64

Sam couldn't believe what she had just heard. "What do you mean, she's gone?"

Harry looked up sharply, caught in the middle of a big bite into the greasy cheeseburger the FBI agents had dropped off for lunch. "Hoosh gone?"

Gavin was just glad he didn't have time to deliver the news in person. Over the phone was bad enough. "I don't know what to say, Ms. Tulley. This whole operation has been one screw up after another from the very start. Now this. And I accept full responsibility for all of it."

"But how in the world could she have disappeared so quickly? And how about her father? Please tell me you at least have *him* in custody –"

Harry had swallowed his bite almost whole and was staring at Sam with alarm. "Who disappeared? Who's in custody?" Sam waived him off.

"I wish I could tell you differently, Ms. Tulley, but no, William got away, too. They both took off in one of the trust's private jets just before sunrise this morning, while the task force was sitting around sipping coffee and congratulating ourselves on the arrests. I was sitting there, too. I nearly broke an arm patting myself on the back, while the Tulleys were jetting away to God knows where and probably laughing at us *behind* our backs. No excuses, ma'am. We took our eyes off the prize at the last minute, and when we looked back it was gone."

"You said they both took off. By that you mean Mary Ellen and her father? What about his wife, Olivia?"

"His wife evidently wasn't part of the plan. Our agents woke her up when they showed up at the Tulley house to serve the arrest warrant. Apparently she wasn't even aware that he had left."

Sam was shattered. Just a few hours earlier she had been promised that it was all over, that Mary Ellen and her father were headed straight for a lifetime in federal prison. Now all they had to show for the heartbreak and danger she had been through were a few piss-ant accountants and lawyers. She shook her head, trying to clear out those thoughts. Nothing could be gained by dwelling on the past. Only the future mattered. "Okay, Gavin, so what's next?" she asked resignedly. "Where do we go from here?"

"I think we have to be realistic about the possibility of capturing the Tulleys anytime soon. It's like trying to hook just one particular catfish in the lake, and in this case the catfish knows how to spot the hook. We may get lucky down the road, like we did with Saddam Hussein, but in the end I wouldn't put any money on our chances." He paused for a moment to let that thought soak in, then continued. "But, on a brighter note, at least some good came out of all this. We didn't get the crooks, but we *will* get the money back that they tried to steal from you. Or most of it, anyway. You can hide cash away in secret numbered accounts, but hard assets, the real wealth that makes up the Ricciardelli trust, well, that just isn't going anywhere."

"And I suppose that we still don't have to worry about our safety anymore, now that they have no profit motive for Maddie's death."

"I would say you're free and clear on that, at this point. So we still have the funeral set for two days from now, and then I think we can shutter up the safe house again and ship you off to be with your daughter." Gavin hesitated. "Speaking of the funeral, that's where I'm headed now. To deliver the bad news in person to Vivienne's family…"

Ouch! Sam had been so focused on her own issues that she had completely forgotten about how Mary Ellen's and William's schemes had impacted the other lives around her. While she at least had the consolation prize of a vast fortune now lying at her daughter's feet, Vivienne's parents no longer even had a daughter. And with the Tulleys lost in the wind, no closure for her death. Once again Sam thought of her old dream, of sitting naked in a law school classroom, exposed to the entire world for who she really was. A fraud. She had been so wrapped up in her own problems, she failed to consider the needs of those around her who were also angry, also hurting. Like Gavin. But maybe she could put some clothes on that girl, if only just this once. "I'm so sorry, Gavin. Please let them know how much I appreciate everything Vivienne did for me. For us. She will never truly be gone from us as long as we remember the sacrifices she made to protect the lives of others, people she barely knew. Vivienne's memory will be in my heart for as long as I live."

"I'll do that, Ms. Tulley. Sam. I'll be sure to tell them that."

"Oh, and Gavin? You shouldn't blame yourself for what happened, either. For any of it. Life just springs its little surprises on us, both the good and the bad, and we need to learn to accept it and move on. That's part of Vivienne's legacy, too. She died to give others a chance to live. It could have been you who died in that house, and it was very nearly me. But the same grim hand of fate that took Vivienne's life spared ours, so we need to honor her by moving forward, not wallowing in second guessing and self pity." *A lesson for me, as well,* she reminded herself. "I for one greatly appreciate everything you have done for my family. If you hadn't jumped in and whisked Maddie off to Siena right after the break in, she would have been sleeping in her bed next to my room when the fire broke out. And there would have been two more people to bury over the next few days. That is part of *your* legacy, Gavin. My life, and the life of my daughter."

"Thank you for that, Sam. I just… thank you." Gavin was deeply touched by Sam's words, by her kindness. It gave him a little more strength to face Vivienne's parents. And then the funeral, with the eyes of thousands of police officers and federal agents staring at him and knowing full well just how badly he had screwed this whole thing up.

65

After the funeral, Harry and Sam decided to swing by the old house one last time to say goodbye. Goodbye to the house, goodbye to each other. He was packed up and headed back to school, and she had a plane to catch the next morning.

They walked gingerly around the edges of the rubble, all that remained of the house and guest house after the fire. The firefighters had given up on saving the house very early on, when it became apparent that the blaze had been intentionally set and there was next to zero chance of winning the battle. Instead, they focused on containing the fire, keeping it from spreading and endangering any of the other houses on the street. Miraculously, the two majestic oak trees in the front yard were still standing, singed a little on the side facing the burning house, but still alive. The firefighters also managed to protect Harry's old truck, a somewhat dubious achievement from his point of view.

The old house still had one last gift remaining, however. The collapse of the third floor early in the fire had rained down bricks and other rubble on Sam's study, and when they pulled back some of the debris they found her old mahogany desk, its legs broken off but still mostly intact. Reaching down and pulling out one special drawer, she found her hidden trove of love letters and cards from Luke.

The day was fairly cool for a Texas summer, with wispy clouds floating across an azure sky, a light breeze coming up from the south. A picture perfect day, and Harry seemed to be enjoying it. He lifted his eyes from the tragedy of the broken mansion and gazed instead at the sprawling grounds, dotted with ancient oak trees and flowering shrubs. At least two idyllic acres in the very center of the village, the perfect location to live out a life of cozy Southern repose. He turned to Sam, breaking the silence as she carefully collected her treasures from the drawer.

"You know, Sam, it would be hard to imagine a better place to have a house than right here, with all of this land around for Maddie and Barley to romp around on, with trees that have stood the test of time for hundreds of years, with an unbelievable view of the downtown and the river, especially up high. It's like having a little Eden of your own…"

Sam turned to gaze behind her, remembering the old third floor vista across the tops of the houses lining the other side of the street, a view that, despite all of her reservations, originally sold her on buying the house. On a day that now seemed so long ago. A far more innocent time.

Harry wasn't finished. "Vivienne's death aside, maybe in the end this fire wasn't all that tragic. Maybe it's an opportunity, a chance to rebuild. To build a new house, a house better suited for a modern world, a house that *you* could design to make it all your own. It's just like that story you once told me, when the cat knocked over your ant farm and destroyed it, and the ants all got away. You can't put this house back together, you can't unburn the fire, but you can take the insurance money, along with all the money you and Maddie will get from Luke's family trust, and you can build an even better house. Build a new ant farm…"

Sam turned to him, completely incredulous. "Hang around here and rebuild this old dinosaur? Are you *kidding* me? I'm going to get as far from this Godforsaken flea-bitten hellhole as I possibly can!" She could see the hurt in his eyes as soon as she said it. "Look, Harry, that's not –"

He gave her a stoic smile, but his face had turned to stone. "No, you don't need to apologize, Sam. I get it. It's just that, well, it's been a great summer together – okay, an *interesting* summer – but now it's time to move on. I have to get back to my final year at Baylor, you have that plane to Italy to catch in the morning. We have to get back to our *real* lives." He suddenly stooped to pick up a rock, examining it very carefully.

"Harry…" Despite her legal training, Sam was finding it very hard to explain what she was thinking. Probably because there was no good way to say it.

Harry tossed the rock back down by his feet. "So is this it? Is this the final goodbye?"

"I… I honestly don't know, Harry." She stepped up to take his now-empty hands in hers. "I honestly don't know what the future holds. For me. For you. For us, maybe. I just know that I have a baby girl who needs her mommy now more than ever. I know that it's been almost two years since Luke's accident, and it's been the longest two years of my life. I need some time to heal, to put all of this nastiness, this craziness behind me. To get back some of that innocence I've lost over those two years."

Harry could no longer control his tears. "Samantha Tulley, you are still the most innocent, the most pure person I have ever met. I know your world is now half a planet away from mine, making sure people like the Tulleys don't continue to steal your daughter blind. I know you feel like you've lost two years with Maddie, although frankly, that's not what I see in her face when she looks at you. And… I know this may be our last true moment together. But if it is, I want to remember it with a full heart."

Sam was crying as well, tears dripping off her chin and onto her blouse. "Well, if that's the case, why the fuck haven't you kissed me already, you idiot?" She pulled his hands behind her waist and, leaning forward, lost herself in his embrace.

66

The sun was just beginning to rise in the east, the clouds below them glowing with a thousand shades of pink and orange. She left the cockpit and wandered back to where her father was seated, staring out the little oval window to his right, lost in thought. The rest of the plane was pitch black, the lights dimmed back and the shades pulled on most of the other windows in the cabin.

"Father, you really should try and get some sleep. We'll be landing soon, and you'll need your strength..."

He turned to face her, and she could see that his eyes were closed. Slowly he opened them, and instead of the dullness of exhaustion, his eyes seemed to glow with a certain fire. A wildness she knew all too well.

"There will be time enough for sleep later, Mary Ellen. But this is not the time to rest. No, just the opposite. It is a time for change, for transformation. For our rebirth."

"Father, everything will be all right. The world is boundless, and with our wealth, with all the money we've stashed away, no one will ever find us."

"But we *want* them to find us, my child." He turned away, staring out the window at the clouds below them. "As it was said

367

in the prophesies, 'Behold, he cometh with clouds; and every eye shall see him, and they also which pierced him: and all kindreds of the earth shall wail because of him'. That is our destiny, Mary Ellen. That is our future."

She sat down beside him, reaching out to grasp his hand, concerned. Frightened. It had been a long time since she had last seen him this way. "It's just the shock, Father. It will take a little getting used to, this new life of ours. But I've planned all of this for a long time. There's no way the American government will ever find us."

He turned back to her, reaching out his other hand to stroke the side of her face. A beautiful face, just like her mother's. "Ah, Mary Ellen, you speak of men, of mere mortals. But who are men in the face of God?" He stood up slowly in front of her, his eyes pinning her, searing her, controlling her as he always had. "But this is all just a beginning, not an end. It has been foretold. Only in death can there be resurrection. Only the darkest night can reveal the true light of the Lord, the dawn that is coming. We are reborn into a new age, a new dawn of man. As it is written, 'I am Alpha and Omega, the beginning and the ending. Behold, I stand at the door and knock: if any man hear my voice, and open the door, I will come in to him, and will sup with him, and he with me. It is time to lay bare the record of the word of God, and of the testimony of Jesus Christ, and of all things that he saw.' '"

William Tulley was standing directly in front of the cabin window, the glow from the rising sun casting a golden halo of light around him, leaving the rest of him in deep shadow. For a moment, he clasped his hands as if in prayer, his face turned upward toward the heavens. Finally, reaching out, he cradled her head softly in his hands and began to speak, his voice so low she struggled to understand him. "The days of the Great Whore are ended. Babylon is fallen. Heaven is opening, and our Redeemer is coming once again to smite the wicked." He looked down at her, smiling crookedly. "And you, my daughter, you shall be the vessel for the Coming. The virgin who brings the Redeemer. I christened you Mary for a reason. You shall be mother to the new Christ child."

Sitting up front in the cockpit, unaware of the drama that was unfolding behind him, the pilot radioed ahead for permission to enter Turkish airspace, pulling back on the throttles a bit to begin the slow descent into Istanbul.

acknowledgments

It would be nice if books emerged instantly and fully formed from their author's minds, like Athena from the head of Zeus, but it just doesn't work like that. At least not for me. This book is the product of years of courtroom experience, six weeks of frenzied writing, then one and a half years of rewrites, rewrites and more rewrites. To get through it all took amazing patience and support from all my family and friends. First of all, to believe that a fifty year old man could shuck a long career in pharmaceutical marketing to become a lawyer. Then believing I could actually write a book that anyone would want to read. And, finally, actually reading all the early versions (ugh!) and offering encouragement and constructive criticism.

I would also like to thank all my awesome law school professors. My advocacy professor, Tracy McCormack, who encouraged me to dip my toe in litigation, and taught me the subtle arts of courtroom showmanship. Jerry Galow, who taught me the wicked doodlebug cross. Robert Hirschorn, who taught me everything I know about voir dire. And especially Dick DeGuerin, who inspired me to become a criminal lawyer, and instilled in me the idea that a criminal defense lawyer's job is to defend not only his client, but also the fundamental right to a fair trial that constitutes the last and best line of protection against an oppressive and despotic government.

This book would be an embarrassment to both me and my forebears if not for the exhaustive efforts of my amazing editor, Kara Vaught. Even after many years of newspaper editing and legal writing, I still had a great deal to learn from her about the nuances of the English language. And thanks to Peter O'Connor for an awesome cover.

Of course, last but certainly not least, my everlasting thanks to Elizabeth, my greatest cheerleader, my inspiration, my best friend forever, and the keeper of my heart.

coming soon

Reflecting the Dead

Revelations, Revolutions